STRONG AS DEATH IS LOVE

THE SONG OF SONGS, RUTH, ESTHER, JONAH, AND DANIEL

ALSO BY ROBERT ALTER

STRONG AS DEATH IS LOVE

THE SONG OF SONGS, RUTH, ESTHER, JONAH, AND DANIEL

A Translation with Commentary

ROBERT ALTER

W·W· Norton & Company   NEW YORK LONDON

For information about permission to reproduce selections from this book, write to
Permissions, W. W. Norton & Company, Inc., 500 Fifth Avenue, New York, NY 10110

For information about special discounts for bulk purchases, please contact
W. W. Norton Special Sales at specialsales@wwnorton.com or 800-233-4830

Manufacturing by RRDonnelley Harrisonburg
Book design by Margaret M. Wagner
Production manager: Julia Druskin

Library of Congress Cataloging-in-Publication Data

Alter, Robert, author.
Strong as death is love : the Song of Songs, Ruth, Esther, Jonah, and Daniel :
a translation with commentary / Robert Alter. — First edition.
pages cm
Includes bibliographical references.
ISBN 978-0-393-24304-8 (hardcover)
1. Love—Biblical teaching. 2. Bible. Song of Solomon—Criticism, interpretation, etc. 3.
Bible. Ruth—Criticism, interpretation, etc. 4. Bible. Esther—Criticism, interpretation,
etc. 5. Bible. Jonah—Criticism, interpretation, etc. 6. Bible. Daniel—Criticism,
interpretation, etc. I. Bible. Song of Solomon. English. II. Bible. Ruth. English. III.
Bible. Esther. English. IV. Bible. Jonah. English. V. Bible. Daniel. English. VI. Title.
BS1199.L66A48 2015
221.5'209—dc23

2014038126

W. W. Norton & Company, Inc.
500 Fifth Avenue, New York, N.Y. 10110
www.wwnorton.com

W. W. Norton & Company Ltd.
Castle House, 75/76 Wells Street, London W1T 3QT

1 2 3 4 5 6 7 8 9 0

for
Carol,
my one and only love

CONTENTS

THE BOOK OF DANIEL

ACKNOWLEDGMENTS

RESEARCH and secretarial costs were provided by the Class of 1937 Chair at the University of California, Berkeley. I am grateful to Jenna Scarpelli for her assiduity and patience in transcribing my handwritten drafts into an electronic text. My friend and colleague Ron Hendel made helpful suggestions for *The Song of Songs*, and I also benefited from students' contributions in a graduate seminar on *The Song of Songs* team-taught with Ron Hendel.

INTRODUCTION

THESE FIVE TEXTS are generally classified by scholars as Late Biblical books. "Late Biblical Books" is by no means a rubric under which texts have been placed in any of the formulations of the biblical canon. The foundational books of the Hebrew Bible were composed (though not yet edited) from the tenth or ninth to the seventh century BCE, with only a few archaic poems coming from an earlier period. The watershed of biblical history was the Babylonian exile, which began after the conquest of Judah and Jerusalem in 586 BCE. Some great prophetic poetry was written in the exile during the sixth century, but its strong stylistic and thematic continuities with pre-exilic writing preclude the classification of "late" for these texts. There were also some psalms written around this time that were included in the canonical collection and probably at least a few proverbs. Late Biblical literature, showing marked differences from the Hebrew writing of the First Commonwealth, was produced from the fifth to the second century BCE, some of it the work of writers in the diaspora, by then under Persian domination, and some of it in the Land of Israel. The two most original and theologically challenging books of Late Biblical literature are Job and Qohelet, both of which I have translated with commentary in a volume entitled *The Wisdom Books*. The short books presented here are, even in their brevity, artful and innovative literary works (perhaps with the exception of Daniel)—beguiling, entertaining, and in some instances perhaps a bit startling.

How do we know that they are late? Esther is manifestly set in the Persian court, as is, retrospectively, Daniel; and Ruth, though it purports to be a story that takes place in the period of the Judges, is concerned with the question of exogamy that much exercised the community in Judah in the mid-fifth century BCE but that was not a pressing issue in earlier times. Beyond any such thematic considerations, the great hallmark of lateness, showing variously in all five of these books, is linguistic.

Biblical Hebrew, like any language, changed through time. The temporal distance between the sundry strands of Genesis or the Book of Samuel and these Late Biblical texts is comparable to the distance between Shakespeare and John Updike. Just as in the four centuries separating Shakespeare from Updike the English language underwent pronounced changes—terms once in common usage replaced by others, palpable modifications of grammar and syntax—the Hebrew through these centuries exhibits a similar set of changes. One of the books in this volume, Ruth, because it purports to take place in the period before the founding of the monarchy around 1000 BCE, deploys an archaizing style that is meant to sound like the literary Hebrew of that era. Flawless archaizing, however, is a very difficult feat to pull off, and so there is a series of small slips, perhaps as many as a dozen, where a word or idiom is used that appears only in Late Biblical Hebrew, never earlier. The Late Biblical character of the Hebrew of Jonah and Esther is more straightforward: one encounters grammatical usages, idioms, and primary items of vocabulary that are distinctively Late Biblical, some of them reflecting the Aramaic that was becoming dominant, and Esther also abounds in Persian loanwords. The Hebrew of the Song of Songs is less overtly late, probably because of the tendency of poetry to be stylistically conservative, but even here there are a few grammatical features and some terms that would not have occurred in the Hebrew in literary usage before 586 BCE.

The Hebrew of the Book of Daniel is surely the oddest instance of linguistic lateness. Roughly the first half of the book, beginning early in Chapter 2, is written in Aramaic. (The only other extended Aramaic section in the Bible is four chapters in the Book of Ezra.) The Aramaic seems perfectly serviceable though not stylistically distinguished, showing, as it does, a strong tendency to formulaic language and mechanical repetitions. Chapter 7 to the end of the book is written in Hebrew—probably because Hebrew is the language of prophecy with which the author (or authors) sought to align his (or their) own work. In keeping with the aim of sounding prophetic, the writer tries to avoid overtly Late Biblical turns of language. It looks suspiciously, however, as if Hebrew were not a vehicle with which he is entirely comfortable: idioms get mangled, terms are sometimes used in problematic senses, and the syntax in a good many instances is awkward or actually garbled. What we have, then, in the Hebrew of Daniel is a Late Biblical writer—indeed, the latest of biblical writers, active, as one can tell from his historical references, in the fourth decade of the second century BCE—who labors to place his own literary production in a Hebrew tradition that goes back to the era before the Babylonian exile but does not succeed very well.

It has often been observed that this late period gave rise to writing that diverged in its views or openly dissented from the biblical texts of the First Commonwealth era. The impulse of dissent is most strikingly evident in the challenges to mainstream biblical ideas laid out in Job and in Qohelet. In the books in this volume, the celebration of erotic love in the Song of Songs and the carnivalesque spirit of Esther, both devoid of theological concerns, are altogether unlike anything found in the antecedent Hebrew literature that has come down to us. What should be added to this common observation about Late Biblical writing is that it reflects a vigorous exploration of new literary forms, and that will be a recurrent focus of the commentary which accompanies these translations. Hebrew narrative before the Babylonian exile is by and large formally conservative. There are some stylistic as well as ideological differences among the four principal strands that make up the Pentateuch, but all these writers share common assumptions (and common literary conventions) about how to tell a story and the purposes to be served by the stories. Nor are there significant differences in these regards between the Pentateuch and the sundry narratives that constitute the Deuteronomistic History, the stretch of books from Joshua to the end of Kings.

By contrast, the works composed from the fifth to the second century BCE reflect an extraordinary efflorescence of new literary genres and techniques. Ruth, which by the author's design seems closest to earlier Hebrew writing, is nevertheless a new kind of narrative—a bucolic idyll in which the profound elements of conflict and ambiguity that define classical Hebrew narrative are rigorously excluded, and the prose itself, with its repeated use of balanced cadences approximating poetry, expresses the harmony of the idyllic world. Jonah, though it purports to be the story of a prophet, deploys fantastic elements to shape a fable about the prophetic calling, making these elements seem different in kind from the stories of miracles that occasionally punctuate earlier Hebrew narrative. Esther is a different kind of fantasy, one of national triumph over powerful forces, which does not employ supernatural intervention. It is

cast in a satiric mold that incorporates farce and is at moments even rau-
cous. This writer's fondness for the descriptive details of imperial pomp
is nothing like antecedent Hebrew literature; and above all, it is a story
framed for sheer entertainment—which goes along with its often-noted
lack of reference to God, Torah, or the Land of Israel. In this crucial
regard, it is a kind of story that would have been inconceivable for the
writers of the First Commonwealth. Daniel is generically distinct from
all its literary antecedents in being an apocalyptic book: in its pages,
prophecy has been transformed into the deciphering of enigmatic coded
visions that indicate precisely what will happen and when it will happen
in an inexorably deterministic system leading to an end-time. And the
Song of Songs is a collection of exuberant love poems exulting in the
delights of the senses—again, with no mention of God—that puts aside
all the concerns of earlier Hebrew literature with covenant, Torah, and
the history of Israel (though allegorical interpretation would put all these
back into the Song). Scrutiny of earlier biblical texts—see especially
Isaiah 5—suggests that there was a genre of Hebrew love poetry centuries before the Song, but it surfaced only at this late moment, perhaps
in part because of the sense of freedom that later Hebrew writers felt to
express themselves in genres strikingly different from the ones that had
till then defined the literature of the emerging canon.

The Song of Songs may provide an object lesson about the nature of
ancient Hebrew literature. There were in all likelihood various modes
of writing going back to the hazy beginnings of the tradition that were
not preserved because they did not serve the ideological ends of the
writers and redactors who were in the process of assembling what would
become the canon. The nine centuries of literary activity that produced
the Hebrew Bible are notable for their arresting variety. In the Late Biblical period, this variety came to define the very horizon of expectations
of the literature. It gave the biblical canon an amplitude and richness it
would not otherwise have had, even in regard to values and worldviews.
And for readers, these late texts provided, and continue to provide, a
range of pleasures and literary experiences not stereotypically associated
with the Bible.

THE SONG OF SONGS

TO THE READER

THE EXTRAORDINARY VARIEGATION of the books of the Hebrew Bible in style, genre, and outlook is one of the most exciting aspects of this anthology that spans nearly a millennium. But even against that background, the Song of Songs stands out in its striking distinctiveness—a distinctiveness that deserves to be called wondrous. The delicate yet frank sensuality of this celebration of young love, without reference to God or covenant or Torah, has lost nothing of its immediate freshness over the centuries: these are among the most beautiful love poems that have come down to us from the whole ancient world. Famously, the erotic nature of the Song constituted a challenge for the framers of the canon, both Jewish and Christian, and their response was to read the poems allegorically—in the case of the early rabbis, as the love between the Holy One and Israel, and in the case of the Church fathers, as the love between Christ and the Church. "If all the writings are holy," Rabbi Akiva proclaimed in a discussion of the Song's canonicity, "the Song of Songs is holy of holies." Both religious traditions, however fervently they clung to this allegorical vision, never succeeded in entirely blocking the erotic power of the text. There are, for example, medieval Hebrew liturgical poems that earnestly follow the theological plot of the allegory yet knowingly or sometimes unwittingly let the young lovers' delight in the carnal consummation of love make its presence felt.

Little is known about the origins of these poems. Different elaborate theories have been proposed about them: that they are wedding poems, that they should be read as drama, that they originated in poems to a pagan love goddess, that they constitute a single architectonic poetic structure, that they are direct adaptations of Egyptian or Mesopotamian love poetry. All such theories should prudently be rejected. The book as a whole has an anthological look, though a case might be made for certain recurrent configurations constituting a kind of unity. It is conceivable that embryonic versions of some of these poems were in oral or perhaps written circulation for centuries, though there is no way of proving that hypothesis. The evidence of the language of the poems—some of the vocabulary and certain grammatical forms—clearly indicates a relatively late date of composition; the fourth century BC seems a reasonable guess, though some would put it a little later. It may be that one or two of the poems were in fact written as wedding poems, but the content of most of them leads one to conclude that the free enjoyment of the pleasures of love and not marriage is what the poets had in view. Several of the poems have an urban setting, with the young woman addressing "the daughters of Jerusalem" or confronted by the town watchmen, but the predominant background of the poems is bucolic or sylvan—luscious gardens, verdant forests, vineyards, rolling hills, and mountains. Solomon is mentioned more than once, but the intention seems to be to draw a contrast between the two young lovers delighting in each other in the vernal lushness of nature and the luxuries of the royal court.

These poets are finely aware of the long tradition of Hebrew poetry, but notably there is little in the way of allusion to earlier Hebrew texts. This is hardly evidence that the poets were unfamiliar with those texts, only that the antecedent biblical literature did not much suit their own purposes.

The formal system of parallelism between versets—that is, parts of the line—that governs Hebrew poetry from its earliest extant texts going back to around 1100 BCE is still very much in evidence, though in quite a few lines the parallelism is looser than in earlier eras. The first line of the book, for example, like a good many after it, is not constructed on semantic parallelism: "Let him kiss me with the kisses of his mouth, / for your loving is better than wine." In this instance, the second verset does not parallel the first but instead explains it. Other lines that appear to diverge from the convention of poetic parallelism actually follow a precedent well attested in earlier Hebrew poetry. Thus the first poetic line of 1:4 reads: "Draw me after you, let us run. / The king has brought me to his chamber." Here, as in many lines in the Prophets, Psalms, and elsewhere, the second verset traces a narrative development of what is introduced in the first: the young woman first declares her eagerness to run off after her lover; in the second verset, they have completed their running and come to his bedchamber, reported in a verb that indicates a completed action. More generally, however, these poets deploy the millennium-old convention of poetic parallelism inventively and vividly. When the beloved describes her dark complexion (1:5) as "like the tents of Kedar, / like Solomon's curtains," she uses the parallelism to make an argument against those who would mock her for her peasant's suntan. Yes, I am dark, she says, like nomads' tents woven from black goat's hair (the name Kedar puns on a Hebrew root that means "dark"), but if I seem to belong to a rough bedouin setting, my darkness is also something lovely, like Solomon's tent hangings, which might well be dyed, in royal fashion, in deep blue or purple.

The predominant use of semantic parallelism in the poetic corpus of the Bible is to concretize, focus, or intensify material from the first verset in the second. This strategy is vividly evident in line after line here. Chapter 8, for example, begins with the following line: "Would that you were a brother to me, / suckling my mother's breasts." It is possible to construe the second verset as a participial phrase, which is done in this translation in part for the sake of readability in English. But it is equally possible that it is a noun phrase, "a suckling of my mother's breasts," which would be in keeping with the procedure of parallelistic verse to substitute in the second verset a paraphrase or epithet for the plain noun (here, "brother") of the first. We should note what is effected through the substitution. The general fraternal relationship marked by "brother" becomes something biological and intimately physical: the beloved fantasizes her lover sucking the same breasts that she has sucked. This fantasy of shared physical closeness in infancy then becomes a vivid anticipation of another kind of physical closeness in adulthood. One can see that the poet had a subtle sense of how the inherited poetic system worked as he put the system to a rather different use from what one finds in the earlier poems that have been preserved in the canon.

Much of the enchantment and the sensual richness of the celebration of love in the Song inhere in its metaphoric language. Some of the metaphors drawn from the animal kingdom and from architecture—teeth as newly bathed ewes, a neck as a tower—may seem a little strange to modern readers, though that probably was not true for the ancient audience. Other figurative comparisons—eyes like doves, breasts like twin gazelles, kisses sweeter than wine—retain all their lovely expressiveness after more than twenty-two centuries. What is remarkable is how consistently the figurative language of these poems evokes the experience of physical love with a delicacy of expression that manifests the poet's constant delight in likening one thing to another. (The Hebrew verb *damah*, "to be like," is repeatedly flaunted.) There is a recurrent shuttling between the metaphor and its referent, in some instances creating a sense of virtual interchangeability between the two that enables the poet to speak candidly of sexual gratification without seeming to do so. In a related kind of poised ambiguity, we often don't know, because of the figurative language, whether we are inside or outside. Here is an exquisite metaphor from the first chapter: "A sachet of myrrh is my lover to me, / all night between my breasts. // A cluster of henna, my lover to me, / in the vineyards of Ein Gedi" (1:13–14). A young woman making herself desirable might possibly wear a sachet of fragrance between her breasts. Reading the lines, we of course realize what the lover, playfully miniaturized as a sachet, is doing in that place, but the realization is nuanced in feeling by the charming metaphor. And the concluding verset, "in the vineyards of Ein Gedi," leaves us pleasantly hovering between possibilities: has the henna of the metaphor been grown at the Ein Gedi oasis overlooking the Dead Sea, or rather, in a slide through the metaphoric to the literal, are the lovers actually enjoying their love in the vineyards of Ein Gedi, as elsewhere vineyards or gardens become their bower?

These ambiguities, always evocative, never arch, between figure and referent are most brilliantly deployed in the relatively long poem that starts at 4:8 and runs to 5:1. The flourishing natural landscape, beginning with the wild and distant mountains of Lebanon, is the apt background for the young lovers, who are themselves vernal, like the world though which they move. But there is a fine transition inaugurated at 4:12 from the literal realm of green things to a figurative one. Now the beloved's body is a "locked garden" filled with luscious fruit and fragrant plants, and she invites her lover to enter the garden and enjoy its fruits. The audience of these lines is of course expected to know exactly what she is talking about, but the delicacy of expression is sustained by the harmonious continuity between outside and inside. This distinctive use of metaphor does not explain everything, but it is surely one of the features of the Song of Songs that makes it among the most beautiful collections of love poetry in the Western tradition.

CHAPTER 1

The Song of Songs, which is Solomon's.

1

Let him kiss me with the kisses of his mouth,
    for your loving is better than wine.

2

---

1. *The Song of Songs.* In biblical idiom this formation indicates a superlative—the best of songs. The exquisite poetry that follows surely justifies the title.

which is Solomon's. The attribution is strictly editorial, following a practice of attributing Late Biblical books to famous figures from earlier Israelite history. The identification is encouraged by the appearance of Solomon's name in verse 5 (see the comment there) and by the reference to "the king" in verse 4 (again, see the comment) and elsewhere.

2. *Let him kiss me.* The Hebrew *yeshaqeini* puns on *yashqeini*, "let him give me drink," since the kisses are likened to wine.

loving. The Hebrew *dodim* suggests lovemaking, a sense already understood in the Middle Ages. The medieval Hebrew poet Yehuda Halevi concludes an allegorical poem clearly based on that Song of Songs with this explicitly sexual line, spoken by the beloved (Israel) to God: "Put your strength in me, for I will give you my loving [*dodai*]." One should note that the young woman begins by imagining her desirable lover from a certain distance, in the third person, and then in the second half of the line closes the gap by addressing him more intimately in the second person.

3   For fragrance your oils are goodly,
                poured oil is your name.
                        And so the young women love you.

4   Draw me after you, let us run.
                The king has brought me to his chamber.
        Let us be glad and rejoice in you.
                Let us extol your loving beyond wine.
                        Rightly do they love you.

---

3. *For fragrance.* The Song of Songs revels in the pleasures of all five senses. This initial poem begins with taste and here moves on to smell. Touch is implied in verse 13, sight in verse 15, and later sound will enter as well.

poured oil. The Hebrew modifier *turaq* is problematic because grammar requires a masculine verb, but the form here is feminine. Some interpreters want to see the word as the name of a kind of oil, but it probably makes more sense to understand it as an image of poured oil emitting a pleasing scent, as the lover's good name projects in public an attractive sense of him. The Hebrew shows wordplay, which also appears in Proverbs, between *shemen,* "oil," and *shem,* "name."

4. *The king.* Here and elsewhere this is a designation for the lover. The beloved is never called queen, perhaps because of the asymmetry between the sexes in the biblical world: he is her glorious king, and she is the one in whom he continually delights, but she is not his queen.

has brought me to his chamber. In a palace, there would be inner chambers, but the chamber of which he speaks is clearly a secluded place in which to make love. Marriage is not mentioned. The Hebrew shows a plural, probably reflecting poetic usage.

Let us. It is noteworthy that she switches back and forth from direct address to third-person reference to her lover. Verse 2 begins with a third-person wish, then moves into intimate address. The "us" here may be the daughters of Jerusalem, introduced explicitly in the next verse, which however begins a new poem.

I am dark but desirable, 5
        O daughters of Jerusalem,
like the tents of Kedar,
        like Solomon's curtains.
Do not look on me for being dark, 6
        for the sun has glared on me.
My mother's sons were incensed with me,
        they made me a keeper of the vineyards.
                My own vineyard I have not kept.

---

5. *desirable.* Though the adjective *na'wah* comes to mean something like "lovely" in standard Hebrew usage, it derives from the verbal stem *'-w-h,* "to desire," and given the erotically fraught world of the Song, that meaning is probably activated here.

the tents of Kedar. Kedar is an Arab tribe, and bedouins till this day make their tents out of black goat hair. The name also puns on the Hebrew root *q-d-r,* "to be dark."

like Solomon's curtains. The curtains are tent hangings. Some scholars revocalize the Hebrew for "Solomon" in order to make it the name of a desert tribe, thus yielding a neater parallelism. But the point of the line is precisely its paradox: I am as dark as a nomad's tent but as desirable as the lovely curtains of a king. This would be an especially effective rejoinder to the elegant urbanite daughters of Jerusalem who might mock her for her suntanned skin, the sign of a peasant.

6. *dark.* Instead of the primary term with which she began, *shehorah,* she now uses the same word with a diminutive suffix, *sheharhoret,* "darkish," "dusky."

My mother's sons. She does not call them "my brothers" but uses a designation that suggests a certain distancing from them. Later, she will invoke a woman's attachment to her mother.

were incensed with me. The Hebrew verb suggests heat, thus linking with the glaring sun of the previous line. The brothers are incensed with her because she has not kept her vineyard, that is, she has not preserved her virginity. She on her part expresses no misgivings—quite the contrary—at having exercised sexual freedom.

they made me a keeper of the vineyards. Her brothers have exiled her from the comforts of home (perhaps an urban home) and made her perform this rough peasant task in order to punish her.

My own vineyard I have not kept. The reference is double—metaphorically, to her virginity, and physically to her complexion, which she has been unable to preserve in its desired fairness while working in the vineyard.

7   Tell me, whom I love so,
          where you pasture your flock at noon,
     lest I go straying
          after the flocks of your companions.
8   —If you do not know, O fairest of women,
          go out in the tracks of the sheep
     and graze your goats
          by the shepherd's shelters.

9   To my mare among Pharaoh's chariots
          I likened you, my friend.

---

7. *whom I love so.* Many translations, following the King James Version, render this as "whom my soul loves," but the Hebrew *nafshi* does not mean "my soul." Rather, it is an intensive alternative to the first-person pronoun. Since English does not have intensive personal pronouns, this translation here and elsewhere compensates by adverbial intensification, "so."

   go straying. The Hebrew *'otiyah* appears to mean "cover up, wrap," a meaning that is problematic both because of the context and because the transitive verb would normally require a grammatical object. It is best construed as a reversal of consonants (whether by usage or scribal error) for *to'ah,* "to wander or go astray."

8. *If you do not know.* This is the first of a series of dialogic exchanges between the lovers. (The switch from her speech to his is indicated in our text by the dash.) In this poem, they are both shepherds, and she has asked him exactly where she may find him lest she wander into the company of his male friends, who might well be tempted to take advantage of her beauty. His response looks like a lover's tease: If you really don't know where to find me, use some ingenuity and follow the tracks of my flock till you come to where I am.

   shelters. Although most translations represent *mishkenot* as "tents," the term is not restricted to tents and could also refer to a lean-to or some similar kind of temporary dwelling.

9. *To my mare among Pharaoh's chariots.* Some scholars think the suffix added to the word for "mare" is not a possessive but an archaic form occasionally used in construct combinations. Ariel and Chana Bloch argue against this on philological grounds, accepted here, and it makes more sense for the lover to claim

Your cheeks are lovely with looped earrings,　　　　　　　10
　　　your neck with beads.
Earrings of gold we will make for you　　　　　　　　　11
　　　with silver filigree.

While the king was on his couch　　　　　　　　　　　12
　　　my nard gave off its scent.
A sachet of myrrh is my lover to me,　　　　　　　　　13
　　　all night between my breasts.

---

possession of the metaphorical mare. Marvin Pope has proposed that the reference of this image is to the strategy of Thutmosis III, at the battle of Qadesh, of sending mares in heat among the enemy cavalry in order to drive them into disarray. Alternatively, since Egypt was known as an exporter of horses, this could simply mean that the beloved, compared to a fine mare, would stand out among the best of horses. Egyptian horses, one should note, were sometimes decked with ornaments around their necks.

10. *looped earrings*. This translation adopts the solution to *torim* proposed by the Blochs, as it does with "silver filigree" at the end of the next verse.

12. *While the king was on his couch / my nard gave off its scent*. This is an appropriately sexy beginning to this richly sensual poem: the lover is lying in bed waiting for her, and as she approaches, she is aware of the fragrance with which she has scented her body. In the next line, it is the lover who metaphorically becomes the fragrance. Nard, or spikenard, was imported to the ancient Near East all the way from the Himalayas, where the plant was grown, so it is clearly a luxury item.

13. *A sachet of myrrh is my lover to me*. The combination of delightfulness and sensuality in this metaphor is one of the hallmarks of the Song of Songs. The lover is playfully miniaturized as a sachet of perfume strung around the neck of the beloved on a cord and resting between her breasts even as their night of sweet physical intimacy is beautifully evoked.

14   A cluster of henna, my lover to me,
           in the vineyards of Ein Gedi.

15   O you are fair, my friend,
           O you are fair, your eyes are doves.
16   —O you are fair, my lover, you are sweet,
           our bed is verdant, too.
17   Our house's beams are cedar,
           our rafters evergreens.

---

14. *in the vineyards of Ein Gedi.* There is an ambiguity here between the metaphorical and the literal that is another characteristic of the poetry of this book. The lover is figuratively a cluster of henna, pressed to the beloved's body, henna being an aromatic plant grown at the oasis of Ein Gedi near the Dead Sea. At the same time, the wording leaves open the possibility that the two lovers are actually together at the oasis.

15. *O you are fair, my friend.* The male lover is speaking, something altogether clear in the Hebrew because "my friend," *ra'yati,* is feminine. In the next line, she answers in kind.

16. *our bed is verdant, too.* Another pleasing ambiguity of the Song is between inside and outside. She probably means to say that the bed on which they will enjoy love's pleasures is a forest floor, but she could be saying that an actual bed inside on which they lie partakes of the verdancy of the flourishing realm of nature outside. The ambiguity continues with the cedar beams and evergreen rafters of the next line, which are either literal, because they are making love in the forest, or metaphorical, because their house is redolent of the green world outside.

17. *Our house's beams.* The Hebrew shows a plural, "houses," but as Yair Zakovitch notes, there are other instances in biblical usage where when two nouns are joined in a construct form, a plural second term converts the first term to a plural, though the sense is actually singular.

CHAPTER 2

I am the rose of Sharon,
  the lily of the valley.
—Like a lily among the thorns
    so is my friend among the young women.

---

1. *rose . . . lily.* Like a good many items of biblical flora, the identification of these two flowers remains uncertain, so it seems sensible to follow the traditional English equivalents here, which may be as good a guess as any others.

2. *Like a lily among the thorns.* This particular poem unfolds through statement and response in a lovers' dialogue. She announces herself as a flower; he goes her one better by answering that she is like a flower among the thorns in comparison to other young women. She then responds by likening him to a fruit-bearing tree, with the contrast between tree and flower neatly corresponding to the anatomical difference between the two sexes.

3   —Like a quince tree among the trees of the forest
                so is my lover among the young men.
         In its shade I delighted to sit
                and its fruit was sweet to my taste

4   He has brought me to the house of wine
                and his banner over me is love.

---

3. *quince tree.* The traditional rendering of "apple tree" cannot be right because apple trees were not cultivated in the ancient Near East. (The term used here would nevertheless become the standard word for "apple" in later Hebrew.) The Blochs opt for "apricot," which does make sense in regard to its succulence, but it remains conjectural. Quince, a harder fruit, has at least a metrical advantage. Quinces have been used in Greece and perhaps elsewhere in the Mediterranean for many centuries to perfume bedsheets, and that association might be in play in the Song of Songs.

its shade . . . its fruit. Because the Hebrew possessive suffix is masculine, it could equally refer to the tree or to its metaphorical referent, the young man. In the apt image, he offers her two things—protection (a standard meaning of "shade" in biblical usage) and sensual pleasure. Fruit, wine, and honey throughout the Song are associated with sexual gratification.

4. *He has brought me to the house of wine.* Egyptian love poetry, which many scholars think is an antecedent to the Song of Songs, often makes a banquet house a place for the lovers' tryst. But since wine is metaphorically identified with sexual pleasure (see 1:2, 4), the house of wine might be entirely metaphorical—that is, the chamber or bower to which the lover has brought his beloved in order to make love to her.

his banner over me is love. Several scholars have argued that the noun here, *degel*, reflects an Akkadian cognate that means "to see," but there is scant evidence in the Hebrew Bible of the use of this word with the sense of sight. Everywhere else, *degel* indicates "a banner or flag." The image would be consonant with a heroic representation of the lover as a strong, even triumphant figure, here leading her to his bower under a flag that signals not tribal or military identity but, quite eloquently, love.

Stay me up with raisin-cakes,   5
      cushion me with quinces
           for I am in a swoon of love.
His left hand beneath my head,   6
      his right hand embracing me.
I make you swear, O daughters of Jerusalem   7
      by the deer or the gazelles of the field,
that you shall not rouse not stir love
      until it pleases.

---

5. *Stay me up with raisin-cakes.* She is faint with desire and so asks for these delicacies to revive her.

I am in a swoon of love. The literal sense of the Hebrew is "lovesick," but that sounds too pathetic, or adolescent, in English. The King James Version "sick of love" sounds like a blunder, or at least has become that for twenty-first-century usage.

6. *His left hand beneath my head, / his right hand embracing me.* The chronological steps of this poem need to be sorted out. First, in verse 4, she recalls a moment when her lover led her off to "the house of wine." Now, however, she is away from him, weak with desire for him (verse 5), and as we learn from verse 7, she is speaking to a group of young women in Jerusalem. This verse, then, is either a flashback to the moment when he embraced her or a wish-fulfillment fantasy of what she now desires.

7. *I make you swear, O daughters of Jerusalem.* The implication seems to be that they have somehow been pestering her with questions about her absent lover: Where is he? If he is as wonderful as you say, why aren't you together with him now? Her rejoinder to such implied challenges is that love will attain its fulfillment in its own good time, and you must not urge its consummation until that time has come.

by the deer or the gazelles of the field. This is a beautiful reflection of the worldview of the Song. Typically, it is God who is invoked in such oaths in the Bible, but God is never mentioned in the book. Instead the young woman invokes beautiful creatures of wild nature, creatures she repeatedly uses as metaphors for her lover.

until it pleases. The Hebrew verb here usually means "to desire" or "to like." The Blochs render this as "until it is ripe," which stretches the sense of the Hebrew term a bit but is quite apt.

8   Hark! Oh, my lover is coming,
          bounding over the mountains,
             leaping over the hills.

9   My lover is like a deer
          or like a stag.
    Oh, he stands behind our wall
          peering through the windows,
             peeping through the crannies.

10   My lover spoke out and said to me:
          "Arise my friend, my fair one, go.

11   For, look, the winter has passed
          the rain has gone away.

---

8. *Hark!* The Hebrew *qol* usually means "voice" or "sound," but it is also some- times an interjection corresponding to "hark" in English. That sense may be more likely here because she would scarcely hear the voice of her lover (unless he were shouting her name or yodeling), and the sound of his footsteps would scarcely be audible as he bounds over the mountains.

9. *Oh, he stands behind our wall / peering through the windows, / peeping through the crannies.* This entire line exemplifies the delicate and witty interplay between tenor and vehicle in the use of metaphor in the Song. The scene can be read two ways. As metaphor, it invites us to imagine a deer that has come leaping down the hills and now stands outside the house, peering in through the window (an occurrence quite familiar to many who live in American sub- urbs near wooded areas). As the referent of the metaphor, it is the vigorous young lover who has come running in his eagerness to be with the beautiful woman he loves, pausing for a moment outside before he crosses the threshold.

11. *the winter has passed.* The love poetry of the Song of Songs is preeminently poetry of the verdant world of spring. Jewish tradition fixed it to be read on the Sabbath of springtime Passover because of the allegorical interpretation in which the two lovers are identified with God and Israel celebrating their nuptials after the exodus from Egypt, which occured in early spring. But the framers of the tradition were also aware of the vernal efflorescence affirmed in the Song, with a good many liturgical poems composed for this Passover Sab- bath invoking the flourishing world of spring.

Buds can be seen in the land,   12
    the nightingale's season has come
        and the turtledove's voice is heard in our land.
The fig tree has put forth its green fruit   13
    and the vines in blossom waft fragrance.
Arise and go, my friend,
    my fair one, go forth."

My dove in the rock's crevices,   14
    in the hollow of the cliff,
show me how you look,
    let me hear your voice,
for your voice is sweet
    and your look desirable.

Seize us the foxes,   15
    the little foxes,
despoiling the vineyards,
    but our vineyards are in bloom.

---

12. *the nightingale's season.* Some interpreters choose to take the Hebrew noun *zamir* as a homonym that means "pruning," but birdsong sounds more appropriate to the mood of the poem.

14. *My dove in the rock's crevices.* In this particular poem, the young woman appears to be playfully hiding from her lover, an act registered in the image of a dove nesting in the rock's crevices.

    the cliff. While the Hebrew *madregah* comes to have the general meaning of "stair," in the context of this line, evoking a scene in nature, it probably refers to a cliff or similar rock formation in which there would be small concavities or cracks in which a dove could hide.

15. *Seize us the foxes.* This verse, like a few others in the Song, is no more than a fragment, and consequently its meaning is uncertain. Since vineyards tend to be metaphorical in the Song (see 1:6) and are figuratively associated with the body of the beloved, one may propose the following reading: there are in the world pesky agents of interference that seek to obstruct love's fulfillment, as foxes despoil a vineyard, but our own special vineyard remains flourishing and intact, our love unimpeded.

16   My lover is mine and I am his,
              who grazes among the lilies.
17   Until morning's breeze blows
              and the shadows flee,
       turn round, be like a deer, my love,
              or like a gazelle
                     on the cloven mountains.

---

16. *who grazes among the lilies.* The implicit metaphor, made explicit in the next verse, is a deer, but the lilies are associated elsewhere with the delights offered by the body of the beloved.

17. *turn round, be like a deer, my love.* This line pivots on still another of the ambiguities in which the poetry of the Song revels. Momentarily, the young woman appears to be sending her lover away to go running across the mountainous landscape. But in the preceding line ("until morning's breeze blows . . .") she clearly invites him to spend the night. The equation between the woman's body and the landscape that appears elsewhere (compare the extended poem in Chapter 4) is manifested here, and "the cloven mountains" are in all likelihood a figurative reference to her breasts.

CHAPTER 3

On my couch at night   1
    I sought him I love so.
        I sought him but did not find him.
Let me rise and go round the town,   2
    in the streets and in the square.
Let me seek him I love so.
    I sought him but did not find him.
The watchmen who go round the town found me.   3
    "Have you seen him I love so?"

---

1. *On my couch at night.* Many interpreters understand this entire sequence as a dream. That reading is plausible but not inevitable since it is perfectly possible that she is tossing in her bed because her lover is not lying by her side and that she then rises to go out and look for him.

2. *Let me rise and go round the town.* This act, whether dreamed or real, is an expression of great daring on the part of the beloved because it would be dangerous for a young woman to go wandering through the streets of the town in the dark of the night. Compare Ruth 3:12, where Boaz keeps Ruth from walking home at night.

3. *The watchmen who go round the town found me.* As yet, she does not find her lover but is found by the watchmen. In the parallel poem in Chapter 5, they attack her. Here they are merely the audience for her plaintive question about her lover's whereabouts.

4   I had barely passed on from them
        when I found him I love so.
            I held him and did not let go
        till I brought him to my mother's house,
            and to the chamber of her who conceived me.

5   I make you swear, O daughters of Jerusalem,
        by the deer or by the gazelles of the field,
    that you shall not stir nor rouse
        love until it pleases.

---

4. *I held him and did not let go.* The lover's response is not registered; nor is there any dialogue between them. All that is reported is her passionate clinging to him and her bringing him to her mother's house. This is, we should note, a young woman who takes the initiative, first daring to go out into the dark streets in search of her lover, then grasping him and leading him to her mother's house.

to my mother's house . . . to the chamber of her who conceived me. This translation preserves the literal sense of the Hebrew in poetic parallelism, the standard term ("mother") is generally used in the first verset, and a substitution—often it is a metaphor or an unusual synonym—is used in the second. The reference to conception here may intimate the sexual act that the young woman has in mind. The figure of the mother often appears in Sumerian love poetry, which could be in the distant background of this poem. In many cultures, it is the mother's role to instruct her daughter about what to do in the act of love, and that may also be a reason for introducing the mother here. Notably, the biblical corpus is dotted with references to the father's house, which is a fixed social unit, but in the Song only the mother's house appears. Another feature of poetic parallelism in the Bible can be observed in the other pair of nouns in this line: quite often, when a spatial term appears in the first verset, the parallel term in the second is a smaller space or an object contained within the space demarcated by the first term. She leads him, then, to the house and then, entering the house, to a chamber within it. This standard procedure of poetic parallelism here indicates a move into secluded intimacy.

5. *I make you swear.* See the comment on 2:9. There the vow she imposes on the daughters of Jerusalem addresses the plight of separation from him, her longing to join him. Here it is a kind of coda to her nocturnal search for her lover, in the end crowned with success—you must not rouse love, she tells the young women, until it is ripe and ready, but now, as I bring my lover to the inner chamber of my mother's house, the moment of ripeness has come.

Who is this coming up from the desert   6
      like a pillar of smoke
perfumed with myrrh and frankincense
      from all the merchant's powders?

Look, Solomon's bed—   7
      sixty warriors round it
         of the warriors of Israel.
All of them wielding the sword   8
      trained in battle,
each with his sword on his thigh
      out of terror in the nights.

---

6. *Who is this coming up from the desert* . . . There is some debate as to whether this verse belongs with the lines that follow. The use of "who," as the Blochs argue, makes it unlikely that it refers to Solomon's bed or to his palanquin, and so the entire verse, two lines of poetry, should probably be seen as an independent fragment. What is clear, however, is that the editor, by placing these two lines here, meant to encourage readers to see a connection with what follows. The image of someone—the Hebrew uses a feminine form—coming up from the desert perfumed, in a grand procession, looks like a reminiscence of the visit of the Queen of Sheba to Solomon, offering an associative link with the figure of Solomon in the poem that runs from verse 7 to the end of the chapter.

7. *Solomon's bed.* The subject of this poem appears to be quite different from the poetry about two pastoral lovers in a sylvan setting that constitutes the bulk of the Song of Songs.

    sixty warriors round it / of the warriors of Israel. This line, together with the next two, looks like a grand epic flourish, describing the formidable array of guards around Solomon in his palace bedchamber. But Yair Zakovitch proposes that the whole sequence is satiric, representing King Solomon quaking in his bed "out of terror in the nights," in striking contrast to the young woman in the preceding poem, who does not hesitate to go out in the night, with no armed guard, in search of her lover.

9   A palanquin did King Solomon make
             from Lebanon wood.
     Its posts he made of silver,
            its padding gold,
     its curtains crimson,
            its inside paved with love
                    by the daughters of Jerusalem.
10   Go out and behold, O daughters of Zion,
            King Solomon in the diadem
                    with which his mother crowned him
            on his wedding day,
                    on the day of his heart's rejoicing.

---

9. *A palanquin.* The Hebrew term *'apiryon* appears only here and is borrowed either from the Greek or the Persian. Some construe it as a fixed royal structure ("pavilion"), but in rabbinic literature, which is only a few centuries removed from our text, it is understood as "palanquin" or, perhaps less grandly, "sedan chair." A palanquin as well as a pavilion would be grandly furnished, and the fact that it has *'amudim*, in some contexts "pillars," is not proof of architectural identity because that word could also mean "posts," as in this translation.

Lebanon wood. This would be expensive cedar wood.

its padding gold. Gold would not make a very comfortable padding, so the reference is probably to padding covered with cloth woven from gold thread.

its inside paved with love. There is no need to emend the noun here. As Zakovitch notes, the sequence here exhibits a familiar biblical pattern of three similar terms and then a switch: silver, gold, crimson, love. The effect of surprise at the end is exquisite.

10. *the diadem.* Though the Hebrew *'atarah* might simply mean "crown," it is not the standard term for a royal crown, and on the evidence of the Talmud, there was a practice to adorn the bridegroom with some sort of special diadem. This might well have been put on by the bridegroom's mother, whereas there are no historical grounds for a procedure in which the mother places the crown of the kingdom on her son.

with which his mother crowned him. As in the previous poem, it is the mother who presides over the nuptials.

on his wedding day. Although no explicit citations occur, it looks as though this poem, evoking the pomp and circumstance of Solomon's wedding day, has in mind Psalm 45, which is an epithalamion for a royal wedding.

CHAPTER 4

O you are fair, my friend,
    O you are fair.
Your eyes are doves
    through the screen of your tresses.
Your hair is like a herd of goats
    that have swept down from Mount Gilead.

1

---

1. *through the screen of your tresses.* The Hebrew says merely "through your tresses," but "the screen of," essentially implied, has been added for poetic legibility. A long interpretive tradition, going back to the Septuagint and embraced by some modern scholars, understands the noun *tsamah* to mean "veil." The Blochs make a compelling philological argument against this construction on three grounds: the form of the noun is one used for body parts; in Isaiah 47:2, this same noun is the object of the verb "to lay bare," which is consistently used for exposing parts of the body, not for the removal of garments; introduction of a veil would interrupt the sequence of references to the beloved's face and body out of which the whole poem is composed. The Blochs also note that covering the beautiful young woman with a veil gives her an aura of modesty, or reflects an inclination to prudery, that is not in keeping with the frank eroticism of the poem. In modern Hebrew, *tsamah*, in accord with the biblical sense of the word, means "braid [of hair]." "Tresses," then, the last word of this line, neatly overlaps with "hair," the first Hebrew word of the very next line.

    a herd of goats / that have swept down from Mount Gilead. The hair of the goats would be black, like the hair of the beloved cascading over her shoulders.

2 Your teeth like a flock of matched ewes
         that have come up from the washing,
   all of them alike,
         and none has lost its young.
3 Like a scarlet thread, your lips,
         and your tongue—desire.
   Like cut pomegranate your cheekbones
         through the screen of your tresses.
4 Like the tower of David your neck
         built gloriously.

---

2. *Your teeth like a flock of matched ewes.* This image, which may look incongruous to the modern eye, would probably have seemed natural to the ancient Hebrew pastoralists. The white plays against the black of the hair, to which a third color, the scarlet of the lips, will be added. In an era millennia before dentistry, most people's teeth would be yellowed and gapped by early middle age, if not sooner. This, then, is an impressive feature of the beloved's beauty: her teeth are perfectly white, like sheep coming out of the water, and every tooth is perfectly matched, with none missing, like the flock of ewes in which "none has lost its young."

3. *and your tongue—desire.* Literally, "your tongue [is] desirable [or lovely]." The metaphoric location later of milk and honey under the tongue, verse 11, suggests that the lover is thinking of openmouthed kisses.

   cheekbones. Though this same word clearly means "temple" (that is, forehead) in the Song of Deborah, Judges 5, there is a long and plausible exegetical tradition, going back at least to Rashi, that understands it as "cheekbones." (Rashi, citing an Old French word, calls it the "apple" of the cheek). The temple would probably be too high on the head because the description is making its way downward, according to the convention of the *wazf*, the vertical celebration of the loved one's beautiful body.

4. *Like the tower of David your neck.* This simile, like a good many others in the poem, is "Oriental," reflecting an aesthetic in which the poet pursues the momentum of the object of comparison, half forgetting the thing to which it is compared. Long necks—think of Nefertiti—were obviously thought of as beautiful.

   built gloriously. The adverbial *letalpiyot* has defied decipherment or convincing etymological explanation. All that is clear is that it constitutes a superlative.

A thousand shields are hung on it,
    all the warriors' bucklers.
Your two breasts are like two fawns,   5
    twins of a gazelle,
        that graze among the lilies.
Till morning's breeze blows   6
    and the shadows flee,
I will go to the mountain of myrrh
    and to the hill of frankincense
You are wholly fair, my friend,   7
    there is no blemish in you.

A thousand shields are hung on it. At this point, the image of the woman disappears in the image of the tower. Nevertheless, the shields hung on the tower allude to links of shining jewelry that the woman wears around her neck.

5. *Your two breasts are like two fawns.* The description continues its vertical descent, though in this particular poem, this is as far down as it will go. After the architectural and military images of the neck, the breasts are represented through soft and gentle animal imagery.

that graze among the lilies. Though the reference is to the fawns, not to the breasts, there is a suggestion that the breasts are surrounded by floral fragrance.

6. *I will go to the mountain of myrrh / and to the hill of frankincense.* In biblical poetry, "mountain" and "hill" are a formulaic pair, with "mountain" (usually in the plural) almost always appearing in the first half of the line and "hill" (again, generally in the plural) in the second half. But the poet here takes advantage of the familiar pair in a subtly erotic metaphor. We have already noted a metaphoric equivalence between mountains and breasts (2:17) in the recurrent evocation of the beloved's body as landscape. (There is one mountain, not two, here in order to match "hill," which in the anatomical hint has to be singular.) If that is intimated here, then the hill would be a smaller anatomical convexity, the *mons veneris*. As elsewhere, the poet manages to be perfectly decorous in his figurative language and yet hint at sexual actualities.

7. *You are wholly fair, my friend . . .* The poem concludes in an envelope structure that invokes the opening line and adds something to it in what amounts to an incremental repetition.

8 With me from Lebanon, bride,
   with me from Lebanon come.
 Gaze from the peak of Amanah,
   from the peak of Senir and Hermon,
 from the lions' dens,
   from the leopards' mountains.
9 You have captured my heart, my sister, bride.
   You have captured my heart with one glance of your eyes,
    with one bead of your necklace.
10 How beautiful your loving, my sister, bride,
   how much better your loving than wine,
    and the scent of your unguents than all perfumes.
11 Nectar your lips drip, bride,
   honey and milk are under your tongue,

---

8. *with me from Lebanon come.* Why Lebanon? It is, of course, a place of deep forests and natural fragrances. It is also far away to the north and wild, a locus of adventure and perhaps danger, as the introduction of lions and leopards at the end of this verse may suggest. This wild setting for the lovers makes a piquant contrast to the enclosed garden in the second part of the poem.

9. *You have captured my heart.* The verb *libavtini* might be an ad hoc invention, derived from *levav*, "heart." The King James Version renders this a bit more strenuously as "ravished my heart."
 one glance of your eyes. The translation adopts the solution of the Blochs. The literal sense is "one of your eyes," which sounds peculiar in English.

11. *Nectar your lips drip.* The Hebrew is a lovely blur of alliteration: *nofet titofna siftotayikh.* The internal rhyme of "lips drip" seeks to provide a small equivalent of this effect. The same sequence of words occurs in Proverbs 5:3, though there the context is negative because the reference is to the lips of a seductress.
 honey and milk are under your tongue. Milk and honey, most readers will recall, are repeatedly associated with the bounty of the Promised Land. Here the order of the two terms is reversed, perhaps because the poet wanted to stress sweetness; and the beloved's open mouth, eager for kisses, becomes the lover's promised land.

and the scent of your robes
    like Lebanon's scent.
A locked garden, my sister, bride,   12
    a locked well, a sealed spring.
Your branches, an orchard of pomegranates   13
    with luscious fruit,
        henna and spikenard,
spikenard and saffron,   14
    cane and cinnamon
        with every tree of frankincense,
myrrh and aloes
    with every choice perfume.

---

and the scent of your robes / like Lebanon's scent. The landscape of Lebanon, where he invited her to roam with him at the beginning of the poem, now clings through simile to the fragrance of her robes.

12. *A locked garden.* This interpretation has triggered, perhaps understandably, reams of mystical-allegorical interpretation. In the first instance, however, the locked garden is the body of the beloved and the sealed spring her intimate part. For the metaphoric equation between spring or well and female sexuality, see Proverbs 5:15–18.

a locked well. The somewhat unusual Hebrew for "well," *gal,* is close to the word for "garden," *gan,* and may be a scribal error. Many manuscripts as well as the Septuagint show *gan* here.

14. *frankincense.* The Hebrew for this fragrance, *levonah,* puns on *levanon,* "Lebanon."

15   A garden spring,
            a garden of fresh water
                    and streams from Lebanon.
16   —Arise, O north, and come, O south,
                    blow on my garden, let its perfumes flow,
       Let my lover come to his garden
                    and eat its luscious fruit.

---

15. *a garden of fresh water.* The first noun here in the Masoretic text is *gal*, which everywhere else means either "pile of stones" or "wave" and which only by a considerable stretch do various translators render as "spring" or "well." (*Gulah*, a word that has this latter meaning, appears in Joshua 15:19 but is far from phonetically the same as *gal*.) Many Hebrew manuscripts as well as three ancient versions show *gan*, "garden," and the inadvertent substitution of *lamed* for *gimel* is one a scribe could easily have made.

and streams from Lebanon. This presumably means fresh-flowing streams like the ones in the mountains of Lebanon. But it is almost as though there were an underground channel leading from the landscape of Lebanon at the beginning of the poem to this enclosed garden far to the south.

16. *blow on my garden, let its perfumes flow.* The delicate dance between outer and inner, between metaphor and its referent, is beautifully performed here. We are invited to envisage a real garden, blooming with luscious fruit and redolent of natural fragrances, in which the beloved awaits her lover. But because the garden is also a metaphor for her body, her invitation to him to enter the garden is a sexual invitation, and the flowing of perfumes a hint of her physical readiness for him.

—I have come to my garden, my sister, bride,   5:1
  I have gathered my myrrh with my perfume,
I have eaten my honeycomb with my honey,
  I have drunk my wine with my milk.
—Eat, friends, and drink,
   be drunk with loving.

5:1. Despite the chapter break, the first verse of Chapter 5 is clearly the conclusion of this poem.

I have gathered my myrrh. The verb *'arah* is a specialized term for "collecting
honey." The lover's declaration in these two lines is a clear statement that he
has heeded her beckoning and entered her garden.

Eat, friends, and drink, / be drunk with loving. This concluding line of the
poem is formally anomalous because a third person is now speaking, urging
the two lovers to revel in the consummation of their love. If we keep in
mind the anthological character of the Song of Songs, we may infer that this
particular poem was originally an epithalamion, and in accordance with the
conventions of this genre of wedding poem, the bride and groom are exhorted
by a wedding guest or by a kind of chorus to enjoy the pleasures of love.

CHAPTER 5

2 I was asleep but my heart was awake:
    Hark! my lover knocks.
—Open for me, my sister, my friend,
    my dove, my perfect one.
For my head is drenched with dew,
    my locks with the drops of the night.
3 —I have put off my gown,
    how can I don it?
I have bathed my feet,
    how can I besmirch them?

---

2. *I was asleep but my heart was awake.* Those who read this poem as a dream take this double indication as a signal of sleeping consciousness. But as with the poem in 3:1–5, it is equally plausible to understand this as an actual state: she sleeps lightly, restlessly, anxiously awaiting the arrival of her lover, who comes in the middle of the night.

Open for me. The clear reference is to the door, but the sexual hint is also palpable.

For my head is drenched with dew. He mentions this as the reason that she must let him in at once, so that he need not linger anymore in the heavy damp of the night. Of course, there is quite a different reason that he so urgently wants her to open the door for him.

3. *I have put off my gown, / how can I don it?* Obviously, she is eager to open for him but momentarily plays this coy game of teasing her lover, which, to her dismay, has the effect of driving him away.

My lover pulled back his hand from the latch,   4
  and my heart raced within me.
I rose to open for my lover.   5
  My hands dripped myrrh
and my fingers liquid myrrh,
  over the handles of the bolt.
I opened for my lover,   6
  but my lover had slipped off, was gone.
    I went faint when he spoke.
I sought him but did not find him.
  I called him but he did not answer.

---

4. *the latch*. This translation adopts an English equivalent for the Hebrew used by several previous translators. The literal meaning of the original is "hole," a relatively large aperture into which a wooden key was introduced to loosen the bolt locking the door.

my heart raced within me. The Hebrew noun means literally "innards," thought to be the seat of strong feelings. The received text reads *'alaw*, "for him," but the Septuagint and many Hebrew manuscripts show *'alay*, literally "for, or upon me," and that is the reading reflected in this translation.

My hands dripped myrrh / and my fingers liquid myrrh, / over the handles of the bolt. The close focus of her hand on the door vividly dramatizes her eagerness to open for her lover. Perhaps those hands are even fumbling in excitement, adding another moment to her delay. The fact that she has perfumed herself suggests that she has been waiting for her lover to join her. The dripping of fragrant unguent over a lock about to be undone subtly hints at the prospect of female arousal, though no metaphorical equation is put forth.

6. *had slipped off, was gone*. The doubling of the verbs expresses the dire finality of his absence as she looks into the night from the open door.

I sought him but did not find him. These words, which also occur in the poem in Chapter 3, point to the fact that she has gone out into the darkened town to look for him, but that narrative fact is made explicit only in the next verse.

7   The watchmen who go round the town found me.
         They struck me, they wounded me.
     They pulled my veil from me,
            the watchmen of the walls.
8   I make you swear, O daughters of Jerusalem,
               should you find my lover, what shall you tell him?
                  that I am in a swoon of love.
9   —How is your lover more than another,
               O fairest among women?
     How is your lover more than another,
            that thus you make us vow?

---

7. *They struck me, they wounded me.* We now realize how dangerous it is for a woman to go out in the streets at night. The watchmen evidently take her for a prostitute, wandering alone at night. (The story of Tamar, in Genesis 38, who disguises herself as a roadside whore, suggests that prostitutes in the ancient Near East sometimes covered their faces because Tamar's father-in-law Judah does not recognize her. In a moment, we will learn that the young woman is wearing a veil.) The watchmen decide to punish her for her brazenness by beating her and humiliating her through the stripping away of her veil.

8. *I make you swear, O daughters of Jerusalem.* One should probably assume narrative continuity with the immediately preceding encounter with the night watchmen. If all this is a dream, then she simply escapes the watchmen and then encounters the daughters of Jerusalem. If it is not a dream, there would have to be a narrative ellipsis: since these young women would not be out in the town in the middle of the night, one would have to infer that, breaking free of the watchmen, she continues to seek her lover through the night and then, still searching, meets the daughters of Jerusalem on the morrow.

9. *How is your lover more than another.* After she has announced that she is positively faint or ill with longing for her lover, as she did in a previous poem (2:5), the daughters of Jerusalem want to know what is so extraordinary about her lover that should drive her to impose this vow and that should trigger such extreme emotions. This question then becomes the pretext for a *wasf*, a celebration of the beauty of the body of the one beloved that moves down from head to legs.

—My lover is shining white and ruddy,   10
             standing out among ten thousand.
His head is purest gold,   11
      his locks are curls
            black as a raven.
His eyes are like doves   12
        by streams of water
bathing in milk,
        dwelling by a pool.
His cheeks are like beds of spices   13
        sprouting aromatic scents.
His lips are lilies,
        dripping liquid myrrh.

---

10. *shining white and ruddy.* This is a little enigmatic: "ruddy" must refer to his complexion because it cannot refer to his hair, which is black (verse 11). Perhaps the word for "shining white," *tsaḥ*, is meant to convey a general sense of dazzling purity in his appearance. That would accord with the image of the lover as a kind of statue that is developed later in the poem.

12. *bathing in milk.* As elsewhere, the realization of the metaphoric image develops its own momentum. Presumably, the milk bath would be the whites of the eyes and the doves the irises.

    dwelling by a pool. The word for "pool" occurs only here. This seems the most plausible construction, though some interpreters relate it to a word that involves the inlaying of jewels.

13. *sprouting aromatic scents.* The Masoretic text has *migdelot*, "towers of," which could be the right reading, though it is hard to imagine flower beds as towers or a beard (if that is what is on his cheeks) as a tower. The Septuagint and the Vulgate read *megadlot*, "growing" or "sprouting," which this translation follows.

14   His arms are coils of gold
            inset with ruby.
      His loins are fine-wrought ivory,
            with sapphire inlaid.
15   His thighs are ivory pillars
            set on pedestals of gold.
      Like Lebanon his look,
            he is choice as the cedars.

---

14. *His arms are coils of gold . . . His loins are fine-wrought ivory.* In contrast to this celebration of her beauty (4:1–7), in which animal imagery and landscape imagery predominate, with one architectural metaphor, the second half of this poem is a cluster of images of jewels and precious substances, appropriately male in their hardness. The lover becomes a kind of statue so resplendent that it seems virtually the statue of a god. As Ron Hendel has suggested to me, this is one of the poetic features of the Song that encourages allegorical readings in which the lover is in fact God.

15. *Like Lebanon his look.* Since Lebanon was so intimately associated with the cedars grown there and exported to surrounding lands, the clear reference of this verset is to the lover's lofty stature.

  he is choice as the cedars. There is a pun in the Hebrew because the word for "choice," *baḥur*, also means "young man."

His mouth is sweetest drink,
    all of him, delight.
This is my lover and this is my friend,
    O daughters of Jerusalem.

---

16. *His mouth is sweetest drink.* The reversion to the mouth does not really violate the vertical movement of the poem downward because it is a kind of summary at the end: the beloved, having canvassed her lover's beauty from head to foot, returns to the physical site of those kisses that epitomize physical intimacy with him and give her such gratification. *Mamtaqim,* "sweetest drink" (which in modern Hebrew means "candy"), is in biblical usage something sweet that is drunk, as its appearance in Nehemiah 8:10 makes clear. This links the phrase with the beginning of the first poem of the Song, in which the lover's kisses are better than wine: the first thing she says about her lover in the whole sequence of poems is also what she says about him, summarizing what she feels, at the end of this poem.

all of him, delight. "All of him" points to the summarizing gesture here: everything I have said of him, from his golden head to the pedestals of gold on which he stands. The word for "delight" is, more literally, "desirable things," "precious things."

This is my lover and this is my friend. This concluding flourish is a direct rejoinder, triumphant after her enthralled description of him, to the question of the daughters of Jerusalem: "How is your lover more than another?"

CHAPTER 6

Where has your lover gone,
    O fairest among women.
Where has your lover turned
    that we might seek him with you?

—My lover has gone down to his garden,
    to the spice beds,

---

1. *Where has your lover gone.* Despite the chapter division (a late medieval intervention in the text), the first three verses of this chapter are in all probability the conclusion of the poem that began at the beginning of Chapter 5. The young woman has roamed through the streets of the town in search of her lover. When she encounters the daughters of Jerusalem (5:8–9), they ask her what it is about her lover that should have made her so overwrought. She responds by praising her lover's beauty (5:10–16). Hearing this, they now ask her: Well, if he is so extraordinary, where is he? We are ready to go out in search with you, so we can see for ourselves if he is really as you say.

2. *My lover has gone down to his garden.* This is an oblique reference to sexual fulfillment. Her body has been vividly equated with a garden of luscious fruit (4:12–5:1). What she is telling them is that there is no need for them to join her in seeking her lover—she has already found him, and he has been with her in rapturous consummation. If this is a true report and not a boast or fantasy, one can reconstruct the following sequence of events, filling in the narrative hiatus between 5:7 and 5:8: after the assault by the watchmen, she continues her search, finds her lover, and spends the night with him; now on the next day, she meets the daughters of Jerusalem, who may know something about her wandering on the previous night; momentarily, she goes along with their assumption that she is distraught because she is looking for her lover; now, at the conclusion of her speech to them, she joyfully announces that she has in fact found him.

to graze in the garden
    and to gather lilies.
I am my lover's and my lover is mine,   3
    who grazes among the lilies.

—You are fair, my friend, as Tirzah,   4
    lovely as Jerusalem,
        daunting as what looms on high.

---

4. *You are fair, my friend.* These words begin a new poem, spoken by the lover. In the understanding on which this translation is based, the poem continues through verse 10.

fair . . . as Tirzah, / lovely as Jerusalem. Tirzah was for a brief time the capital of the northern kingdom of Israel as Jerusalem was capital of the southern kingdom of Judah. By the time this poem was composed, Tirzah and the northern kingdom had long vanished, so this city as a byword for beauty was either a distant memory or reflects an old line of poetry (or perhaps a proverbial saying) in this poem that was written centuries later.

daunting as what looms on high. The adjective *'ayumah* suggests something like "inspiring awe or trepidation," an emotion that a man might well feel in beholding the ravishing beauty of the woman he desires. The happy solution of "daunting" is borrowed from the Blochs. The simile (a single word in the Hebrew, *kanigdalot*) has perplexed interpreters. It is derived from the same root as *dagul,* "standing out," in 5:10. The Blochs make an elaborate argument that this is a poetic epithet for the stars and hence render the term in their translation as "the stars in their courses." That is a lovely flourish but makes the word more explicitly stellar than the Hebrew warrants because there is no set equation between the root *d-g-l* and stars in biblical usage. It may be preferable to preserve the resonant ambiguity of the Hebrew: she is daunting as something grand and lofty, which might indeed be the stars or might be the two cities just mentioned, both set on promontories.

5   Turn away your eyes from me,
        for they have overwhelmed me.
    Your hair is like a herd of goats
        that have swept down from Mount Gilead.

6   Your teeth are like a flock of ewes
        that have come up from the washing,
    all of them alike
        and none has lost its young.

7   Like cut pomegranate your cheekbones
        through the screen of your tresses.

8   Sixty are there queens
        and eighty concubines
           and young women beyond number.

---

5. *Turn away your eyes from me, / for they have overwhelmed me.* This line transforms the daunting beauty of the previous line into a vividly concrete response to her.

Your hair is like a herd of goats . . . This line, together with everything in verses 6 and 7, is a reprise of 4:1–3, though here 4:3a does not appear, and the pomegranate image comes at the end instead of at the beginning. This sort of verbatim recurrence of lines may reflect the anthological nature of the Song of Songs, in which two or more lines of poetry might have migrated from one poem to another. For elucidation of this line and of verses 6 and 7, see the comments on 4:1–3.

8. *Sixty are there queens.* The Hebrew style here reflects a kind of epic flourish, and the syntactic inversion of the translation seeks to emulate that effect. (One may note that the Hebrew for "they," *heimah,* shows an extra syllable at the end, a form of the word usually reserved for poetry; "are there" in the translation is meant as a stylistic equivalent.) The ascent from sixty to eighty to "beyond number" follows a structural procedure in biblical poetry, in which when a number is introduced in the first verset, it is somehow increased in the second (and here, in the third as well).

concubines. Following "queens," these are probably the king's concubines. The poet could have Solomon in mind.

young women. The Hebrew is *'alamot,* which others translate as "maidens." That choice is in keeping with the quasi-epic style of the line, but the English term could imply virginity, which is not true of the Hebrew. The first two versets invoke a large number of royal consorts; this third adds the whole vast set of nubile young women—all of whom cannot compare to the one and only beloved.

Just one is my dove, my pure one,   9
     just one to her mother,
          dazzling to her who bore her.
The girls saw her and called her happy,
     queens and concubines, and they praised her.
Who is this espied like the dawn,   10
     fair as the moon,
dazzling as the sun,
     daunting as what looms on high?

---

9. *her mother . . . her who bore her.* The parallelism in these two versets follows the standard procedure of biblical poetry in which the normal term is used in first verset, and in the following verset a metaphoric or paraphrastic substitution or an unusual synonym is employed. Again in keeping with biblical poetics, the second term here concretizes the general designation "mother" by focusing on the act of birth, as if the mother were saying: This dazzling beauty has come out of my womb!

dazzling. The Hebrew *barah* means both "pure" and "bright," but the sense of brightness may be more salient here because of the imagery of brilliance in the next verse, where *barah* again appears.

The girls. Literally, "daughters."

queens and concubines. The sequence reverses the order of verse 9: it begins with the general category of "girls" (*banot*) and then proceeds to queens and concubines.

10. *dawn . . . moon . . . sun.* Zakovitch proposes that at dawn both sun and moon can be visible. In any case, the progression moves, as one would expect in biblical poetry, from pale light (the moon) to intense light (the sun). The words for both "sun" and "moon" are feminine, in contrast to their more common synonyms in earlier biblical Hebrew, and the grammatical gender makes them more apt as similes for the beautiful young woman.

11   To the walnut garden I went down
        to see the buds of the brook,
    to see if the vine had blossomed,
        if the pomegranate trees were in flower.
12   I scarcely knew myself,
        she set me in the noblest chariot.

---

11. *To the walnut garden I went down.* This verse and the next, no longer a celebration of the beauty of the beloved, appear to be a new poem or, given their brevity, the fragment of a poem. As elsewhere, there is a studied ambiguity between literal and figurative, outside and inside. At first, the lover's declaration looks like a straightforward report of having gone down into a garden to enjoy the spring landscape, and in light of the vernal ambience of the Song, this is a perfectly plausible reading. The next verse, however, invites us to see the garden as a metaphor.

12. *I scarcely knew myself.* The idiom suggests ecstatic confusion. Shalom Paul has likened it to an Akkadian expression that refers to a condition of mental confoundment.

    she set me in the noblest chariot. The Hebrew collocation 'ami-nadiv is a famous crux. Literally, it would seem to mean "my people-noble." The combination nedivey-'am, "the people's nobles," appears a number of times in biblical poetry, especially archaic poetry (for example, in the Song of the Well, Numbers 21:18, and in the Song of Deborah, Judges 5). The Blochs propose emending the text by reversing the order of the two words; Zakovitch reads it as having the same meaning as nediv-'am even though the order is reversed. The word for "chariot" is in the plural, but plural for singular, perhaps as an epic gesture, is not uncommon in biblical poetry. But what is this chariot? Especially given the statement of ecstasy in the first half of the line, the contention of the Blochs that the noble chariot in which she places him is her body seems convincing. Retrospectively, then, we conclude that the garden of the previous verse is, like the garden in Chapter 4 and above in 6:2, also a metaphor for the beloved's body.

CHAPTER 7

Turn back, turn back, O Shulamite,
    turn back, that we may behold you.
—Why should you behold the Shulamite
    in the dance of the double rows?

---

1. *Turn back, turn back.* The imperative verb *shuvi* does not mean "turn around," as it is understood in some translations. The Shulamite has been dancing and evidently has begun to move away from the group of other dancers, so now these plural speakers—a kind of chorus—invite her to dance again.

Shulamite. The meaning of her name has been disputed. The most probable derivation is from *Shalem*, a shortened form of "Jerusalem," though one should not exclude a punning association with Solomon (*Shelomoh* in Hebrew) and with the verbal root that suggests wholeness.

Why should you behold. This seems to be the speech of a second group. The poem, then, would be composed of an antiphonal exchange between two (presumably male) choruses.

the dance of the double rows. Or "the dance of the double camps." Its choreography is beyond retrieval, but one may imagine two rows of dancers with the Shulamite as the star performer moving between them. The two rows may even be the two choruses.

2   —How fair your feet in sandals,
                O daughter of a nobleman.
        The curves of your thighs like wrought rings,
                the handiwork of a master.
3   Your navel a crescent bowl,
                let mixed wine never lack!
        Your belly a mound of wheat
                hedged about with lilies.
4   Your two breasts like two fawns,
                twins of a gazelle.

---

2. *How fair your feet in sandals*. Though the first Hebrew noun can also mean "steps," the poem is focused on her body parts, not on her movements. As has often been observed, this particular poem in praise of the beauty of the beloved moves from feet to head rather than the other way around because the chorus is watching her dancing; and their eyes are first caught by her moving feet. The antiphonal voice has just challenged this group with a question—why should we gaze on the Shulamite?—and now an answer is provided in the celebration of her beauty.

The curves of your thighs like wrought rings. In this instance, the beauty of the lovely woman is first likened to exquisite artifacts, as in her celebration earlier of her lover's beauty, and only afterward to growing things, animals, and architectural elements. It is worth noting that her thighs, navel, and breasts appear to be visible as she dances, so she may be wearing some sort of diaphanous dress or skimpy tunic. That would give special point to the entreaty, "Turn back, turn back, . . . that we may behold you."

3. *Your navel a crescent bowl*. Sometimes, as Freud famously said of cigars, a navel is just a navel, despite the inclination of some interpreters to see it as an image of a different body part. Nevertheless, the filling of a receptacle with liquid has a certain erotic resonance. But the intention of the line is more general: just as the crescent concavity of her navel should always be filled, she is never to be arid and empty.

mixed wine. The ancient Hebrews, like the Greeks, often mixed strong wine with water.

a mound of wheat. One should note that this poetics has no particular commitment to metaphoric consistency. In the previous line, the navel was likened to a finely crafted bowl; now the belly around it is compared to a mound of wheat. Visually, the two lines trace a counterpoint between the navel's concavity and the gentle convex curve of the belly.

Your neck like an ivory tower,   5
    your eyes like pools in Heshbon
        by the gate of the town of grandees.
Your nose like the tower of Lebanon
    looking out toward Damascus.

---

5. *your eyes like pools in Heshbon.* Heshbon is a Moabite city. Perhaps it was proverbial for its beauty, though if that is the case, the tradition has been lost to us. The simple exoticism of a distant place may have appealed to the poet, as with Lebanon and Damascus.

the town of grandees. The Hebrew *bat-rabim* is literally "daughter of the great ones" or, equally possible, "daughter of the many." These two words are often construed as a place-name, but this translation follows the argument of the Blochs that "daughter" is an epithet for the town (cities are often imagined as women in biblical languages) and that *rabim* has the meaning it sometimes shows elsewhere of "important persons," "masters." It would be in accordance with the use of parallelism in biblical poetry for the poet to introduce a poetic epithet for a place-name that appears in the preceding verset.

Your nose like the tower of Lebanon. Even more than the image of the neck as a tower, this simile is likely to seem incongruous to modern readers, but it reflects both the value set on a long, architecturally elegant nose as a sign of beauty and the tendency of this poetry to follow the momentum of the term of comparison in the simile.

6 Your head upon you like Mount Carmel,
   and the locks of your head are purple.
    A king is caught in the tangle.
7 How fair you are, how sweet,
   O Love, among delights!

8 Your stature was like a palm tree
   and your breasts were like the clusters.
9 I thought: I will climb the palm,
   I will grasp its stalks,

---

6. *like Mount Carmel.* Mount Carmel, overlooking the site of present-day downtown Haifa, is lofty and wooded and thus is an appropriate image for the grandeur of the Shulamite's head. Because the word "mount" does not appear in front of "Carmel" in the Hebrew, some interpreters have taken *karmel* as a homonym that means "farmland," but surely a luxuriant high place is a more apt image for the head. The word is also close to *karmil*, "purple," and so may punningly point toward the color that appears in the next verset, though a different term is used for the color.

the locks of your head are purple. What is probably meant is a black sheen that has purple highlights, but the color is also chosen because *'argaman* is associated with royal raiments, which would be an appropriate link for this "daughter of a nobleman."

A king is caught in the tangle. The king is probably an epithet for the lover, as in 2:4. The other noun in this clause, *rehatim*, is obscure. It might refer to the beams of a loom. The translation choice of "tangle" is dictated by context.

7. *O Love.* The word for "love," *'ahavah*, is capitalized in the translation because it cannot be a designation for the human object of love. Love itself is said to be the sweetest of delights.

8. *Your stature.* These words signal the beginning of a new poem, in which the lover recalls contemplating the fine stature of his beloved and longing to embrace her.

and let your breasts be like grape clusters,
            and the scent of your breath like quince,
and your mouth like goodly wine.   10
            —It flows to my lover smoothly,
                  stirring sleepers' lips to speak.
I am my lover's   11
            and for me his desire.

Come my lover,   12
            Let us go out to the field,
                  spend the night in the henna.
                        There will I give my love to you.

---

9. *let your breasts be like grape clusters.* As he evokes physical intimacy, the comparison moves from date palm to grapes, perhaps because of the general association of wine with kisses and lovemaking.

the scent of your breath like quince. This second verset exhibits the general tendency of poetic parallelism in the Bible to move from a large object or space to something smaller. The word for "breath" is literally "nose," but by metonymy that becomes in biblical usage a term for "breath."

10. *your mouth.* Literally, "your palate."

It flows to my lover smoothly. She now responds to him in midsentence (her response is indicated here typographically by the initial dash). Though the verb used usually means simply "go," in conjunction with this adverb it has the sense of "flow." The "it" appears to refer to the goodly wine of the mouth that he has just mentioned: yes, she says, it is delectable wine that flows straight to my lover, exciting those who sleep to speech where actual wine might be a soporific.

11. *I am my lover's / and for me his desire.* This line is plausibly read as her summarizing affirmation of their love after she has evoked in the previous line the potent effect of her kisses. Some interpreters, however, prefer to see it as the initial line of the next poem.

12. *the henna.* The Hebrew *kefarim* has a homonym that means "villages," which is also possible here, but it seems more likely, as the next verse indicates, that she is inviting him to spend a night in the open air, and *kefarim* in the sense of "henna" is associated earlier with love's pleasures.

13   Let us rise early in the vineyards.
          We shall see if the vine is in flower,
    if the blossoms have opened,
          if the pomegranate trees have budded.

14   The mandrakes give off fragrance
          and at our door all luscious fruit,
    fresh picked and stored as well,
          I have laid up for you, my love.

---

14. *mandrakes.* This plant was thought to be an aphrodisiac, as is evident in the story of the mandrakes found by Reuben (Genesis 30:14–16). It is also quite obvious in the Hebrew that *duda'im*, "mandrakes," plays on *dodai*, "my love" (in the sense of "lovemaking") that she has just used. Either the phonetic closeness of the two words led to the belief that mandrakes were aphrodisiac, or the belief in their power to stimulate desire generated the name for the plant.

give off. The use of this verb pointedly picks up "give" at the end of the previous line.

our door. The Hebrew shows a plural, again a poetic usage.

all luscious fruit . . . I have laid up for you, my love. This is still another instance of the delightfully teasing play between outside and inside, literal and figurative, in which the Song abounds. She has invited him to look at the blossoming world with her. Now they come back to her house, where she announces that she has set aside delicious fruit for him, which could be taken literally. But the concluding verset strongly intimates that the fruit is the delectable pleasures of love that she has scrupulously kept for him alone—"stored" (literally, "old") because she has carefully held these for him, "fresh picked" (literally, "new") because these fruits will have the freshness of the spontaneous gifts of her body.

CHAPTER 8

W ould that you were a brother to me,
     suckling my mother's breasts.
I would find you in the street, would kiss you,
     and they would show no scorn for me.

1

---

1. *suckling my mother's breasts.* This could also be read as a noun phrase: "a suckling of my mother's breasts." That construction would be in keeping with the logic of the biblical parallelism, where the general term in the first verset (here "brother") is followed by some sort of epithet or paraphrase as the equivalent in the second. Second-verset equivalents usually concretize the term that appears in the first. In this instance, we are given the sensual concreteness of the lover sucking the breasts of the beloved's mother, which then is a kind of prolepsis of kissing or sucking the breasts of his beloved.

I would find you in the street. There may be an echo of her desperate search through the streets to find her lover in 3:1–4. In the fantasy of a fraternal bond here, of course, since they are brother and sister, they are free to embrace in full public view, without censure. Her desire for him is so imperative that she wishes she could have unimpeded access to his embraces even when they are out in the streets.

2 I would lead you, I would bring you
   to my mother's house, she would teach me.
 I would give you spiced wine to drink,
   from my pomegranate wine.

3 His left hand beneath my head,
   his right hand embracing me.

4 I make you swear, O daughters of Jerusalem,
   that you shall not rouse nor stir love
    until it pleases.

---

2. *I would lead you, I would bring you*. As elsewhere, it is she who plays an unabashedly active role. The implied narrative sequence is that after having encountered him in the street and having kissed him, she takes him by the hand and leads him back to her mother's house, where they can make love.

she would teach me. Though emendations have often been proposed for this word in the received text, it makes sense as it stands. In many cultures, as several commentators have argued, it is the traditional duty of the mother to instruct her daughter in the art of love, and it looks as if that is what the young woman has in mind here. That role resonates with the initial image of the fantasy, in which the mother's breasts suckle the lover.

spiced wine . . . my pomegranate wine. In biblical Israel and elsewhere in the ancient Mediterranean, spices were sometimes added to wine. As in previous poems in the Song, the wine is a metaphor for the pleasures of love that she now offers him.

3. *His left hand beneath my head / his right hand embracing me.* This line, which repeats 2:6, is a discreet expression of the sexual consummation that she has promised in the previous line or might even refer to their embrace after the consummation. This poem becomes a nice companion piece to the poem in 2:4–7. There it was the lover who brought the beloved to the bedchamber; here it is she who brings him. The parallelism strongly suggests that "the house of wine" in 2:4 is an epithet for the private place where they make love, as here; in her mother's house, she offers him her "spiced wine."

4. *I make you swear, O daughters of Jerusalem . . .* This recurring line, in the present context, concluding this particular poem, suggests something like the following: I make you swear not to interfere and not to urge love's fulfillment before the time is ripe; now I have enjoyed that ripeness in the intimate privacy that is only for me and my lover.

Who is this coming up from the desert   5
    leaning on her lover?

Under the quince tree I roused you.
    There your mother conceived you,
        there she who bore you conceived you.

---

5. *Who is this coming up from the desert / leaning on her lover?* This line, the first verset replicating 3:6a, sounds like the beginning of a poem that has been lost. The next, triadic line is also a fragment lacking context. Although there are occasional brief fragments earlier in the book, two fragments in immediate sequence here may reflect a quandary of the editor as he came to the end of his collection of poems: in the material at his disposal, he had a couple of snippets of poems, perhaps on torn pieces of parchment, that he did not want to discard either because he felt that they had authoritative status or because he saw them as good lines of poetry.

Under the quince tree I roused you. The quince, if that is what the Hebrew *tapuaḥ* is, was earlier associated (2:5) with reviving the young woman faint with passion. Here it is she who addresses him, as the grammatical forms of the Hebrew makes clear. The verb "rouse"—again the woman take sexual initiative—is probably intended in an erotic sense. Thus Rashi: "she says this seeking her lover's affection . . . and it is the language of the wife of one's youth rousing her lover at night as he slumbers, embracing him and kissing him."

There your mother conceived you. This verset and the one that follows are enigmatic. Elaborate explanations have been proposed, from mythological to zoological. The simplest possibility is that an act of love was once consummated under this tree, and the young woman now proposes a new consummation—in a way, a reenactment. The editorial placement of this line here was probably encouraged by the role of the mother in verses 1 and 2 above.

she who bore you. The vocalization of the Masoretic text indicates a verb, "she bore you" (*yeladetkha*), but the conventions of parallelism would lead us to expect a poetic substitution for the noun "mother" in the preceding verset (thus the translation supposes *yoladetkha*), and this is in fact the vocalization reflected in the Septuagint and in one version of the Syriac.

6   Set me as a seal on your heart,
         as a seal on your arm.
   For strong as death is love,
         fierce as Sheol is jealousy.
   Its sparks are fiery sparks,
         a fearsome flame.

7   Many waters cannot
        put out love
             nor rivers sweep it away.
   Should a man give
        all the wealth of his house for love,
            they would surely scorn him.

---

6. *Set me as a seal on your heart, / as a seal on your arm.* Some commentators see this line as still another fragment, but it works perfectly well as the initial line of the poem that follows.

fierce as Sheol is jealousy. Many modern interpreters prefer to understand the noun *qin'ah* as "passion," but most of its biblical usages indicate jealousy, which makes perfectly good sense here.

a fearsome flame. The word for "flame" has the theophoric suffix *yah*, but this translation follows the scholarly consensus that it is used here as an intensifier, with no theological implication. This would be consistent with the rest of the Song of Songs, where God is neither mentioned nor at issue in the poems.

7. *Many waters cannot / put out love.* The "many waters" may have some mythological resonance as the primordial waters of creation and (as in Psalms) of the great cosmic sea. This poem differs somewhat from the others in the collection because it is less a direct address by one of the lovers to the other than a celebration of the power of love, though this does not preclude the possibility, if verse 6a is the beginning of the poem, that it is spoken by the beloved to her lover.

We have a little sister   8
      and she has no breasts.
What shall we do for our sister
      on the day she is spoken for?
If she is a wall,   9
      we will build on her a silver turret.
If she is a door,
      we will besiege her with cedar boards.

---

8. *We have a little sister.* This poem, too, differs from the others: here a group of brothers, acting as a kind of chorus, contemplates, perhaps apprehensively, the conjugal future of their prepubescent sister. We may be invited to recall the spiteful brothers who punished their sexually active sister by making her a keeper of vineyards (1:6). It is quite possible that this verse and the one that follows amount to a flashback: the decidedly nubile sister (verse 10) thinks back to the moment when her brothers were nervous about her approaching puberty.

and she has no breasts. The supple, beautiful breasts of the young woman are a recurrent feature of the love poems.

9. *If she is a wall.* The reference is probably to being closed off from the dangers of the potential suitors or seducers. (The locked garden of Chapter 4 is a partial analogy.)

we will build on her a silver turret. Though the precise meaning of the Hebrew noun is in dispute, it is most plausibly understood in this context as some sort of ornament, perhaps to be given as a reward for her protecting her virginity. Zakovitch cites the Talmudic "city of gold," an ornament worn by brides, as a possible analogue.

we will besiege her with cedar boards. This verset is obscure. The most likely sense is an expression of hostility by the brothers toward their sister, as in 1:6. That is, if she is a door, which unlike a wall opens up to let people in, instead of bedecking her with silver ornaments, we will lay siege against her with siege engines made of cedar wood. Despite the efforts of some interpreters to understand the verb here as indicating something less hostile, the plain meaning of *tsur 'al* is "to lay siege against." The brothers, then, cast themselves as guardians of the family honor, prepared to punish their sister if she betrays it.

10   —I am a wall
                and my breasts are like towers.
        Then I was in his eyes
                like a town that finds peace.

11   A vineyard Solomon had
                in the Vale of Wealth.
        He gave the vineyard to the keepers:
                each would get from its fruit
                        a thousand silver shekels.

---

10. *I am a wall / and my breasts are like towers.* She now offers a vigorous rejoinder to the remembered speech of her brothers. She is a wall, she knows perfectly well how to protect herself from unwanted suitors; and contrary to the moment years earlier when she was a physically undeveloped little sister, she is a sexually mature woman with palpably prominent breasts of which she is proud.

in his eyes. The implied antecedent to "his" must be her one true lover.

like a town that finds peace. The Hebrew merely has "like one [feminine] who finds peace." Towns are invariably feminine in biblical Hebrew and are sometimes referred to as mother or daughter or personified as a woman. In the context of "wall" (the term for the wall of a city, not of a house) in the previous line, it seems plausible that she who finds peace is the city. To complete the walled city metaphor of her rejoinder to her brothers: for her lover the town opens its gates, allowing him to enter peacefully—there is neither siege nor conflict, only a happy welcoming.

11. *the Vale of Wealth.* The Hebrew *ba'al hamon* definitely looks like a place-name, but it is probably meant to be thematically significant. For this reason, the name is translated rather than transliterated. *Ba'al* does not actually mean "vale" but is a component of many biblical place-names, probably because the Canaanite god Baal was once worshipped at these places. The word for "wealth," *hamon*, is phonetically akin to *hon*, "wealth" in verse 7.

a thousand silver shekels. The Hebrew only says "a thousand silver."

My vineyard is my own.   12
     You can have the thousand, Solomon,
          and two hundred for the keepers of its fruit.

You who dwell in the garden,   13
     friends listen for your voice.
         Let me hear it.

---

12. *My vineyard is my own.* Given the way "vineyard" is used in 1:6 and "garden" elsewhere, she is almost certainly referring to the precious treasures of her body. Vineyards, of course, were economically important in ancient Israel. The idea that her private vineyard is worth far more than King Solomon's large revenue-producing vineyard is clearly in keeping with "Should a man give / all the wealth of his house for love, / they would surely scorn him."

13. *You who dwell in the garden.* The conjugated verb is feminine, so we know it is the lover addressing the young woman. As with a few other nouns in the Song, the Hebrew for "garden" shows a poetic plural. The beloved, as in Chapters 4 and 5, is in a garden and is also herself a garden.

friends listen for your voice. This is a little obscure. The probable meaning is that friends—his, hers, anyone amicably disposed—are eager to hear her sweet voice, as is the lover himself in 2:14.

Let me hear it. But he seems to want her to speak for him alone. The single Hebrew word represented by these four English words is really not metrically sufficient to constitute a verset in a line of poetry, and the syntax is somewhat problematic. All of this makes the whole line look textually suspect.

14   —Flee my lover and be like a deer
            or like a gazelle
                    on the spice mountains.

---

14. *Flee my lover and be like a deer.* It is appropriate that the book ends with a lovers' dialogue. He speaks one line of poetry (verse 13), and she answers with an antithetical line of poetry (verse 14). Both lines are triadic, a kind of line often used in biblical poetry to mark some sort of closure.

on the spice mountains. Like so much in the Song, this phrase and the imperative verb that precedes it point in two directions. Again, the purposeful ambiguity between outside and inside, literal and figurative, is invoked. Ostensibly, she is saying that he must run away to the distant mountains (perhaps after a night of love, though that is by no means clear). But her breasts have been represented figuratively as mountains, and "spice mountains" (or more literally, "mountains of fragrances") would be an apt designation for them. This entire line recalls 2:17 (see the comment on that verse), with *harey besamim*, "spice mountains," similar in form to *harey bater*, "cloven mountains," in 2:17. In what might be understood as a lover's teasing invitation, she urges him to run away—to the amorous haven of her waiting body.

THE BOOK OF RUTH

TO THE READER

Is RUTH IN FACT a Late Biblical book? Although this is the consensus of biblical scholars, there are some vocal dissenters. These tend to take at face value the assertion of the opening verse that we are reading a story that goes back to the period of the Judges—an assertion that led, as perhaps the author of Ruth intended, to the placement of the book between Judges and Samuel in the Septuagint and consequently in the Christian canonical order of the Bible. Some of the dissenters evoke the pure classical style of Ruth that in many ways sounds like the Hebrew of the early first millennium BCE.

But style is actually the clearest evidence of the lateness of Ruth. The writer took pains to create a narrative prose redolent of the early centuries of Israelite history, but it is very difficult to execute such a project of archaizing without occasional telltale slips, as one can see in the Hebrew of the frame story of Job. Here, there are at least a dozen terms that reflect distinctive Late Biblical usage—as, for example, the verbs used for taking a wife (1:7), for wait or hope (1:13), and for removing a sandal (4:7), and another ten idiomatic collocations occur that never appear in earlier biblical texts.

The other strong sign of Ruth's composition in the period after the return from Babylonian exile in the fifth century BCE is its genre. The book is still another manifestation of the veritable explosion of new narrative genres that characterizes the Late Biblical period. For all the polemic thrust of this text (to which we will turn momentarily), it is basically an idyll, quite unlike any of the narratives written during the First Temple period. The setting is bucolic—Bethlehem is a small town, scarcely a city, and the action of the two central chapters takes place outside the town, in the fields and on the threshing floor. Harvesting

and agriculture are a palpable presence in the story. Unlike the narratives from Genesis to Kings, where even pastoral settings are riven
with tensions and often punctuated by violence, the world of Ruth is
a placid bucolic world, where landowner and workers greet each other
decorously with blessings in the name of the LORD, and where traditional practices such as the levirate marriage and leaving unpicked ears
of grain for the poor are punctiliously observed. The idyllic nature of
the book is especially evident in its characters. In the earlier biblical
narratives, character is repeatedly seen to be fraught with inner conflict and moral ambiguity. Even such presumably exemplary figures in
the national history as Jacob, Joseph, David, and Solomon exhibit serious weaknesses, sometimes behaving in the most morally questionable
ways. In Ruth, by contrast, there are no bad people. Orpah, who turns
back to Moab, leaving Naomi, is devoted to her mother-in-law and is
merely following Naomi's exhortation. She is a good person, only less
good than Ruth. The unnamed kinsman of the last chapter is also not
a bad person, merely less exemplary than Boaz in his unwillingness to
take on a Moabite wife with all that might entail. In sum, this idyllic
narrative is one of the few truly successful stories in any literature that
concentrates almost exclusively on good people.

Ruth's Moabite origins have led many interpreters—convincingly, in
my view—to see this story as a quiet polemic against the opposition of
Ezra and Nehemiah to intermarriage with the surrounding peoples when
the Judeans returned to their land in the fifth century BCE. The author
may have picked up a hint from 1 Samuel 23:4, where David, said here
to be Ruth's great-grandson, is reputed to have placed his parents under
the protection of the king of Moab to keep them safe from Saul. Readers
should note that for biblical Israel, Moab is an extreme negative case of
a foreign people. A perennial enemy, its origins, according to the story of
Lot's daughter in Genesis 19, are in an act of incest. The Torah actually
bans any sort of intercourse, social, cultic, or sexual, with the Moabites.
Against this background of hostility, Moab in this story provides refuge
for the family of Elimelech fleeing from famine (like Abraham, Isaac,
and Jacob), and the two Moabite daughters-in-law are faithful, loving
women, with Ruth's moral nobility altogether exemplary. It is this that
Boaz is aware of from the outset, and he is in no way put off by Ruth's
identity as a Moabite, unlike the kinsman who declines to perform the

levirate obligation. Ruth is a perfectly virtuous Moabite—'*eshet ḥayil*, a "worthy woman"—who becomes the progenitrix of the royal line of the Judean kingdom. It is hard not to see in the boldly iconoclastic invention of this plot an argument against the exclusionary policy on foreign wives propagated by Ezra and Nehemiah. This would also make the fifth century BCE, at the moment when intermarriage was an urgent issue, a plausible time for the composition of the book.

It is remarkable that a story in all likelihood framed for a polemic purpose should be so beguiling. Charm is not a characteristic that one normally associates with biblical narrative, but this idyll is charming from beginning to end, understandably making it one of the most perennially popular biblical books. If the writer set out to make Ruth the Moabite a thoroughly good person in order to implement his argument for openness to exogamy, he also had a rare gift for making good characters convincing, manifested from the very beginning in Naomi's solicitous speech to her daughters-in-law and then in Ruth's unforgettable pledge of devotion to her. This author was finely aware of the conventions of earlier biblical narrative as he was sensitive to the prose style of his predecessors, but he subtly adapted those conventions to his own artistic and thematic ends. He clearly is familiar with the betrothal type-scene that plays an important role in Genesis and early Exodus, but in his canny version, it is a young woman, not a young man, who encounters her future spouse near a well in a foreign land, and the foreign land, paradoxically, is Judah, which she will then make her homeland, "coming back" with Naomi to a place where she has never been.

Another recurrent device of classical biblical narratives is the use of the first piece of dialogue assigned to a character to define the distinctive nature of the character. That procedure is splendidly realized in Ruth's first speech, addressed to Naomi, in Chapter 1. The lyric suasive force of her speech should be noticed, for it is the first signal instance of one of the appealing features of the prose of the Book of Ruth. Earlier biblical narrative often introduces brief poetic insets into the prose—formal poems, sometimes just a line or two in length, that mark a portentous juncture of the story, a blessing or a prayer or an elegy (the valedictory words of Rebekah's family to her as she leaves to become Isaac's bride, Jacob's cadenced cry of dismay when he believes Joseph has been torn apart by a wild beast). In Ruth, on the other hand, the dialogue repeatedly glides into parallel structures that have a strong rhythmic quality and sound rather like verse but do not entirely scan as formal poetry. Naomi's relatively long speech to her daughters-in-law abounds in loose parallel structures and emphatic repetitions, culminating in one parallelism that actually scans as verse in the Hebrew: "would you wait for them till they grew up? / For them would you be deprived of husbands?" Ruth's beautifully cadenced response is still closer to poetry: "For wherever you go, I will go / and wherever you lodge, I will lodge. / Your people is my people, / and your god is my god."

These gestures toward poetry continue to mark the speech of the characters down to the words of blessing of the townswomen near the end of the last chapter. The balance, the rhythmic poise, the stately symmetries of the language are an apt manifestation of the harmonious world of the Book of Ruth: the characters express a kind of moral confidence ultimately stemming from a sense of the rightness of the traditional values of loyalty, love, and charity and of the sustaining force of providence even in the face of adversity. All this taken together, consummated with the most finely managed artistry, makes the Book of Ruth one of literature's most touching stories with a happy ending.

CHAPTER 1

And it happened in the days when the judges ruled that there was a famine in the land, and a man went from Bethlehem to sojourn in the plains of Moab, he and his wife and his two sons. And the man's name was Elimelech, and his wife's name was Naomi, and the names of his two sons were Mahlon and Chilion, Ephrathites from Bethlehem of Judah.

---

1. *when the judges ruled.* The "judges" (*shoftim*) are tribal chieftains, as in the Book of Judges. This initial notice led the Septuagint, and the Christian canon afterward, to place the Book of Ruth in the Former Prophets, after Judges.

2. *And the man's name.* All the names appear to have symbolic meaning, though perhaps that is not entirely certain. Elimelech means "my God is king." Naomi, as she herself points out in 1:20, suggests "sweet" or "pleasant." Unlike these two names, which have some sort of general currency, the two sons' names, Mahlon and Chilion, mean "sickness" and "destruction" and so are manifestly schematic names pointing to the fate of their bearers and would not have been used in reality.

Bethlehem of Judah. "Bethlehem" signifies "house of bread," a meaning that will be fully activated in the grain harvest during which the main action takes place. Because it is a generic name for any town in a region where grain is cultivated, the writer stipulates "of Judah" to distinguish it from at least one other Bethlehem.

3 And they came to the plains of Moab and they were there. And Elimelech,
4 Naomi's husband, died, and she, together with her two sons, was left. And
they took for themselves Moabite wives. The name of one was Orpah and
5 the name of the other Ruth. And they dwelled there some ten years. And
the two of them, Mahlon and Chilion, died as well, and the woman was
6 left of her two children and of her husband. And she rose, she and her
daughters-in-law, and turned back from the plains of Moab, for she had
heard in the plains of Moab that the LORD had singled out His people to
7 give them bread. And she went out from the place where she had been,
with her two daughters-in-law, and they went on the way to go back to the
8 land of Judah. And Naomi said to her two daughters-in-law: "Go back,
each of you to her mother's house. May the LORD do kindness with you
9 as you have done with the dead and with me. May the LORD grant that
you find a settled place, each of you in the house of her husband." And

---

4. *Orpah*. Orpah points to the word for "nape," another name dictated by plot
function, because in the end she necessarily turns her back on Naomi to head
back to Moab. Elsewhere, turning the nape is a sign of flight; here it merely
focuses on Naomi's vision of Orpah as she turns around, after all a devoted
daughter-in-law only following her mother-in-law's exhortation.

Ruth. There is some uncertainty about the meaning of this name. It might
be a defective spelling of *re'ut*, "friendship," or it might derive from the verbal
stem *r-w-h*, which suggests "well-watered" or "fertile." It is also possible that
the name has no thematic meaning.

dwelled. First they came merely to "sojourn." Now they "dwell" in Moab for
a decade, threatening to become expatriates.

6. *turned back*. The whole story turns on four thematic key words—three are
verbs, *lashuv*, "to go back or return," *lalekhet*, "to go," *lidboq*, "to cling." These
verbs, as we shall see, will acquire complicated and even paradoxical meanings.
The fourth term is a noun, *ḥesed*, "kindness" (but also implying something like
"faithfulness" or "loyalty"). The word first appears in verse 8.

bread. This Hebrew term, *leḥem*, is probably a synecdoche for "food" as it
often is elsewhere, though there is special emphasis on bread because of the
barley harvest in the fields around Bethlehem.

9. *a settled place*. The literal meaning of the Hebrew word is "rest." In combination with *naḥalah*, "inheritance," the word *menuḥah* implies "settling down
somewhere in comfort and security."

she kissed them, and they raised their voice and wept. And they said to 10
her, "But with you we will go back to your people." And Naomi said, "Go 11
back, my daughters, why should you go with me? Do I still have sons in
my womb who could be husbands to you? Go back, my daughters, go, for 12
I am too old to have a husband. Even had I thought 'I have hope. This
very night I shall have a husband and bear sons,' would you wait for them 13
till they grew up? For them would you be deprived of husbands? No, my
daughters, for it is far more bitter for me than for you because the LORD's
hand has come out against me." And they raised their voice and wept once 14
more, and Orpah kissed her mother-in-law, but Ruth clung to her. And 15
she said "Look, your sister-in-law has gone back to her people. Go back

---

11. *Do I still have sons in my womb who could be husbands to you?* Naomi here
refers explicitly to the practice of *yibum*, levirate marriage: when a husband
dies, leaving no male offspring, one of his brothers is obliged to marry the
widow and beget children with her, serving as a kind of proxy for his deceased
brother. The obligation of levirate marriage is at issue in the story of Tamar
in Genesis 38. It is worth noting that she becomes the progenitrix of the line
that will lead to David, like Ruth, who is only three generations removed from
David. In Chapter 4 here the practice of *yibum* is extended beyond brothers-
in-law to kinsmen, which differs from Genesis.

13. *would you wait for them till they grew up? For them would you be deprived
of husbands?* These clauses are the first manifestation of a pronounced tendency in Ruth to cast dialogue in cadenced parallel statements that are loose
approximations of parallelistic poetry. This approximation will become tighter
in Ruth's first speech.
    bitter. In verse 20, Naomi will explicitly say this is the antonym to her name.
    the LORD's hand has come out against me. The wording suggests something
close to an attack.

14. *Orpah kissed her mother-in-law.* In context, the obvious implication is that
this is a farewell kiss as she turns her "nape," *'oref,* to Naomi and heads home.
She is a good woman but less resolute than Ruth.

15. *Go back.* This is the plain meaning of this verb, for Moab is Ruth's place of
origin; then, paradoxically, she will be said to "go back" to Judah, a land where
she has never been.

16 after your sister-in-law." And Ruth said, "Do not entreat me to forsake
you, to turn back from you. For wherever you go, I will go. And wherever
you lodge, I will lodge. Your people is my people, and your god is my god.
17 Wherever you die, I will die, and there will I be buried. So may the LORD
18 do to me or even more, for only death will part you and me." And she saw
that she was insisting on going with her, and she ceased speaking to her.
19 And the two of them went until they came to Bethlehem, and it happened
as they came to Bethlehem that the whole town was astir over them, and
20 the women said, "Is this Naomi?" And she said, "Do not call me Naomi.

---

16. *lodge.* The verb *lun* means "to spend the night while traveling or wandering,"
so Ruth scarcely envisages a comfortable and stable lot in following Naomi.

Your people is my people, and your god is my god. There was no real process
of conversion in the ancient Near East. If a person considered residence in a
different country, he or she would in the natural course of things embrace the
worship of the local god or gods. One should therefore not imagine that Ruth
has become a theological monotheist, only that she is recognizing that if she
follows Naomi to her people in Judah, she will also adopt the god of the country.

17. *Wherever you die, I will die, and there will I be buried.* Ruth's moving speech,
with its fine resonance of parallel clauses, appropriately ends on the note of
death: she will always remain with Naomi in the trajectory of a whole life until
death. The procedure of biblical narrative of defining a character by his or her
initial speech is vividly deployed here, showing Ruth as the perfect embodi-
ment of loyalty and love for her mother-in-law.

19. *the whole town.* This is a perfect illustration of the fact that biblical *'ir*
usually means "town," not "city." Bethlehem, far from being a walled city, is a
modest agricultural town with small cultivated fields on its outskirts.

was astir. It would have been a notable event in this small town that Naomi,
having entirely disappeared for ten years, should suddenly reappear, with a
young woman in tow. This would have triggered gossip and speculation among
the townswomen. The women focus on Naomi, not paying attention to the
young woman with her.

the women. The Hebrew merely says "they," but the plural verb is conjugated
in the feminine. It is noteworthy that throughout the first chapter women alone
have been active characters, the men briefly introduced only to die. This is
surely a point of departure from the patriarchal norm of classical Hebrew narrative, where there are some strong female characters but the men predominate.

Call me Mara, for Shaddai has dealt great bitterness to me. I went out full, 21
and empty did the Lord bring me back. Why should you call me Naomi
when the Lord has borne witness against me and Shaddai has done me
harm?" And Naomi came back, and her daughter-in-law with her who was 22
coming back from the plains of Moab. And they had come to Bethlehem
at the beginning of the barley harvest.

---

20. *Mara* This name would mean "bitter," the antithesis of the sweetness suggested by the name Naomi.

21. *the Lord has borne witness against me and Shaddai has done me harm.* These
two parallel clauses are entirely scannable as poetry, with three accented syl-
lables in each half of the line in Hebrew. Because of the poetic requirement of
synonymous substitution, Naomi, after invoking the standard term, "the Lord"
(YHWH) in the first verse, uses a poetic or archaic alternative in the second
verse, "Shaddai" (in traditional translations, "the Almighty"). In fact, elsewhere
"Shaddai" unattached to *'el,* "God," appears only in poetry.

22. *Naomi came back, and her daughter-in-law with her who was coming back.*
The paradox here is thematically pointed. Naomi is of course coming back to
her homeland. Ruth is "coming back from the plains of Moab," which is her
homeland, because she is united in purpose with Naomi and has in a sense
already made the land of Judah, to which she comes for the first time, her new
homeland. This paradox will be further enriched by the allusion in the next
chapter to Abraham's migration from a land in the east to Canaan.
    And they had come to Bethlehem at the beginning of the barley harvest. This
notation clearly sets the agricultural scene where all the subsequent action will
unfold. The harvesting bears out the word Naomi heard in Moab that the Lord
had remembered his people to give them bread, and the fertility of the land also
adumbrates Ruth's destined fertility.

CHAPTER 2

1 And Naomi had a kinsman through her husband, a man of worth from
2 the clan of Elimelech, and his name was Boaz. And Ruth the Moabite
said to Naomi, "Let me go, pray, to the field, and glean from among the
ears of grain after I find favor in his eyes." And she said to her, "Go, my

---

1. *a man of worth.* The original meaning of *gibor ḥayil* is "valiant warrior," but
in the idyllic setting of the Book of Ruth, its meaning is extended to an entirely
pacific sense—a landholder of substantial means. It is the same designation
that is applied to the "worthy woman" of Proverbs 31:8, and later this feminine
form of the epithet will be attached to Ruth.

his name was Boaz. Though the meaning of the name is not altogether trans-
parent, and though it may not be meant to be symbolic, a tradition going back
to Late Antiquity associates it with a Hebrew root signifying "strength."

2. *Ruth the Moabite.* She is explicitly identified as a Moabite to underscore the
seeming contradiction of a foreign woman going out to take advantage of the Israelite law (Leviticus 19:9–10) enjoining agriculturalists to leave what the reapers
failed to garner for the poor to pick up.

after I find favor in his eyes. Ruth exercises a kind of nervous reticence in
regard to Naomi's prosperous relative, who has no doubt been pointed out to
her by her mother-in-law, in not mentioning him by name. She realizes that
she will be dependent on Boaz's goodwill and so says she will not glean until
he has shown himself favorable toward her. In the event, she begins gleaning
before that happens.

daughter." And she went and came and gleaned in the field behind the 3
reapers, and it chanced that she came upon the plot of Boaz, who was
from the clan of Elimelech. And look, Boaz was coming from Bethle- 4
hem, and he said to the reapers, "May the LORD be with you!" and they
said, "May the LORD bless you!" And Boaz said to his lad who was 5
stationed over the reapers, "Whose is this young woman?" And the lad 6
stationed over the reapers answered and said, "She is a young Moabite
woman who has come back with Naomi from the plain of Moab. And 7

---

3. *it chanced that she came upon the plot of Boaz.* This is hardly an accident
because that is precisely where she intended to go. The peculiar formulation
may be meant to suggest that there is a concordance between human initiative
and God's providence.

4. *And look, Boaz was coming from Bethlehem.* His home would be in town and
the cultivated fields he owns outside the town.

May the LORD be with you! The exchange of greetings here perfectly expresses
the harmonious and traditional world of the Book of Ruth: master and workmen
bless each other cordially in the name of the LORD.

5. *lad.* Though the Hebrew noun *na'ar* does designate a young man, it is very
often extended, as here, to refer to anyone in a position of subservience. Boaz's
overseer of the reapers is surely not a stripling and may well be a man of mature
years.

Whose is this young woman? We now learn that the widow Ruth is young,
appearing to Boaz as a *na'arah*, a nubile young woman. He of course does not
know until his overseer tells him that she is a Moabite. The use of "whose"
reflects his assumption that she must be under the authority of her father's
house.

6. *has come back.* In the words of the overseer, Ruth's emigration from Moab is
again assimilated to Naomi's coming back to Judah.

she said, 'Let me glean, pray, and gather from among the sheaves
behind the reapers.' And she has come and stood since the morning
8 till now. She has barely stayed in the house." And Boaz said to Ruth,
"Have you not heard, my daughter—do not go to glean in another field,
and also do not pass on from here, and so shall you cling to my young
9 women. Your eyes be on the field in which they reap and go after them.
Have I not charged the lads not to touch you? Should you be thirsty,
you shall go to the pitchers and drink from what the lads draw from
10 the well." And she fell on her face and bowed to the ground and said

---

7. *gather from among the sheaves*. She would not be picking up sheaves but
rather ears of grain that had fallen from the sheaves.

she has come and stood since the morning till now. This is obviously testimony
to Ruth's assiduousness at her task of gleaning.

She has barely stayed in the house. The Hebrew text, which reads literally,
"This is her staying in the house a bit," seems garbled, and so the translation is
no more than a guess.

8. *Have you not heard, my daughter*. This form of address appears to imply that
Boaz is a mature man, perhaps a decade or two older than Ruth, who may be
in her early twenties.

and so shall you cling to my young women. First Ruth clings to Naomi. Now,
in this thematically fraught word, which will be repeated, she is enjoined to
cling to Boaz's servant girls.

9. *Your eyes be on the field*. "Be" is merely implied in the Hebrew.

Have I not charged the lads not to touch you? A nubile young woman (and,
probably, an attractive one) might well be subjected to sexual advances from
these farmhands.

drink from what the lads draw from the well. "The well" is merely implied by
the verb, which is used only for drawing water from a well. What we have here
is a piquant reversal of the traditional betrothal type-scene: instead of a future
bridegroom encountering a young woman, *na'arah*, at a well in a foreign land,
there is a young woman, *na'arah*, in a land foreign to her but homeland to the
others, for whom *ne'arim* will draw water.

to him, "Why should I find favor in your eyes to recognize me when I
am a foreigner?" And Boaz answered and said, "It was indeed told me, 11
all that you did for your mother-in-law after your husband's death, and
that you left your mother and your father and the land of your birth to
come to a people that you did not know in time past. May the LORD 12
requite your actions and may your reward be complete from the LORD
God of Israel under Whose wings you have come to shelter." And she 13
said, "May I find favor in the eyes of my lord, for you have comforted
me and have spoken to the heart of your servant when I could scarcely
be like one of your slave girls." And Boaz said to her at mealtime, 14
"Come here and eat of the bread and dip your crust in vinegar." And
she sat alongside the reapers, and he bundled together roasted grain

---

10. *when I am a foreigner.* These words are fraught with poignancy and thematic point. As a foreigner, Ruth feels she has no right to expect favors from
the Judahites. In fact, the plot will manifest how she "clings" to this new community and becomes an integral part of it.

11. *you left your mother and your father and the land of your birth.* These words
are the most significant literary allusion in the book. They explicitly echo God's
first words to Abraham in Genesis 12:11, "Go forth from your land and your
birth place and your father's house." Now it is a woman, and a Moabite, who
reenacts Abraham's long trek from the East to Canaan. She will become a
founding mother of the nation as he was the founding father. Ruth's paradoxical
journey outward from home that proves to be a "going back" to home has been
aptly summarized by Herbert Marks: these "brief chapters outline the two principal archetypes of Western narrative, the Abrahamic myth of definitive rupture
and the Odysseian myth of ultimate return, the journey home."

14. *mealtime.* The meal after the arrival of a stranger at a well in a foreign land
is still another motif of the betrothal type-scene.
      dip your crust in vinegar. This homey detail neatly catches the pastoral qual-
ity of the idyll.

15 for her, and she ate and was sated and left some over. And she rose to
glean, and Boaz charged his lads, saying, "Among the sheaves, too, she
16 may glean, and you shall not harass her. And also she may certainly
take her share from the loose ears of grain and glean, and you shall
17 not chide her." And she gleaned in the field till evening and beat out
18 what she had gleaned, and it came to almost an *ephah* of barley. And
she carried it and came to the town, and her mother-in-law saw what
she had gleaned. And she took out and gave to her what she had left
19 over after being sated. And her mother-in-law said to her, "Where did
you glean today and where did you work? May he who recognized you
be blessed!" And she told her mother-in-law how she had worked with
him, and she said, "The name of the man with whom I worked today

---

15. *Among the sheaves, too, she may glean.* Boaz makes a point of offering Ruth
the opportunity to collect a generous abundance of grain, not just solitary ears
left by the reapers in the standing barley.

16. *take her share.* The use of the verb *sh-l-l* here is unusual because it usually
means "to take booty." The evident idea is that she will have a windfall of good
takings, like someone who reaps booty after a victory.

17. *beat out what she had gleaned.* This would be to get rid of the chaff.

18. *what she had left over after being sated.* This refers to what she left over from
the midday meal, as reported in verse 14. What she gives to Naomi here is not
the garnered grain but prepared food. This story that began in hunger now
manifests an abundance of food.

19. *recognized.* The sense of the verb is obviously to single out or show special
attention, as in verse 10 above. But it is a key verb in the Jospeh story, and there
is an underlying sense in which Boaz "recognizes" Ruth as a true daughter of
Naomi and a fit mate for himself.

is Boaz." And Naomi said to her daughter-in-law, "Blessed is he to the 20
LORD, Who has not forsaken His kindness with the living and with
the dead!" And Naomi said to her, "The man is related to us, he is of
our redeeming kin." And Ruth the Moabite said, "Moreover, he said to 21
me, 'To the lads who are mine shall you cling until they finish all the
harvest that is mine.'" And Naomi said to Ruth her daughter-in-law, 22
"It is good, my daughter, that you shall go out with his young women,
and that they not trouble you in another field." And she clung to Boaz's 23
young women to glean till the barley harvest and the wheat harvest
were finished. And she stayed with her mother-in-law.

---

20. *Who has not forsaken His kindness with the living and with the dead!* All this
echoes, with perfect thematic appropriateness, Orpah's and Ruth's exemplary
behavior observed by Naomi in 1:8.

he is of our redeeming kin. "Redeemer" throughout the story signifies a legal,
familial function. If a childless woman is widowed, a male kin can "redeem"
her through marriage, assuring that through him her inheritance will not be
lost and providing her offspring. Naomi is careful to say "of our redeeming kin,"
properly implying that there may be other candidates in the family, as proves
the case in Chapter 4.

22. *trouble you.* The verb here has almost a sense of "interfere with," but that
British usage is a little too explicitly sexual to adopt in the translation.

CHAPTER 3

1 And Naomi her mother-in-law said to her, "My daughter, shall I not
2 seek for you a settled place for you, that it be well for you? And now, is
not Boaz our kinsman with whose young women you were winnowing
3 barley at the threshing floor tonight? And you must bathe and anoint
yourself and put on your garments and go down to the threshing floor.
Do not let yourself be known to the man till he has finished eating and
4 drinking. And it will be, when he lies down, that you will know the
place where he lies down, and you shall come and uncover his feet and

---

1. *a settled place*. See the note on 1:10. In both instances, Naomi associates the
Hebrew term *manoaḥ* with the security and tranquillity of married life.

3. *you must bathe and anoint yourself and put on your garments*. These instructions initiate a chain of details in the nocturnal encounter between Ruth and
Boaz that almost teasingly hint at an erotic experience, but such an experience
is pointedly not consummated. Here Ruth is enjoined to wash her body and
anoint it (perhaps with fragrant oils) and dress herself (perhaps finely).

Do not let yourself be known to the man. The verb "to know" is reiterated in
the episode. In its active form, it can have a sexual meaning in biblical usage,
so it plays a role in the erotic tease of the narrative.

till he has finished eating and drinking. In this, Naomi is calculating that Boaz
will be in a good mood after eating and drinking, a calculation confirmed in
verse 6, when these two verbs are followed by "he was of good cheer."

4. *uncover his feet*. Alternately, the Hebrew noun could mean "the place of his
feet." In any case, it is an odd detail. Since the verb of uncovering is the one
used in biblical prohibitions of uncovering the nakedness of someone—that is,
engaging in sexual intercourse—the erotic tease of the narrative is again manifested. (But the proposal of some interpreters that "feet" is a euphemism for
the penis is highly dubious.) Ruth lies down not alongside Boaz but at his feet,

lie down, and as for him, he shall tell you what you should do." And she 5
said to her, "Whatever you say to me I will do." And she went down to 6
the threshing floor and did all that her mother-in-law charged her. And 7
Boaz ate and drank, and he was of good cheer, and he came and lay
down at the edge of the stack of barley. And she came stealthily and
uncovered his feet and lay down. And it happened at midnight that the 8
man trembled and twisted round, and, look, a woman was lying at his
feet. And he said, "Who are you?" And she said, "I am Ruth your servant. 9

---

an expression of her lower social status and of the subservient role of wives in
relation to their husbands in biblical society. The uncovering may simply be an
act to show that someone is present, and so when Boaz awakens in the middle
of the night, perhaps what first startles him—though it is unreported—is his
exposed feet, after which he realizes that a woman is present.

he shall tell you what you should do. Naomi certainly appears to leave open
the possibility that Boaz will ask Ruth to have sex with him, though she is
counting on the likelihood that he will instead virtuously devise a plan to do
social and matrimonial justice to his kinswoman by marriage.

7. *she came stealthily.* The implication of the adverb is not a surreptitious act
but an entrance on tiptoe, so as not to wake Boaz.

8. *trembled and twisted round.* Since only after this does he see that a woman
is there on the threshing floor with him, one may infer that the momentary
physical contortion is from suddenly awaking in the night, perhaps even from
a nightmare.

9. *Who are you?* The question is brusque, unadorned by any polite form of
address, as if to say: Woman, what are you doing here on my threshing floor in
the middle of the night? He of course has met Ruth during the day, but in the
dark of the night he does not immediately recognize her, especially after just
having awakened.

May you spread your wing over your servant, for you are a redeeming

10   kinsman." And he said, "Blessed are you to the LORD, my daughter. You
have done better in your latest kindness than in the first, not going after

11   the young men, whether poor or rich. And now, my daughter, do not be
afraid. Whatever you say I will do for you, for all my people's town knows

12   that you are a worthy woman. And now, though in fact I am redeeming

---

spread your wing. The Hebrew *kanaf* means both "wing" and "corner of a garment," and most translations render it in the latter sense because the reference
is to a man. But Ruth is echoing Boaz's words in 2:12, "the LORD God of Israel
under Whose wings you have come to shelter," and as a metaphor, a man can
certainly extend a sheltering wing. Zakovitch observes, citing both Rashi and
Ezekiel 15:8, that sheltering wings can be a symbol of marriage. In that case,
Ruth delicately avoids explicit reference to marriage, instead using an image
that also has the more general connotation of shelter.

a redeeming kinsman. Not "the" redeemer, because she knows there may be
another candidate for the role.

10. *your latest kindness.* The immediate context suggests that the more salient
meaning of *ḥesed* here is "act of loyalty."

the first. Though this might mean Ruth's loyalty to Naomi in Moab, the
mention that follows of her not going after the young men makes it more likely
that he is referring to her discretion during the day in keeping a distance from
the young men.

whether poor or rich. Ruth stayed away from everyone in the group of glean-
ers, regardless of social standing.

11. *Whatever you say I will do for you.* These words pointedly echo Ruth's to
Naomi in verse 5. Though she has placed herself in a posture of subservience
to him, he now affirms that he is prepared to do whatever she bids him.

all my people's town. The literal sense of the Hebrew is "all my people's gate,"
but "gate" is a synecdoche for the town, because it is both the entrance to the
town and the area where courts of justice were held when the town's elders
convened.

a worthy woman. This feminine equivalent of the epithet earlier used for
Boaz, "a man of worth," intimates that the two are perfectly suitable mates.

kin, there is also a redeeming kin closer than I. Spend the night here, 13
and it shall be in the morning, should he redeem you, he will do well
to redeem, and if he does not want to redeem you, I myself will redeem
you, as the LORD lives. Lie here till morning." And she lay at his feet till 14
morning and arose before a man could recognize his fellow man. And
he said, "Let it not be known that a woman came to the threshing floor."
And he said, "Give me the shawl that you have and hold it out." And she 15
held it out, and he measured out six shares of barley and he set it on her,
and she came into the town. And she came to her mother-in-law, and 16
her mother-in-law said, "How is it with you, my daughter?" And she told

---

13. *Spend the night here*. There is both a practical and a symbolic reason for
Boaz's urging Ruth to spend the night with him on the threshing floor. He is
concerned that it might be dangerous for her to make her way back through
the town in the dark of night—in the event, she will leave at the first crack of
dawn, when just a bit of light shows but not enough to distinguish one face
from another (verse 14). But the night spent together is also an adumbration of
marital union, though here, in the most likely reading, still unconsummated.
The verb used for "spend the night" is the same in Ruth's "wherever you lodge,
I will lodge," though this "lodging" is one that cannot be together with Naomi.

he will do well to redeem. The redemption of the widowed kinswoman is his
prerogative and his obligation, so if the relative chooses to do it, Boaz can only
lend his assent and approval.

I myself. In the Hebrew, the otherwise unrequired first-person pronoun is
added as a strong emphasis on the part of the speaker.

14. *Let it not be known that a woman came*. Boaz is, of course, concerned for
Ruth's reputation.

15. *six shares of barley*. The Hebrew simply says "six barley," not specifying the
unit of measure, but it would have to be relatively small for Ruth to carry it.

and he set it on her. Boaz evidently wraps up the measure of barley in the
shawl and then places it either on Ruth's shoulder or on her head.

16. *How is it with you*. The Hebrew appears to say "who are you," but *mi*, usually "who," as in Boaz's words in verse 8, also sometimes means "what" or "how."

17 her all that the man had done for her. And she said, "These six shares
of barley he gave me, for he said, 'You should not come empty handed
18 to your mother-in-law.'" And she said, "Stay, my daughter, till you know
how the matter will fall out, for the man will not rest if he does not settle
the matter today."

---

17. *You should not come empty handed.* The Book of Ruth is all about the transition from emptiness to fullness—from famine to abundance, from bereave-
ment and childlessness to marriage and children. Naomi has told the women of
the town "I went out full, and empty did the Lord bring me back" (1:21), and
now the same Hebrew word *reiqah* appears in Ruth's report of Boaz's speech
to her. The fullness of the shawl bearing the barley is a hint of the fullness of
offspring that Ruth will enjoy and bring to Naomi.

18. *Stay, my daughter.* This reiterated form of address is a token of Naomi's
constant affection for Ruth.

the man will not rest. Now that the two women have taken this initiative,
the responsibility for action lies with Boaz, and Naomi trusts his dependability,
and his good faith.

CHAPTER 4

And Boaz had gone up to the gate, and he sat down there, and look, the 1
redeeming kin of whom Boaz spoke was passing by, and he said, "Turn
aside, sit down here, So and So." And he turned aside and sat down.
And he took ten men of the town elders and said, "Sit down here," and 2
they sat down. And he said to the redeeming kin, "Naomi, who came 3
back from the plain of Moab, sold the parcel of the field that was our
brother Elimelech's. And as for me, I thought, I shall alert you, saying, 4
'Acquire it in the presence of those seated here and in the presence of
my people's elders.' If you would redeem, redeem, and if you will not

---

1. *the gate.* The town gate, with some sort of square or plaza in front of it, is
both the principal public place of the town and the site where courts of justice
are held. Boaz exploits both these aspects of the gate, first taking a seat there
in the expectation, which proves correct, that the redeemer-kin is likely to pass
through this frequented space; then convening a quorum of the elders to serve
as witnesses to the legal act that will be executed.

sit down here, So and So. The Hebrew *peloni 'almoni*, which appears twice
elsewhere in the Bible, seems to derive from *pele'*, "mystery" (so Rashi proposes), and the root *'-l-m*, suggesting "mute." The point of refusing this character a name is that by declining to exercise his obligation of redemption, he
essentially withdraws from playing any role in the plot except to stand aside
for Boaz. One notes that he immediately assents to Boaz's command to take a
seat, as do the elders in the next verse—both testifying to Boaz's authority in
the community.

3. *Naomi . . . sold the parcel of the field that was our brother Elimelech's.* Presumably, she was compelled to do this in her destitution. Zakovitch observes that
since a widow does not inherit her husband, this would have to be after the
death of Mahlon and Chilion, for a mother can inherit her sons.

redeem, tell me, that I may know that there is none except you to redeem
5 and I am after you." And he said, "I will redeem." And Boaz said, "On
the day you acquire the field from Naomi, you will also acquire Ruth
6 the Moabite to raise up the name of the dead man on his estate." And

---

4. *if you will not redeem.* The received text shows "if he will not redeem," but
many Hebrew manuscripts as well as the Septuagint, the Vulgate, and the
Peshitta have the more coherent second-person singular.

   there is none except you to redeem. Mr. So and So is the only known kin of
Naomi besides Boaz, so his refusing to redeem will clear the way for Boaz.

   I will redeem. At this point the kinsman imagines that the redemption solely
involves acquiring the parcel of land so that it can be restored to the possession
of Naomi's clan, to which he belongs. Since Naomi has been left without offspring, he thinks that by providing the purchase price, he will retain permanent
possession of the parcel of land.

5. *On the day you acquire.* As Zakovitch notes, this idiom puts temporal pressure
on the kinsman because it refers to this very day when they are sitting before
the gate in the presence of the elders and the townspeople.

   you will also acquire Ruth the Moabite to raise up the name of the dead man.
This is the more challenging aspect of the obligation of redemption that until
now Boaz has held in reserve—the duty of *yibum* or levirate marriage (see Deuteronomy 25:6). When a man dies without male offspring, his brother is obliged
to marry the widow ("levirate" derives from the Latin *levir*, "brother-in-law") and,
acting as a kind of proxy for the deceased, beget a child with the widow, who
will thus continue the name of the dead brother. In this case, the kinsman is
not actually the brother of Ruth's dead husband but his relative (perhaps, a first
cousin), and the Hebrew word *'ah* means both "brother" and "kinsman." The
received text here reads "from," *me'et*, "Ruth," but this is almost surely a scribal
error for *'et*, the sign of a direct object in Hebrew. One should note that Boaz
makes a point of identifying Ruth as a Moabite, calculating that this will trouble
the kinsman, for the Moabites are not merely foreigners but traditional enemies
with whom contact has been proscribed. The introduction of the levirate obligation also pointedly recalls the story of Tamar and the sons of Judah in Genesis 38.
One son marries her and dies, leaving Tamar childless. The same fate befalls his
brother after marrying her, leading Judah to withhold his third son from carrying
out the levirate duty. Tamar, like Ruth, is a foreigner (in her case, a Canaanite),
and when she contrives through deception to conceive twins by Judah, Perez
and Zerah, she becomes the progenitrix of the line that will lead to Boaz, as we
are reminded in the genealogical notice at the end of the book (verses 18–21).

the redeeming kin said, "I cannot redeem, lest I spoil my estate. You—
redeem my obligation of redemption, for I cannot redeem." And thus it ₇
was in former times in Israel concerning redemption and concerning
exchange to fulfill every condition: a man would remove his sandal and
give it to his fellow man. And this was the practice in Israel. And the ₈
redeemer said, "You—acquire it," and he removed his sandal. And Boaz ₉
said to the elders and to all the people, "You are witnesses today that

---

6. *I cannot redeem, lest I spoil my estate.* He leaves unstated why this should
be the case. Many commentators conclude that he does not want to contami-
nate his family by introducing a Moabite woman. The Midrash Ruth Rabba
proposes that he fears he will suffer the fate of Mahlon and Chilion, who died
after marrying Ruth and Orpah. In any case, if he begets a son with Ruth, the
estate will stand in the name of her dead husband, not of the kinsman, as is
indeed the aim of the levirate law.

7. *And thus it was in former times in Israel.* This formula (compare 1 Samuel 9:9)
clearly indicates that the writer and his audience are removed in time from the
era when the levirate obligation was practiced, and it is thus another reflection
of the lateness of the book.
    to fulfill every condition. The language here is explicitly legal.
    a man would remove his sandal and give it to his fellow man. There is no
certainty as to who gives the sandal to whom or what exactly it signifies. In
the enunciation of the levirate law in Deuteronomy 25:9, it is the widow who
removes the sandal from the brother-in-law who has refused to marry her, and
she then spits in his face, so the removal of the sandal in Deuteronomy is
clearly a sign of disgrace. (There the verb is *ḥalats*; here, in the Late Biblical
usage, it is *shalaf*, a term that in earlier Hebrew refers only to "the unsheathing
of a sword.") In our text, there is no indication of disgrace. The removal of the
sandal seems to be a legal ritual for the transfer of an obligation, or of property—perhaps from the kinsmen to Boaz. The seeming confusion here about
the details of the *yibum* ritual may reflect the writer's distance from the time
when it was practiced.

8. *You—acquire.* By emphatically designating Boaz with the second-person pronoun before the verb in the imperative, the kinsman relinquishes all rights of
redemption to Boaz.

I have acquired all that was Elimelech's and all that was Chilion's and
10 Mahlon's from the hand of Naomi. And also Ruth the Moabite, wife of
Mahlon, I have acquired for myself as wife, to raise up the name of the
dead on his estate, that the name of the dead be not be cut off from his
11 brothers and from the gate of his place. You are witnesses today." And all
the people who were in the gate and the elders said, "We are witnesses.
May the LORD make the woman coming into your house like Rachel and
like Leah, both of whom built the house of Israel. And do worthy things
12 in Ephrathah and proclaim a name in Bethlehem. And may your house
be like the house of Perez to whom Tamar gave birth by Judah, from

---

9. *I have acquired all that was Elimelech's.* Since Naomi has sold her late husband's land, Boaz is declaring that he is about to pay whatever sum is required for buying back the property.

Chilion's . . . Mahlon's. Zakovitch shrewdly observes the way the difference in the meaning of the two names plays out in the story. "Chilion" implies utter destruction, and with no offspring, this son's name will be lost. "Mahlon" suggests a lesser condition of illness, and his name will be revived through Ruth.

10. *Ruth the Moabite.* If this national epithet put off the kinsman, Boaz on his part unambiguously affirms his readiness to marry the foreign woman.

from the gate of his place. This combination of terms is unusual but is dictated by the fact that they are assembled in the square in front of the gate.

11. *like Rachel and like Leah.* Their blessing transforms Ruth into a kind of adopted matriarch.

do worthy things in Ephrathah and proclaim a name in Bethlehem. In a benedictory flourish, their speech glides into formal verse, though it is unusual that the standard designation, "Bethlehem," appears in the second half of the line, and the less common synonym, "Ephrathah," in the first half. The phrase "do worthy things" incorporates the same term, *hayil*, that occurs in the designation of Ruth as a "worthy woman."

12. *Perez to whom Tamar gave birth by Judah.* The underlying allusion to the story of Judah and Tamar is now made explicit.

the seed that this young woman will give you." And Boaz took Ruth the   13
Moabite, and she became his wife, and he came to bed with her and the
Lord granted her conception and she bore a son. And the women said to   14
Naomi, "Blessed is the Lord, Who has not deprived you of a redeemer
today, and let his name be proclaimed in Israel. And may he be a restorer   15
of life for you and a support for your old age, as your daughter-in-law,
whom you love, has borne him, who has been better to you than seven
sons." And Naomi took the child and placed him in her lap and became   16
a nurse for him. And the neighbor women called a name for him, saying,   17
"A son is born to Naomi," and they called his name Obed—he was the
father of Jesse father of David.

---

13. *The Lord granted her conception.* The phrase does not ordinarily occur in
reports of conjugal union and conception. It is probably dictated by the fact
that Ruth had remained childless in her years of marriage to Mahlon.

14. *And the women said.* The story began with three women (and three dead
men), then with the unflagging loyalty and love between two women. When
Naomi and Ruth arrived in Bethlehem, they were greeted by a bevy of aston-
ished, and gossiping, women. Now the women become a chorus to celebrate
the birth of Naomi's grandchild.

16. *And Naomi took the child and placed him in her lap and became a nurse for
him.* To cuddle the child and become a caregiver for him is, of course, a natural
expression of a grandmother's love, but it also strongly suggests how the child
has become a vivid replacement for the two sons Naomi has lost. It is by no
means necessary to see this act, as some interpreters have done, as a formal ceremony of adoption, and it would be both odd and unnerving for a grandmother
to adopt her grandchild while his mother was alive.

17. *the neighbor women.* This designation, as Zakovitch, with his characteristic sensitivity to nuances of word choice, observes, points to a closeness to
Naomi in this group that does not characterize the more general chorus of
townswomen.
    and they called his name Obed. Only here is the name given to a child by
neither father nor mother but by neighbor women. It is probably a reflection
of the importance of the community of women in the story. The name Obed,
which occurs elsewhere, means "worshipper" and is probably a shortened form
of Obadiah, "worshipper, or servant, of the Lord."

18,19 And this is the lineage of Perez. Perez begat Hezron. And Hezron begat
20 Ram and Ram begat Aminadab. And Aminadab begat Nahshon, and
21 Nahshon begat Salmah. And Salmah begat Boaz, and Boaz begat Obed.
22 And Obed begat Jesse, and Jesse begat David.

---

18. *And this is the lineage of Perez.* In careful emulation of the Book of Genesis, the writer weaves together narration with genealogy to pointed thematic
purpose. Here he aligns the son Ruth bears both back to Judah's son, Perez,
and forward to the founder of the divinely authorized dynasty, David. As with
some other genealogical lists, there are exactly ten generations from Perez to
David. Ruth the Moabite, who "comes back" to the region of Judah and, in the
words of her vow to her mother-in-law, takes Naomi's God as her own, at the
end becomes the great-grandmother of David king of Israel.

THE BOOK OF ESTHER

TO THE READER

Of THE SEVERAL BIBLICAL BOOKS that test the limits of the canon, Esther may well be the most anomalous. It is the only scriptural text of which no scrap has been uncovered at Qumran. The pious Dead Sea sectarians might well have looked askance at it not merely because it never mentions the name of God but also because its narrative world is fundamentally secular. The Jews of the Persian empire are said here to have different "rules" from their neighbors, but these rules—the Persian loanword *dat* is used, which means "regulation" or "governing decree"—are in no way identified as divine commandments, and issues of faith or covenant are not at all part of this story. Nor, quite notably, is the Land of Israel. The likely date of the book's composition would be sometime late in the fifth century BCE or perhaps slightly later: any date after the demise of the Persian empire in the fourth century is highly improbable because by then the fictional activities of a Persian court would have been of little interest to Hebrew audiences, and the abundant borrowings of Persian words would have been unintelligible. In all likelihood, then, the book was written not long after the return to Zion authorized by the Persian emperor Artaxerxes and led by Ezra and Nehemiah in the middle of the fifth century, but this momentous event does not exist for the author of Esther, who envisages life in the diaspora as a normal and even permanent condition.

The most unusual aspect of Esther, for a book that made it into the biblical canon, is that it offers strong evidence of having been written primarily for entertainment. It has variously been described as a farce, a burlesque, a satire, a fairy tale, and a carnivalesque narrative, and it is often quite funny, with sly sexual comedy playing a significant role. The portrait of King Ahasuerus and the Persian court makes no pretense of serious correspondence to historical reality, as the original audience surely must have known. The Persian emperors were famous for their tolerance toward ethnic minorities—a policy clearly enunciated in the Cyrus Cylinder—and so Ahasuerus's accepting Haman's plan to massacre all the Jews of the realm is a manifest fantasy. And though the repeated attention in the book to imperial bureaucratic procedure and the written document (*ketav*) as its principal instrument does reflect something about the Persian system of governance, and the emphasis on luxury and banquets also corresponds to what we know of the Persian court, there could have been no actual legal stipulation like the one mentioned here that all royal decrees were absolutely irrevocable.

Ahasuerus, though he consents to a genocidal scheme, is basically a well-meaning, often obtuse, figure of fun. He repeatedly has a dim sense of what is going on around him. In the early chapters, he barely speaks, instead following the counsel of his courtiers like a marionette, and to the end he is an easy mark for manipulation. The writer even introduces a couple of arch hints that may lead us to wonder about his virility as well as about his intelligence.

What could have motivated this sort of narrative invention? Political grounds for the satiric representation of a Persian emperor seem unlikely. Ahasuerus is assigned the role he plays because of the necessities of the gratifying national fantasy contrived by the writer. The reigning queen Vashti, unwilling to expose her female charms to the eyes of her husband's drunken companions, must be removed, at the urging of one of those very companions, in order to make way for Esther, the beautiful Jewish commoner who becomes queen and saves her people. Her meteoric rise to royal grandeur, which then enables the ascent of her adoptive father Mordecai to the position of vice-regent, leans on the literary precedent of the Joseph story, as has often been observed. Here, however, the rags-to-riches story of Joseph is compounded by the threat to the lives of Mordecai, Esther, and all their people, and they must foil the plot of a nefarious enemy—said, altogether unrealistically, to be a descendant of Israel's arch-enemies, the Amalekites—whom Mordecai at the end will replace as the king's first minister.

Reversal is the key to the plot of Esther. In the first verse of Chapter 9, this pattern is actually spelled out in two Hebrew words, *wenahafokh hu'*, "on the contrary" or "it was the opposite." Instead of Haman's minions killing the Jews, it is the Jews who kill them. Instead of Mordecai's being impaled on the stake that Haman has erected for him, it is Haman and then his sons who are executed and impaled. Instead of Haman parading in regal grandeur on the king's own horse, it is Mordecai who is accorded that signal honor. And at the end, it is Mordecai, not Haman, who exercises power of the realm as vice-regent, adorned in regal finery. The carnivalesque character of the story is evident in all this. In the carnival, hierarchies are (temporarily) reversed; the lowly get to play the roles of those above them, typically through masks and costumes, as Mordecai, having donned sackcloth in the hour of impending disaster, appears at the end in indigo and white, a golden diadem, and a wrap of crimson linen. The penultimate chapter of the book is largely devoted to fixing the date and practice of the carnivalesque holiday of Purim (which generally falls in March, around the same time as Mardi Gras). Though this chapter is often seen as an epilogue, it is quite possible that the entire story was invented in order to provide an as-if historical justification for a day of feasting and drinking and merrymaking, already embraced by the Jews, that has no warrant among the festivals stipulated in the Torah.

The peculiarities of the Book of Esther's narrative world are matched by the peculiarities of its Hebrew style. As one would expect, it shows a number of the characteristics of Late Biblical Hebrew, with certain terms, as in other Late Biblical books, anticipating usages of the rabbinic Hebrew that would begin to emerge toward the end of the biblical period. But it should also be said that in contrast to other Late Biblical books, Esther exhibits a noticeable degree of stylistic looseness. Infinitives are often used where conjugated forms of the verb seem to be required, a procedure not evidenced elsewhere in Late Biblical Hebrew. Agreement between subject and verb is often ignored. The careful tense distinction of classical Hebrew between perfect and imperfect forms of the verb is entirely relaxed, and at some points the writer appears to be a little uncertain as to how to handle Hebrew verb tenses. And from time to time there are run-on sentences that sprawl over several verses without a great deal of syntactic coherence.

Yet, as novelists such as Balzac and Dreiser demonstrate, it is possible to tell a very effective story with a sometimes-ragged style. The author of Esther, unlike his Hebrew predecessors in the First Commonwealth period, revels in catalogs of descriptive details and delights in invoking the pomp and luxury of the imperial court where Esther's and Mordecai's destiny of greatness will in the end be splendidly realized. Here, for example, at the very beginning, is the setting for the king's "seven-day banquet in the garden court of the king's pavilion—white linen, indigo cotton fastened with cords of fine crimson cloth on silver cylinders and marble columns, gold and silver couches on a paving of alabaster and marble, and mother-of-pearl and black pearl." And beyond the descriptions, the writer deploys lively wit and an apt sense of comic timing in the dialogues that reveal a subtle Esther, a resolute Mordecai, a fumbling Ahasuerus, and a menacing but finally sputtering Haman. It is not hard to understand how this delightful story, devoid though it is of spiritual concerns and covenantal gravity, became canonical. It of course provided the warrant for a festive early spring celebration that few wanted to give up. But even apart from the holiday, as a story it was for its early audiences, as it would continue to be, both highly amusing and gratifying, at once a vivid satire and a tale of national triumph that offered to diaspora Jews a pleasing vision of safety from imagined enemies and a grand entrée to the corridors of power.

CHAPTER 1

And it happened in the days of Ahasuerus, the Ahasuerus who was 1
king from India to Cush, one hundred and twenty-seven provinces.
In those days, when Ahasuerus was seated on his royal throne which 2
was in Shushan the capital, in the third year of his reign, he made a 3
great banquet in his presence for all his ministers and his servants, the
freeholders of Persia and Media, the noblemen and the ministers of
the provinces, when he showed the wealth of his kingdom's glory and 4
the worth of the splendor of his greatness many days—a hundred and
eighty days. And when these days had gone by, the king made a banquet 5

---

1. *Ahasuerus*. The name is derived from that of the Persian emperor called
Xerxes by Herodotus. He reigned from 486 to 465. Beyond the name, there is
scarcely any historical connection between the actual emperor and the king of
this fantasy world of our text.

    Cush. In all likelihood, this is Nubia, so the empire stretches from the south-
west to the far northeast.

    one hundred and twenty-seven provinces. This is the first in a series of flam-
boyant numerical exaggerations in the story.

3. *freeholders*. The Hebrew term *ḥayil* means "military force" but also refers to
wealth, as in Ruth, and the latter meaning is more likely here.

4. *a hundred and eighty days*. The lavish banquet, then, for the royal bureaucracy
goes on for approximately half a solar year. This does not seem to be an empire
in which much business gets done.

for all the people who were in Shushan the capital, from the greatest to the least, a seven-day banquet in the garden court of the king's
6 pavilion—white linen, indigo cotton fastened with cords of fine crimson
cloth on silver cylinders and marble columns, gold and silver couches on
a paving of alabaster and marble, and mother-of-pearl and black pearl.
7 And drink was proffered in golden vessels and vessels of various kinds,
8 an abundant royal wine in kingly fashion. And the drinking was according to royal rule, there was no compulsion, for thus had the king decreed
to all the officials in his house, to let every man act according to his will.
9 Vashti, too, made a banquet in the royal house that was Ahasuerus's.

---

5. *for all the people.* After the six months of royal feasting, the king prepares a
second banquet just one week long for the general populace.

in the garden court of the king's pavilion. Either the king did not want to give
the throngs access to the palace proper, or there were so many of them that an
open space was required. In any case, the garden with its pavilion accords well
with all the imperial luxury.

6. *white linen, indigo cotton fastened with cords of fine crimson cloth . . .* This
lengthy catalog of sumptuous items is one of the markers of Esther's distinctive style. There is nothing like it in the spareness of earlier biblical narrative.
(The furnishings of Solomon's temple and palace in 1 Kings are hardly the
same thing because they constitute an inventory and are not an integral part
of the narrative.)

indigo cotton . . . fine crimson cloth. The Hebrew appears to say "cotton and
indigo," "fine cloth and scarlet," but it makes no sense to put two colors in a
list of sumptuous fabrics, so both terms should be instances of hendyadis, two
words joined by "and" that refer to a single concept.

black pearl. This is no more than an interpretive guess for the precious stone
indicated by the Hebrew *soheret.*

8. *And the drinking was according to royal rule.* "Royal rule" incorporates the
recurrent word *dat,* one of many Persian loanwords.

there was no compulsion. What this may mean is that according to royal
practice, the guests were free to drink as little or as much as they chose, as the
last phrase of the sentence indicates.

9. *Vashti, too, made a banquet.* The context suggests that this was a banquet for
women alone.

On the seventh day, when the king was of good cheer through the wine, 10
he said to Mehuman, Bizzetha, Hashbona, Bigetha, Agabtha, Zethan,
and Carcas, the seven eunuchs who served in the presence of king Ahasuerus, to bring Queen Vashti before the king with the royal crown, to 11
show her beauty to the peoples and the ministers, for she was comely
to look at. And Queen Vashti refused to come according to the word of 12
the king by the eunuchs, and the king was very furious, and his rage
flared up within him. And the king said to the sages, experts in protocol, 13
for thus was the king's practice before all the experts in rule and law,
and those closest to him were Carchena, Shethar, Admantha, Tash- 14
ish, Meres, Marsena, and Memucan, the seven ministers of Persia and
Media—according to the rule, what to do with Queen Vashti because 15

---

10. *the king was of good cheer.* The Hebrew expression (literally, "when his heart
was good") regularly occurs in the Bible to express the elevated state caused
by drinking.

   Mehuman, Bizzetha . . . These seven Persian names—rather mangled in
Hebrew transliteration—matched by the names of the seven ministers in verse
14, are part of the writer's effort to endow his story with vivid Persian local color.
There may also be an intended comic effect in the string of foreign names.

11. *to show her beauty.* The Midrash imagines this is an order for her to parade
naked before the male revelers. This could conceivably be what actually is
hinted, but even if it is not, the midrashic interpretation nevertheless enters
into the carnivalesque spirit of sensuality and dissipation that characterizes
the story.

13. *experts in protocol.* The literal meaning is "knowers of the times," but the
end of the verse argues for this sense. One notes that the sentence beginning
here sprawls over two relatively long verses, another departure from the stylistic
norms of First Commonwealth Hebrew narrative.

16 she had not obeyed the king's dictate by the eunuchs. And Memucan
said before the king and the ministers: "Not only against the king has
Queen Vashti done wrong but against all the ministers and all the peo-
17 ples that are in all the provinces of King Ahasuerus. For the queen's act
will go out to all the women to hold their husbands in contempt in their
eyes, when they will say, 'King Ahasuerus said to bring Vashti before
18 him and she did not come.' And this very day, the noblewomen of Persia
and Media will say to all the king's nobles that they heard of the queen's
19 act, and there will be a full measure of contempt and fury. If it please
the king, let the royal decree go out from before him and be written in
the rules of Persia and Media, not to the transgressed, that Vashti not
come into the presence of King Ahasuerus, and her queenship be given

---

16. *Not only against the king has Queen Vashti done wrong.* This long speech of
a courtier's counsel stands in instructive contrast to the lack of any dialogue
assigned to Ahasuerus up to this point. He is a man who likes to show off his
riches and his wife's beauty, and who likes to party, and who becomes furious
when his wishes are thwarted. Beyond this, he exhibits scant sense of how
to act and appears to be readily manipulable. Manipulation is precisely what
Memucan proceeds to do through his shrewd rhetoric, playing on male solidar-
ity and a male sense of vulnerability in the face of the rebellious wives. Thus
Vashti is cast as a perverse woman who will subvert male authority throughout
the empire.

18. *And this very day.* This choice of phrase makes it sound imperative for the
emperor to take action against Vashti immediately.
   contempt and fury. The contempt is that of the wives shown to their husbands. The fury may be the response of the husbands. In any case, Memucan
conjures up a state of moral anarchy if uppity women are not put in their place.

19. *go out.* As with Vashti's act of rebellion, things "go out," radiate from the
center in Shushan to the far reaches of the empire.
   and be written in the rules of Persia and Media. Again, the key word *dat*
appears. This satiric narrative is all about an elaborately rule-bound imperial
bureaucracy, where as it will later emerge—against all historical plausibility—a
royal decree once issued cannot be revoked.

to another better than she. And let the king's edict that he will issue 20
be heard throughout his kingdom, large though it is, and let all wives
accord worth to their husbands, from the greatest to the least." And the 21
thing was good in the eyes of the king and the ministers, and the king
did according to Memucan's word And he sent out ministers to all the 22
provinces of the king, to every single province in its own writing and to
every single people in its own language, that every man should rule in
his home and speak his people's language.

---

20. *edict.* This is another Persian loanword intended to invoke the procedures
and official channels of the Persian empire. The Hebrew form of the word,
pitgam, would later come to mean "aphorism."

be heard throughout his kingdom, large though it is. This is another instance
of projecting power from the center at Shushan to the far ends of a vast empire.
In fact, the difficulty of exercising royal power will be an important issue in
the story.

accord worth. The Hebrew *yeqar*, one of numerous Aramaic usages in the
story, means "worth," "honor," "respect."

21. *in the eyes of the king and the ministers.* Evidently, Ahasuerus needs the
express support of his courtiers before he can confidently embrace Memucan's
counsel or anybody's.

22. *in its own writing.* This vast multiethnic empire would have incorporated
groups with different systems of writing and, as the next phrase makes clear,
different languages, and the emperor wants to make sure that his decree will be
clearly understood wherever it is proclaimed, from India to Cush.

and speak his people's language. This final phrase may be out of place, and,
in fact, the sundry versions of the Septuagint simply omit it. However, it may
mean that the husband, having heard the royal decree in his own language,
proceeds to convey its contents to his wife in that language, which is presumably also her language, so that there should be no mistake about what has been
decreed.

CHAPTER 2

₁ After these things, when King Ahasuerus's wrath subsided, he recalled
₂ Vashti and what she had done and what was decreed about her. And the
king's lads, his servants, said, "Let virgins comely to look at be sought
₃ out for the king. And let the king appoint officials in all provinces of his
kingdom, and every young virgin woman comely to look at be gathered
in Shushan at the women's house by Hegai the king's eunuch, keeper of

---

1. *when King Ahasuerus's wrath subsided, he recalled Vashti and what she had
done.* These words may indicate ambivalence on the part of the king. His wrath
has subsided, and he remembers Vashti, perhaps conscious of the fact that he
remains without a queen, but he also remembers her disobedience. He may
well be hesitant about what to do, which would then invite the detailed advice
of his courtiers that begins in the next verse.

2. *Let virgins comely to look at be sought out for the king.* The pattern introduced
in the first chapter is repeated here: others speak at considerable length while
there is no reported speech for the king. This contrast creates the impression
that Ahasuerus is a passive ruler, led around by his advisers.

3. *and every young virgin woman comely to look at be gathered in Shushan.* The
fairy-tale character of the story becomes especially clear here. Every beautiful
virgin from all the provinces of the vast empire is to be sought out and brought
to the capital.
   the women's house. This is, of course, the royal harem, but the translation
follows the Hebrew, which does not use a specialized term.
   the king's eunuch. Though the term *saris* often refers to a high-ranking official who has not been castrated, as in Genesis 39:1, putting actual eunuchs in
charge of a harem was a general practice, for obvious reasons.

the women, and let them be given unguents. And the young woman who 4
will be pleasing in the eyes of the king shall rule in Vashti's stead." And
the thing was pleasing in the eyes of the king, and so did he do. There 5
was a Jew in Shushan the capital, and his name was Mordecai son of
Jair son of Shimei son of Kish, a Benjaminite man, who had been exiled 6
from Jerusalem with the group of exiles that was exiled with Jeconiah
king of Judah, whom Nebuchadnezzar king of Babylon had exiled. And 7
he became guardian to Hadassah, which is to say, Esther, his uncle's
daughter, for she had no father or mother. And the young woman was
comely in features and comely to look at, and when her father and her
mother died, Mordecai had taken her as his daughter. And it happened 8

---

unguents The frequent choice by translators of "cosmetics" for this term is
misconceived. Even in this fairy-tale world, putting on cosmetics for six months
running (see verse 12) would be extremely odd. The idea is rather that the
young virgins are steeped at length in substances that will make their bodies
supple and fragrant.

4. *the thing was pleasing in the eyes of the king.* It is no accident that a phrase
from the end of the courtier's counsel to the king is repeated in the report of
his response to the counsel: he is seen to be perfectly malleable to the words
and advice of those around him in the court.

5. *Mordecai son of Jair.* His father has a good Hebrew name, but his own name
is derived from that of the Babylonian god Marduk, a reflection of the degree
to which the Judeans exiled to Babylonia had adapted themselves to the new
culture. Similarly, Esther (who also is given a Hebrew name, Hadassah) has a
name deriving from that of the Babylonian goddess Ishtar.

7. *his uncle's daughter.* They are, then, first cousins. Though Mordecai assumes
a paternal role, actually adopting the orphaned Esther, they are in fact, respectively, a younger and older member of the same generation—Esther perhaps in
her late teens, Mordecai conceivably in his thirties.
    comely in features and comely to look at. This doubling of the epithet for
beauty may suggest that she is lovelier than all the other assembled virgins.
The same double epithet is applied to Joseph (Genesis 39:6), and its use here
probably signals the general allusion to the Joseph story: in both cases, we have
an extraordinarily beautiful Hebrew who ends up in a position of grandeur and
power in the royal court.

when the king's word and his rule were heard, and many young women were gathered in Shushan the capital by Hegai, that Esther was taken
9 into the king's house by Hegai, keeper of the women. And the young woman was pleasing in his eyes, and she won favor before him, and he hastened to bring her unguents and her share of food to give to her and the seven young women who were fit to give her from the king's house, and he singled her out and her young women for good treatment in the
10 women's house. Esther did not tell who were her people and her kin, for
11 Mordecai had charged her not to tell. And every single day Mordecai would go walking in front of the women's court to know how Esther
12 fared and what would be done for her. And when each young woman's turn came to come to the king, at the conclusion of her having twelve months, according to the women's rule, for thus would the days of their unguents be completed—six months in oil of myrrh and six months in
13 perfumes and women's unguents—and in this fashion would the young woman come to the king, whatever she would say would be granted her

---

9. *And the young woman was pleasing in his eyes.* This is again like Joseph, who finds favor in the eyes of everyone he encounters (see Genesis 38:4 and 23).

10. *for Mordecai had charged her not to tell.* Mordecai does not hesitate to send his adoptive daughter to the king's bed—that is clearly the culmination of the selection process for the new queen—and he calculates that her potential proximity to the throne might prove useful to their people.

11. *Mordecai would go walking in front of the women's court.* He was of course prohibited from entering the harem.

12. *six months in oil of myrrh and six months in perfumes and women's unguents.* This is another fantastic detail of the fairy-tale plot: each of these beautiful virgins spends a full year steeping herself in fragrant oil, perfumes, and unguents, so that when she comes to the bed of the king, her body will in every one of its cells be in a state of perfect erotic attractiveness.

to take with her from the women's house to the house of the king. In 14
the evening she would come, and in the morning she would go back to
the women's house again in the hands of Shaashgaz, the king's eunuch,
keeper of the concubines. She would not come again to the king unless
the king desired her and she was called by name. And when the turn 15
came of Esther daughter of Abihail, Mordecai's uncle, whom he had
taken as his daughter, to come to the king, she asked nothing but what
Hegai the king's eunuch would say. And Esther found favor in the eyes
of all who saw her. And Esther was taken to King Ahasuerus, to his royal 16
house, in the tenth month, which is the month of Teveth, in the seventh
year of his reign. And the king loved Esther more than all the women, 17
and she won grace and favor before him more than all the virgins, and he
put the royal crown on her head and made her queen in Vashti's stead.
And the king made a great banquet for all his ministers and his servants, 18
Esther's banquet, and he granted relief of taxes for the provinces, and

---

14. *In the evening she would come, and in the morning she would go back.* The
selection process, then, comes down to trial by sexual intercourse: with which
of these virgins will the king be truly satisfied? The image of the king as an
indefatigable sexual athlete bedding virgins night after night is intrinsically
comic, but it is also undercut by a sly hint that points in the opposite direction.

again. The Hebrew *sheni*—seemingly "second"—looks odd. If it really modi-
fies "house," it should have a definite article in front of it, which it does not,
and it would be strange for there to be two different harems. This translation
emends the word to *shenit,* "again," or "a second time."

16. *the month of Teveth.* These names of the months, which became standard
in later Hebrew usage, entered the language in the Babylonian period from the
language of the surrounding culture.

17. *And the king loved Esther more than all the women.* The reason for his love is
not spelled out. Perhaps it was just her winning ways, as indicated at the end of
verse 16. But if sexual performance is the crucial test, how would one inexpe-
rienced virgin distinguish herself from the others? We are left wondering about
this, but the arch double meaning of one detail at the beginning of Chapter 5
raises the suspicion that this passive and not very competent king may have a
problem with virility. If that is the case, the beautiful and understanding Esther
might possibly be the one virgin who helps him overcome his difficulties.

19 he gave gifts in kingly fashion. And when the virgins gathered a second
20 time, with Mordecai sitting in the king's gate, Esther was not telling
who were her kin and her people, as Mordecai had charged her, and
21 Esther did what Mordecai said, for she was under his guardianship. In
those days, when Mordecai was sitting in the king's gate, Bigetha and
Theresh, two of the king's eunuchs, of the guardians of the threshold,
22 became furious and sought to lay hands on King Ahasuerus. And the
matter became known to Mordecai and he told Esther, and Esther spoke
23 to the king in Mordecai's name. And the matter was searched out and
found to be so, and the two of them were impaled on stakes, and it was
written down in the Book of Acts before the king.

---

21. *became furious.* This is the general meaning of the Hebrew verb *qatsaf,* and
there is no evidence that it has a technical political sense, such as "became
disaffected." Something, then, that Ahasuerus has done or some general policy
of the king infuriates the two eunuchs. In light of the figure Ahasuerus has cut,
this would not be entirely surprising.

23. *impaled on stakes.* The Hebrew appears to say "were hanged on a tree," but
the historical evidence points to impalement, not hanging, as the customary
form of execution in the ancient Near East. In many instances, the condemned
person was put to death in some other fashion and his impaled body was then
displayed as a form of humiliation.

it was written down in the Book of Acts. The Book of Acts, on the model of the
designation repeatedly used in the Book of Kings, would be royal annals. The
mention of the recording of the event prepares the background for the reading
out loud of this episode to the insomniac king in Chapter 6.

CHAPTER 3

After these things King Ahasuerus elevated Haman son of Hammeda- 1
tha the Agagite and raised him up and seated him higher than all the
ministers who were with him. And all the king's servants who were in 2
the king's gate would kneel and bow down to Haman, for thus had the
king charged concerning him, but Mordecai would not kneel and would
not bow down. And the king's servants who were in the king's gate said 3

---

1. *King Ahasuerus elevated Haman.* No reason is given for this act. In light of the
very bad character that Haman goes on to exhibit, the king's decision to grant
him special power suggests extremely poor judgment on the part of Ahasuerus.

the Agagite. Agag is the Amalekite king whom Saul is supposed to kill in
1 Samuel 15. Obviously, no one in the actual Persian court could have been
related to the Amalekites, but the ethnic identification is introduced in order to
align Haman with the traditional arch-enemies of the people of Israel.

2. *all the king's servants who were in the king's gate.* These are all members of
the court, probably high-ranking imperial officials.

but Mordecai would not kneel. The reason given for his refusal beginning
in Late Antiquity is religious: as a Jew, he would not prostrate himself before
flesh and blood. But that is not self-evident in the text, and Mordecai might
well have personal or political motives, refusing to bow down to someone he
despises and who he thinks is not entitled to be vice-regent.

4 to Mordecai, "Why do you flout the king's command?" And it happened
as they said this to him day after day and he did not heed them, they
told it to Haman to see whether Mordecai's words would stand, for he
5 had told them that he was a Jew. And Haman saw that Mordecai was
not kneeling and not bowing down to him, and Haman brimmed with
6 wrath. And he scorned to lay hands on Mordecai alone, for they had
told him who Mordecai's people were, and Haman sought to destroy
all the Jews, Mordecai's people, who were in all Ahasuerus's kingdom.
7 In the first month, which is the month of Nissan, in the twelfth year of
King Ahasuerus's reign, he cast a *pur*, which is a lot, for every day in the
month and every month of the twelve, and it fell on the month of Adar.
8 And Haman said to King Ahasuerus: "There is a certain people, scat-
tered and separate from the peoples in all the provinces of your king-

---

4. *to see whether Mordecai's words would stand.* The meaning of this clause is
ambiguous. If the reason for Mordecai's refusal to bow to Haman is religious—
Jews don't bow to people—then "for he had told him that he was a Jew" explains
his action. Alternately, Mordecai may have categorically refused to bow without
offering any religious justification. In that case, his stubborn refusal is compounded by the fact that he has announced his belonging to an ethnic group
perceived as different.

6. *Haman sought to destroy all the Jews.* This resolution of genocide reflects the
fairy-tale vehicle of the narrative and could scarcely represent an actual option
of policy in the Persian empire, known for its toleration of minorities.

7. *in the twelfth year of King Ahasuerus's reign.* Esther, then, would have been
queen for five years at this point.
   pur. This is a Persian loanword, and thus it is immediately glossed by the
Hebrew word for "lot," *goral.* The Hebrew plural form of the word, Purim,
becomes the name of the carnivalesque holiday for which the Book of Esther
serves as rationale.
   it fell on the month of Adar. Adar corresponds approximately to March, placing Purim around the same time as Mardi Gras and other carnivalesque festivals marking the end of winter. No day is given in this verse, though one version
of the Septuagint shows "on the thirteenth day of the month," and that phrase
may have dropped out through an error in scribal transcription.

dom, and their rules are different from every people's and they do not observe the king's rules, and it does not pay for the king to leave them in peace. If it please the king, let it be written to wipe them out, and ten 9 thousand talents of silver will I measure out to the court overseers to bring into the king's treasury." And the king removed his ring from his 10 hand and gave it to Haman son of Hammedatha the Agagite, foe of the Jews. And the king said to Haman, "The silver is yours and the people's, 11 to do with it as is good in your eyes." And the king's scribes were called 12 together in the first month on its thirteenth day, and it was written as all that Haman had charged to the king's satraps and the governors in every single province according to their system of writing and to the ministers of every single people and every single province according to their language. In the name of King Ahasuerus was it written, and it was sealed with the king's ring. And missives were sent out by the hand 13

---

8. *their rules are different.* The Book of Esther reflects a repeated preoccupation with rules, appropriately using the Persian loanword *dat.* The royal court constantly issues rules that have to be strictly observed. The Jews have different rules, and they are called that, not "commandments," and may well be ethnic practices rather than an absolutely religious regimen.

9. *ten thousand talents of silver will I measure out.* This is an extravagant amount, hundreds of tons of silver. Haman's evident intent is to persuade the king to authorize the massacre by this huge gift to the royal treasuries, which is virtually a bribe. Haman would have had to be fabulously rich, which might be the reason Ahasuerus elevated him to the position of viceroy.

10. *And the king removed his ring from his hand and gave it to Haman.* In this, he confers full royal authority upon Haman to carry out his murderous plan.

11. *The silver is yours.* The king refuses the extravagant gift. Keep the silver, he says, and do with it whatever you want—perhaps large expenses will be incurred in carrying out the massacre throughout the vast empire.

12. *according to their system of writing.* Just as different ethnic groups in the empire have different languages, they also use different scripts.
   sealed with the king's ring. This is the ring Ahasuerus gave to Haman.

of couriers to all the king's provinces—to destroy, and kill and wipe out
all the Jews, from young lad to old man, babes and women, on a single
day, on the thirteenth day of the twelfth month, which is the month of
14 Adar, and to take their spoils. A copy of the writing to be given as rule in
every single province, manifested to all the peoples, to be ready for this
15 day. The couriers went out rushed by the king's word, and the rule was
given out in Shushan the capital. And the king and Haman sat down to
drink, and the city of Shushan was confounded.

---

13. *to destroy, and kill and wipe out.* The multiplication of synonyms for killing
clearly emphasizes the total annihilation that Haman aims for.
  and to take their spoils. This would be an additional motivation for the killers.

14. *A copy of the writing to be given as rule.* The term for "copy," *patshegen*, is
still another Persian loanword. The narrative bristles with language representing the punctilious observance of imperial bureaucratic procedure. The writer
may well have been struck by the elaborate bureaucracy of the Persian empire,
though needless to say, no such decree for the massacre of an entire population
within the empire was ever issued.

15. *And the king and Haman sat down to drink.* While the couriers sent out by
Haman are feverishly racing across the empire with the orders for the massacre,
the king and Haman sit at their ease in the capital, drinking. Indeed, drinking
is the chief activity in which we see the king engaged, both at the beginning of
the story and afterward.
  and the city of Shushan was confounded. The murderous decree, of course,
would have been public knowledge, and the Jews of Shushan were to be mas-
sacred, just like the Jews elsewhere in the empire. The inhabitants of Shushan
may not necessarily be sympathetic toward the Jews—after all, they have been
enjoined by Haman's decree to carry out the massacre and stand to gain from
it the property of the victims—but it is nevertheless an act so extreme that it
leaves them in a state of confusion. We have, then, three very different postures
as the disaster looms: Haman and the king complacently drinking, the populace
of Shushan confounded, and (implicitly) the Jews in a state of trepidation in
the face of imminent destruction.

CHAPTER 4

And Mordecai knew all that had been done, and Mordecai rent his gar- 1
ments and donned sackcloth and ashes and went out into the city and
cried out loudly and bitterly. And he came as far as in front of the king's 2
gate, for one could not enter the king's gate in clothing of sackcloth. And 3
in every single province, where the king's word and his rule reached,
the Jews were in great mourning—and fasting and weeping and dirges,
sackcloth and ashes were laid out for the multitudes. And Esther's young 4
women and her eunuchs came and told her, and the queen was badly
shaken. And she sent garments to clothe Mordecai and to remove his

---

2. *And he came as far as in front of the king's gate.* Though some of the Hebrew
usage in Esther is a little slack, here the writer's choice of phrase is quite
precise: Mordecai makes his way toward Esther as far as he can come, which
is the square in front of the palace, but he can go no farther because of his
unseemly garments.

3. *fasting and weeping and dirges.* Facing destruction, they undertake a fast, a
customary procedure to entreat God in a moment of collective distress, but in
this thoroughly secular tale no turning to God is mentioned. Mordecai on his
part is not yet reported to be fasting, only crying out bitterly.
    sackcloth and ashes were laid out. The verb used here usually refers to making
up a bed. Perhaps in this case it applies to clothing, or the meaning might be
that the people slept in bedding of sackcloth and ashes.

4. *she sent garments to clothe Mordecai.* She would like to speak to him face to
face, but he can enter the palace only if he removes his sackcloth and puts on
proper clothing.

5 sackcloth from him, but he did not accept them. And Esther called to
   Hatach, of the king's eunuchs whom he had stationed before her, and
   she charged him concerning Mordecai to find out what was this and
6 for what was this. And Hatach went out to Mordecai in the city square
7 that was in front of the king's gate. And Mordecai told him all that
   had befallen him and the matter of the silver that Haman had meant
   to weigh out to the king's treasuries for the Jews, to wipe them out.
8 And the copy of the writing of the rule that was given out in Shushan
   to destroy them he gave to him to show to Esther, to tell her, and to
   charge her to come to the king to plead with him and to entreat him
9 for her people. And Hatach came and told Mordecai's words to Esther.
10 And Esther said to Hatach and charged him to convey to Mordecai:

---

5. *to find out what was this and for what was this.* Her inquiry is puzzling, for
having been informed of Haman's decree, she surely knows why Mordecai has
put on the garb of mourning. Perhaps she simply wonders why he needs to
adopt this particular outward expression of grief and, evidently, to persist in it.

6. *And Hatach went out to Mordecai.* The introduction of an intermediary
suggests a potential distance or division between the adoptive father and his
adoptive daughter, and, in fact, a certain tension will emerge in the exchange
between them.

7. *the matter of the silver that Haman had meant to weigh out.* Although the
king had refused this offer and so it might seem moot, Mordecai cites Haman's
readiness to pay a vast fortune as a reflection of his utter determination to wipe
out the Jews—literally at any price.

8. *the copy of the writing of the rule.* This is not only another expression of the
story's preoccupation with imperial bureaucratic procedures but is also a piece
of "documentary evidence" of the dire decree with which Mordecai wants to
confront Esther.

10. *charged him to convey to Mordecai.* The Hebrew uses an elliptical expression, "charged him to Mordecai."

"All the king's servants and the people of the king's provinces know that 11
every man and woman who comes into the inner court without having
been called, the single rule is to put to death unless the king reach out
to him the golden scepter. And as for me, I have not been called to come
to the king thirty days now." And they told Esther's words to Mordecai. 12
And Mordecai said in response to Esther: "Do not imagine to escape of 13
all the Jews in the house of the king. For if you indeed remain silent, 14
relief and rescue will come to the Jews from elsewhere, and you and

---

11. *All the king's servants and the people of the king's provinces know.* The knowledge of this court practice is universal in the empire, so Mordecai must surely
be quite aware of it. His urging Esther, then, to go before the king, she suggests,
might well lead to her instant death.

the single rule is to put to death. Josephus vividly imagines court officials
armed with axes standing by the king, ready to chop off the head of anyone who
presumes to enter the royal presence uninvited.

unless the king reach out to him the golden scepter. This is obviously a gesture
symbolizing the conferral of royal favor. But in light of the sexualized atmo-
sphere of the tale, and the oblique hint of a question about royal sexual performance in the nightly testing of the beautiful virgins, it seems legitimate to
suggest that a sexual double meaning is lurking here: if the phallic royal scepter
is extended when the queen appears, she will know that she is in the king's
good graces.

And as for me, I have not been called to come to the king thirty days now. Her
very wording emphasizes the length of this period. It is surely a long time to
leave a beautiful young wife neglected in the women's quarters. From what we
know about Ahasuerus, he is unlikely to have been preoccupied with affairs of
state. Could the flagging of interest in Esther be the result of uncertainty about
his sexual capability?

13. *Do not imagine to escape of all the Jews in the house of the king.* This response,
through the mediation of Hatach, is close to a rebuke: don't think an exception
will be made for you and that you will be able to save your own skin. In fact,
Esther's Jewish identity is not known in the court, but Mordecai seems to imply
that somehow Haman's ruthless henchmen will ferret it out.

14. *relief and rescue will come to the Jews from elsewhere.* The early rabbis understood this to be God, but the expression is quite vague, and as throughout the
book, God is not mentioned.

your father's house will perish. And who knows whether for just a time
15 like this you have attained royalty?" And Esther said in response to Mor-
16 decai, "Go, assemble all the Jews who are in Shushan, and fast on my
behalf, and do not eat nor drink three days, night and day. And I, too,
with my young women, shall fast in this fashion. And so, I shall come to
17 the king not according to rule, and if I perish, I perish." And Mordecai
moved on and did all that Esther had charged him.

---

16. *fast on my behalf.* This is slightly odd because they are already fasting. The
difference may be that the fast is now to be especially on behalf of Esther, who
is about to endanger her life for her people, and it is also a very long fast—three
whole days and nights.

    and if I perish, I perish. These words express a kind of stoic resolution: I know
I have to do this, however dangerous; if I succeed, it will be a great triumph,
but otherwise, I am prepared to accept my grim fate.

CHAPTER 5

And it happened on the third day that Esther donned royal garb 1
and stood in the inner court of the king's house opposite the king's
house, with the king sitting on his royal throne in the royal house
opposite the entrance to the house. And it happened when the king 2
saw Queen Esther standing in the court, that she found favor in his
eyes, and he reached out to Esther the golden scepter that was in his
hand, and Esther approached and touched the top of the scepter. And 3

---

1. *the third day.* This is obviously at the end of three days of fasting decreed by
Esther. The narrative will now swiftly move from fasting to feasting.

donned royal garb. As a counterpoint to Mordecai's sackcloth, which prevents
him from entering the palace, Esther is careful to put on her queenly robes,
and perhaps a crown as well, when she enters the throne room unbidden. The
word "royal," *malkhut,* is repeated as a designation (not strictly necessary) of
the throne, highlighting this meeting as an encounter between king and queen.

opposite the entrance to the house. Thus, as Esther approaches the inner
court, she can see the king and vice versa.

2. *she found favor in his eyes.* However much he has neglected her during the
past thirty-three days, the sight of beautiful Esther in her splendid royal robes
stirs feelings of affection in him.

he reached out to Esther the golden scepter. This is the crucial gesture signal-
ing his favorable acceptance of her uninvited appearance.

Esther approached and touched the top of the scepter. The literal sense is
"head of the scepter." A sexual undermeaning here is not to be excluded.

the king said to her, "What troubles you, Queen Esther, and what is
your request? Up to half the kingdom, and it will be granted to you!"
4 And Esther said, "If it please the king, let the king and Haman come
5 today to the banquet that I have prepared for him." And the king said,
"Hurry to Haman to do Esther's bidding." And the king and Haman
6 came to the banquet that Esther had prepared. And the king said
to Esther at the wine banquet, "What is your petition, and it will be
granted to you, and what is your request? Up to half the kingdom, and
7 it will be done!" And Queen Esther answered and said, "My petition

---

3. *What troubles you.* The king sees that his royal consort is agitated about
something. Shrewdly, she does not reveal the source of her agitation yet but
instead extends a social invitation.

Up to half the kingdom. Ahasuerus, feared by Esther as a distant royal husband who might sentence her to die, is suddenly, as he beholds his beautiful
wife, extravagantly uxorious in what he is prepared to give her. Once again he
is easily manipulated. But all she asks is that he agree to be her dinner guest
a second time.

4. *to the banquet that I have prepared.* Counting on a favorable response, she
has actually prepared the feast before coming to the king. Time, of course, is an
urgent consideration because the date of the scheduled massacre is approaching. Lavish banquets are the very language of this Persian court. The story
began with banquets, and now a pivotal moment will take place through one
banquet leading to a second one.

5. *Hurry to Haman to do Esther's bidding.* An invitation to a private feast with
the queen and king would of course be very attractive to Haman. Nevertheless,
he is seen "to do Esther's bidding," manipulated in a scheme she has devised.

6. *the wine banquet.* This designation, which is new in the story, suggests that
drinking is even more important than eating at these regal banquets. The wine
will put the king in "good cheer."

and my request, if I have found favor in the eyes of the king and if it 8
please the king to grant my petition and to fulfill my request, let the
king and Haman come to the banquet that I shall prepare for them,
and tomorrow I shall do according to the king's bidding." And Haman 9
went out that day happy and of good cheer, and when Haman saw
Mordecai in the king's gate, and he had not arisen and had not stirred
for him, Haman brimmed with wrath against Mordecai. And Haman 10
held himself in check and came to his house, and sent and brought his
friends and Zeresh his wife. And Haman recounted to them the glory 11
of his wealth and his many sons and all in which the king had elevated
him, and how he had raised him up over the noblemen and the ser-

---

8. *let the king and Haman come to the banquet that I shall prepare for them.*
Esther lulls Haman into a false sense of security and also leads the king for
the moment to imagine she may have nothing to ask of him but attendance at
another lavish "wine banquet." She also wants to make sure that the king will be
in a receptive mood by plying him with drink and food on two successive days.

and tomorrow I shall do according to the king's bidding. She saves this for the
end of her response: Yes, I do have a further request, which the king has bidden
me to state, and I shall announce it at the feast on the morrow.

9. *happy and of good cheer.* He is obviously happy to think himself the special
object of the queen's favor, and "of good cheer," here as elsewhere, indicates the
euphoric mood induced by drinking. But a moment later, the sight of Mordecai
not deigning to arise in deference to his presence (not to speak of his refusal to
bow down to the king's ministers) will change his good mood to wrath.

10. *Haman held himself in check.* He does not want to rant and rage in public
but waits until he returns home, when he can consult his intimates about a
plan of revenge.

11. *Haman recounted to them the glory of his wealth.* Haman's wealth is surely
a familiar story (one recalls the immense treasure he was prepared to offer the
king), but he cannot resist bragging about it to his household and his friends.

and his many sons. Throughout the Bible, and in ancient Near Eastern culture in general, producing many sons is a sign, like wealth, of having achieved
successful standing in the world. The sons, each given a name, will appear at
the end of the story in their humiliating public execution.

and all in which the king had elevated him. Here he reverts to what was
reported in 3:1. Again, Haman is bragging about something everyone knows.

12 vants of the king. And Haman said, "Queen Esther brought with the
king to the banquet that she prepared only me, and tomorrow, too, I
13 am invited by her with the king. But all this is not worth my while so
14 long as I see Mordecai the Jew sitting in the king's gate." And Zeresh his
wife together with all his friends said to him, "Let them set up a stake
fifty cubits high, and in the morning say to the king that Mordecai be
impaled on it, and come with the king to the banquet happy." And the
thing pleased Haman, and he set up the stake.

---

12. *only me.* On top of all the grand things Haman has just enumerated, he has
just now been the object of the queen's unique favor.

with the king. This phrase, occurring twice here in Haman's boast, expresses
his self-gratifying illusion that he has been placed virtually on par with the king.

13. *sitting.* That is, Mordecai's refusal to rise in defiance.

14. *And Zeresh his wife together with all his friends said to him.* It is unclear
whether Haman expected to elicit this vengeful proposal from them or whether
he was turning to them for a suggestion about how he should practically implement his anger against the defiant Mordecai. In any case, the murderous counsel they offer him indicates that he is a man who keeps very bad company.

a stake fifty cubits high. This would be roughly sixty feet high, higher, in fact,
than the palace itself. The height, like much else in the story (the hundreds of
beautiful virgins, the vast sum Haman is prepared to give Ahasuerus) is altogether hyperbolic, an expression of Haman's rage against Mordecai rather than
a practical stipulation of how a corpse should be publicly displayed.

in the morning. This would be the morning of the very day on which Haman
has been invited to a second banquet by Esther, who, unbeknownst to him, is
Mordecai's kinswoman and adopted daughter.

impaled. As before, the term probably indicates that the person is to be
executed first and then the body exposed for humiliation on the high pole.

come with the king. Zeresh aptly picks up on the phrase her husband has
used twice, recognizing that it expresses his gratified sense of uniquely privileged closeness to the throne.

happy. Just as he came out of the first banquet happy at having been accorded
such special social honor in the court, he will enter the second banquet happy
that he has just destroyed his hated enemy.

CHAPTER 6

That night the king could not sleep, and he ordered to bring the annals, 1
the Book of Acts, and that they be read to the king. And he found it 2
written that Mordecai had told about Bigetha and Theresh, the two
eunuchs of the king, the guardians of the threshold, who had sought to
lay hands on King Ahasuerus. And the king said, "What honor and gran- 3
deur were done for Mordecai on account of this?" And the king's lads,
his attendants, said, "Nothing was done for him." And the king said, 4
"Who is in the court?" And Haman had come into the outer court in
the king's house to say to the king to impale Mordecai on the stake that
he had readied for him. And the king's lads said to him, "Look, Haman 5

---

1. *could not sleep.* The literal sense of the Hebrew is "his sleep wandered."
This vivid expression became the standard idiom for insomnia in later Hebrew.
The king's sleeplessness at this juncture in the plot is a narrative convenience,
so that he can discover Mordecai's act of loyalty when the annals are read to
him, but the insomnia might be "motivated" by his excited curiosity about what
Esther will reveal to him at the banquet the next day.

4. *Haman had come into the outer court . . . to say to the king to impale Mordecai.*
It is now early in the morning, and Haman has arrived bright and early so that
he can proceed promptly to the execution of Mordecai before the banquet later
in the day. Everything that follows is the unfolding of a series of comic reversals:
the man whom Haman thinks he is about to kill proves to be the man whom
the king honors; Haman himself, the comic villain, instead of being the object
of royal honor, as he imagines, is forced into the humiliating role of honoring
the very man he hates.

6 is standing in the court." And the king said, "Let him come in." And
Haman came, and the king said to him, "What should be done for the
man whom the king desires to honor?" And Haman said in his heart, "To
7 whom would the king desire to do honor more than to me?" And Haman
8 said to the king, "The man whom the king desires to honor, let them
bring royal raiment that the king has worn and a horse on which the king
9 has ridden, and set a royal crown on his head, and give the raiment and
the horse into the hands of a man of the king's nobles, the courtiers, and
let them dress the man whom the king desires to honor and ride him on
the horse through the city square and call out before him, 'Thus shall
10 be done to the man whom the king desires to honor.'" And the king said

---

6. *What should be done . . . ?* As before, Ahasuerus is at a loss to know what to
do—surely an appropriate means of honoring Mordecai should not have been
beyond him—and again turns for counsel to someone in his court. The advice
Haman gives him will prove to be Haman's own comeuppance.

To whom would the king desire to do honor more than to me? This delusion
is entirely in keeping with the self-congratulatory frame of mind in which he
reported to his wife and intimates his grand social success in being invited to a
private banquet by the queen.

8. *royal raiment that the king has worn and a horse on which the king has ridden.*
Haman's delusions of grandeur bring him dangerously close to claiming the
throne for himself, as the Midrash properly recognizes: he wants raiment,
horse, and crown that are not merely regal but that the king has actually used,
thus putting himself in metonymic contact with the body of the king—in a way,
becoming the king. All this royal grandeur, of course, will be accorded instead
to his enemy Mordecai.

9. *courtiers.* The Hebrew uses still another Persian loanword, *partemim.* Such
linguistic "local color" is appropriate since Haman would have made fluent use
of all the set designations for the sundry officials in the Persian court.

Thus shall be done . . . The repetition of this entire clause, without varia-
tion, makes it a kind of refrain in this episode. The implementation of the
king's desire to honor a particular man will be carried out, item after item, but
the object of the honor will not be the one whom the grandiose deviser of the
honor imagines.

to Haman, "Hurry, take the raiment and the horse as you have spoken, and do this for Mordecai the Jew, who is sitting in the king's gate. Omit nothing from all you have spoken." And Haman took the raiment and 11 the horse and dressed Mordecai and rode him on the horse through the city square and called out before him, "Thus shall be done to the man whom the king desires to honor." And Mordecai returned to the king's 12 gate, and Haman was thrust back to his house, mournful and distraught.

---

10. *Hurry.* The element of hastening is prominent throughout this swiftly paced tale. Haman hurries to the palace first thing in the morning in order to get royal authorization to impale his enemy as soon as possible. Ahasuerus hurries to carry out Haman's plan for according honor, perhaps mindful of the fact that he has a banquet to attend later in the day. At the end of this episode, the king's eunuchs hurry to bring Haman, fresh from his public humiliation in honoring Mordecai, to the banquet.

who is sitting in the king's gate. This neutral observation on the part of the king touches on what galls Haman, that the seated Mordecai has refused to stand in deference to him.

Omit nothing from all you have spoken. This stipulation provides a rationale, in the king's own command, for the exact repetition in the language of the narrative report, of everything Haman has proposed. The one item that is in fact omitted is placing the crown on his head—perhaps, one may surmise, because the king himself does not mention it, thinking that this would be going too far.

12. *Mordecai returned to the king's gate.* Mordecai's sitting in front of the palace is a kind of vigil. He continues to wait and see how things will fall out for his threatened people, and all the regal honor just accorded him has not turned his head or deflected him from this task.

13 And Haman recounted to Zeresh his wife and to all his friends what had befallen him. And his wise men and Zeresh his wife said to him, "If Mordecai is of the seed of the Jews, before whom you have begun to fall, you shall not prevail over him but you shall surely fall before him."

14 While they were still speaking, the king's eunuchs arrived and hastened to bring Haman to the banquet that Esther had prepared.

---

13. *If Mordecai is of the seed of the Jews . . . you shall not prevail over him.* This response is scarcely in keeping with their counsel on the previous day to impale Mordecai, but it reflects the nationalist comic fantasy that is the vehicle of this story. Haman has already identified Mordecai to them as "the Jew." Now they appear not entirely certain whether he is of Jewish stock, but if he is, they are convinced that he is destined to defeat Haman because they recognize some special indomitable power in "the seed of the Jews." That recognition was not in evidence when they advised Haman to have Mordecai executed.

14. *hastened to bring Haman to the banquet that Esther had prepared.* The banquet is also a trap for Haman. He is, then, rushing from humiliating frustration to fatal defeat, on the verge of "falling" before the seed of the Jews, as his wife and counselors have just predicted.

CHAPTER 7

And the king and Haman came to drink with Esther. And the king [1,2] said to Esther again on the second day of the wine banquet, "What is your petition, Queen Esther, and it will be granted you? Up to half the kingdom and it will be done!" And Queen Esther answered and said, [3] "If I have found favor in the eyes of the king, and if it please the king, let my life be granted me in my petition and my people's in my request.

---

1. *came to drink.* At this second feast, the primacy of drinking is made clear at the outset, and in the next verse the social occasion will be immediately designated as "the wine banquet." It may be a calculation of Esther's to ply Ahasuerus with drink in order to be sure that he is especially favorably disposed toward her when she makes her shocking revelation.

2. *What is your petition . . .* In contrast to the general technique of earlier biblical narrative, which is to introduce small but significant changes in what looks like verbatim repetition, the Book of Esther uses exact repetition as a kind of narrative refrain, much like the frame story of Job, another Late Biblical composition.

3. *let my life be granted me.* When she finally states the content of her petition, she does it with strategic effort, pointedly startling the king by saying that her own life is in imminent danger, something he had no reason to suspect. In the immediately following sentence, she adds "my people," now revealing to him for the first time that she is a Jew. On the evidence of the subsequent narrative events, that revelation does not trouble him.

4 For we have been sold, I and my people, to be destroyed, to be killed,
and to be wiped out. And had we been sold to be male slaves and slave
girls, I would have remained silent, for the foe is not worth bothering the
5 king." And King Ahasuerus said, and he said to Queen Esther, "Who is it
6 and where is he, whose heart has prompted him to do this?" And Esther
said, "A man foe and enemy, this evil Haman." And Haman was terrified

---

4. *we have been sold.* The sense of the idiom is "given over," but she may also be
alluding to the extravagant price in silver that Haman offered in order to secure
permission to kill the Jews, and actual sale will be at issue when she mentions
the hypothetical alternative of slavery.

to be destroyed, to be killed, and to be wiped out. These verbs pick up the language of the genocidal decree devised by Haman. They also reflect the rather
loose Hebrew grammar of this text, for classical Hebrew would require passive
infinitive forms, but active infinitives ("to destroy," "to kill," "to wipe out") are
used here.

for the foe is not worth bothering the king. Some understand *tsar,* "foe," to
mean *tsarah,* "trouble," but this same word is picked up in verse 6 to designate
Haman.

5. *And King Ahasuerus said, and he said to Queen Esther.* Adele Berlin has
proposed that the repetition of the verb "said" is meant to indicate hesitation
on the king's part. Such usage, however, would be unique in biblical narrative;
there may be a scribal error here, perhaps a simple inadvertent duplication (dit-
tography). Some scholars emend the first "he said" to "hurried," a verb that in
Hebrew shares two of three consonants with the verb for "said."

where is he. The Hebrew could also be construed as "who is he" (a mere
repetition), but there is probably an ironic effect in the king's asking (clueless,
as usual) where the scoundrel is when he is standing before him.

6. *A man foe and enemy, this evil Haman.* Esther continues to weigh her utter-
ances shrewdly, saving the revelation of the would-be murderer and his stigma-
tizing label for the end of her speech.

before the king and the queen. And the king arose in his wrath from   7
the wine banquet to the pavilion garden, and Haman stood to plead for
his life to Queen Esther, for he saw that the evil was fixed against him
by the king. And the king came back from the pavilion garden to the   8
house of the wine banquet, and Haman was fallen on the couch where
Esther was, and the king said, "Is it also to force the queen with me
in the house?" The word had scarcely issued from the king's mouth,
and Haman's face turned pale. And Harbona, one of the eunuchs, said   9

---

7. *And the king arose in his wrath from the wine banquet to the pavilion garden.*
He is so furious after discovering that his most trusted minister has plotted
to kill his queen that he scarcely knows what to do—at many instances he
scarcely knows what to do—and so he walks out into the garden to pace back
and forth. This is, of course, also a narrative convenience, so that Haman can
be alone with Esther.

8. *Haman was fallen on the couch where Esther was.* The guests at the wine
banquet would have been reclining on couches. Haman has prostrated himself
on Esther's couch in pleading for his life. But the verb "fall" makes this a literal
realization of Zeresh's dire prophecy, "You shall surely fall before him" (in this
case, not before Mordecai but before his adoptive daughter).

Is it also to force the queen with me in the house? The sexual comedy of the
Book of Esther becomes particularly acute at this moment. Ahasuerus, seeing
Haman sprawled out on Esther's couch, briefly imagines that his first minister
is attempting to rape the queen, in the king's very presence. The misapprehen-
sion may be sharpened by his own uneasy awareness that he has failed to invite
the beautiful queen to his bedchamber for a month. One should also keep in
mind that to sexually possess the king's consort is to lay claim to the throne, as
Absalom does in cohabiting with David's concubines on the palace roof in
full view of the people. Such presumption to kingship accords with Haman's
frustrated plan to wear the king's raiment and crown and ride the king's horse.

turned pale. The precise meaning of the Hebrew term is in dispute, but it
clearly indicates that he is distraught.

before the king, "Look, there is actually a stake that Haman has prepared for Mordecai, who spoke good on behalf of the king, standing in
Haman's house, fifty cubits high." And the king said, "Impale him on it."
10 And they impaled Haman on the stake that he had readied for Mordecai, and the king's wrath subsided.

---

9. *Look, there is actually a stake that Haman has prepared for Mordecai.* Again,
it is someone in the court, in this case one of the palace eunuchs, who needs
to propose to the king an appropriate course of action. In the fairy-tale logic of
this narrative, that action is a neat reversal: the very instrument of the would-be
executioner is used to execute him.

10. *And they impaled Haman on the stake.* In the rapid pace of this narrative,
justice is immediately carried out, perhaps on the same day.
    and the king's wrath subsided. Haman's murderous project, which would have
involved the death of the queen, would have to be seen by Ahasuerus as an
act of base betrayal on the part of his most trusted minister, so the king's anger
abates only when Haman is put to death.

CHAPTER 8

On that day King Ahasuerus gave to Queen Esther the house of Haman, 1
foe of the Jews, and Mordecai came before the king, for Esther had told
what he was to her. And the king removed his ring that he had taken 2
away from Haman and gave it to Mordecai, and Esther placed Mordecai over the house of Haman. And Esther spoke once again before the 3
king and fell at his feet and wept and pleaded with him to take away the
evil of Haman the Agagite and his scheme that he had hatched against

---

1. *and Mordecai came before the king.* Repeatedly, the writer is careful to use
the preposition "before," rather than "to," in relation to the king because a
person comes before—that is, into the presence of—the august personage of a
monarch. This is the first moment in the story when Mordecai and Ahasuerus
actually meet.

for Esther had told what he was to her. This crucial revelation on her part
was not previously reported in the narrative but is introduced now in order to
explain Mordecai's appearance before the king.

2. *And the king removed his ring.* The passing of the signet ring, token of conferral of the king's power on its bearer, marks the neatly antithetical reversal
of positions—Haman is now dead, and Mordecai assumes the position he had
enjoyed.

3. *And Esther spoke once again.* The king would assume that he has granted her
all she could want, but now she has still another urgent petition. If Ahasuerus
were more alert, he might have understood on his own that there remains a
grave problem because of the irreversibility of the royal decree.

4 the Jews. And the king reached out the golden scepter to Esther, and
5 Esther arose and stood before the king. And she said, "If it please the
king and if I have found favor before him and if the thing be fit before
the king and I be pleasing in his eyes, let it be written to turn back the
missives, the scheme of Haman son of Hammedatha the Agagite, which
6 he wrote to destroy the Jews who are in all the king's provinces. For
how could I behold the evil that would befall my people and how could
7 I behold the destruction of my birth-kin?" And King Ahasuerus said to
Queen Esther and to Mordecai the Jew, "Look, I have given the house
of Haman to Esther, and him they have impaled on a stake for his having

---

4. *And the king reached out the golden scepter to Esther.* Since she has already
been granted the privilege to present her petition to the king, she fears that
this new request will seem presumptuous and be rebuffed, so again she needs
the extending of the golden scepter as the sign that the king has granted her
permission to speak.

Esther arose and stood before the king. Since she has prostrated herself in
supplication, she needs to rise in order to speak.

5. *let it be written.* As previously in the story, scrupulous attention is paid to
empirical bureaucratic procedure enacted through written documents. The
verbal stem k-t-b and its cognate noun ketav (in its two senses of "script" or
"system of writing" and "writ") are emphatically repeated.

7. *Ahasuerus said to Queen Esther and to Mordecai the Jew.* She, too, is a Jew, as
she has now made perfectly clear, but in the eyes of Ahasuerus her royal status
remains primary, and the identifying title "Queen" is repeated in the story again
and again.

Look, I have given the house of Haman to Esther, and him they have impaled.
Ahasuerus, perhaps with a small hint of impatience, notes that he has already
done a great deal for Esther and her kinsman, but in the next verse he goes on
to say that he will leave it to them to deal with what remains a sticky situation.

laid hands on the Jews. And as for you, write concerning the Jews what 8
is good in your eyes in the king's name, and seal it with the king's ring,
for a writ that has been written in the king's name and sealed with the
king's ring one cannot turn back." And the king's scribes were called 9
together at that time, in the third month which is the month of Sivan,
on the twenty-third day therein, and it was written as all that Mordecai
had charged to the Jews and to the satraps and the governors and the
ministers of the provinces from India to Cush, one hundred and twenty-
seven provinces, every province according to its own system of writing
and every people according to its language, and to the Jews, according
to their system of writing and according to their language. And he wrote 10
in the name of King Ahasuerus and sealed it with the king's ring and
sent missives by the hand of couriers on horseback riding mail-horses
bred of swift steeds: That the king has granted to the Jews who were in 11

---

8. *for a writ that has been written in the king's name and sealed with the king's
ring one cannot turn back.* This crucial point is distinctly part of the fantasy
world reflected in the plot of this book. The Persian empire—and indeed any
empire—could scarcely have been governed on the basis of absolutely irrevocable decrees. That supposition, however, enables another of the story's sym-
metrical antitheses: just as Haman sent out written decrees to the far reaches of
the empire to destroy all the Jews, Mordecai now will send out written decrees
authorizing the Jews to attack and kill their would-be destroyers.

9. *from India to Cush.* As at the beginning of the book, we are reminded of the
vastness of the empire.

10. *And he wrote in the name of King Ahasuerus.* The king has enjoined both
Esther and Mordecai to implement the writing of messages bearing the full
authority of the throne, but in the event, it is Mordecai, quickly assuming the
powers of vice-regent and equipped with the king's signet ring, who does the
writing, or rather, instructs the scribes to write the documents in all the different languages of the realm.
    riding mail-horses bred of swift steeds. The exact meaning of the three unusual
terms for horses (at least one of them a Persian loanword) is unclear, but there
is an evident implication that they are fast horses. Herodotus noted the speed
and efficiency of the Persian imperial mail system.

every single city to assemble and defend their lives, to destroy, and to
kill and to wipe out the whole force of every people and province that
was assaulting them, even children and women, and to take their booty,
12 on a single day, in all the provinces of King Ahasuerus, on the thirteenth
13 day of the twelfth month, which is the month of Adar, the copy of the
writ to be given as a rule in every single province, manifest to all the
peoples, and for the Jews to be ready for this day to take vengeance of
14 their enemies. The couriers riding the mail-horses went out rushing
urgently by the king's command, and the rule was given out in Shushan

---

11. *to assemble.* Perhaps previously they had been denied the right to assemble,
which would mean to group forces in self-defense.

to destroy, and to kill and to wipe out. These are precisely the terms used in
Haman's plan to extirpate the Jews.

even children and women. "Even" has been added in the translation to clarify
the meaning. The annihilation of the entire population—again what Haman
had envisaged for the Jews—is, needless to say, horrendous, though it accords
with the practice of *herem,* the total "ban," that was not uncommon in ancient
Near Eastern warfare and that figures prominently in Joshua, a text our writer
may have in mind here.

14. *rushing urgently by the king's command.* The king's command in itself
imparts urgency to their mission, but they need to hurry in order to bring the
royal message to distant parts of the empire before the day appointed for the
destruction of the Jews. The hurrying also reinforces the overall breakneck
speed of the narrative.

and the rule was given out in Shushan the capital. This clause needs to be
added so that we will be sure to know that the decree was also promulgated in
Shushan, where there was no necessity to send out mounted couriers.

the capital. And Mordecai came out before the king in royal garb, indigo   15
and white, and a great golden diadem and a wrap of crimson linen. And
the city of Shushan was merry and rejoicing. For the Jews there was   16

---

15. *And Mordecai came out before the king in royal garb.* This is an obvious realization of Haman's fantasy that *he* should be dressed in royal garb, and now, in
Mordecai's case, it is going to be his habitual attire as vice-regent, not merely
the finery worn for a ceremony to honor him. In Chapter 6, the king quietly
deleted Haman's inclusion of the crown in his list of royal accoutrements. Here
Mordecai is said to wear an *'atarah,* "diadem," which is nearly a crown but
perhaps a bit less than *keter,* the word Haman used. Behind Mordecai's being
clothed in regal garments (earlier he was in sackcloth) lies the Joseph story, in
which the former Hebrew prisoner is dressed by Pharaoh in regal clothing after
he is invested with power as vice-regent.

the city of Shushan was merry and rejoicing. This reiterated theme at the end
of the story accords with its carnivalesque character and with its aptness as the
founding narrative of a carnivalesque holiday, Purim.

17 light and joy and gladness and honor. In every single province and in every single city, where the king's command and his rule reached, there was joy and gladness for the Jews, banquet and holiday, and many of the peoples of the land were passing as Jews, for the fear of the Jews had fallen upon them.

---

17. *banquet and holiday.* The story that began with banqueting ends with banqueting. In all its recurrent cases, the term used is *mishteh*, which emphasizes drinking (and intoxication will become a theme of the holiday of Purim). The Hebrew for "holiday," *yom tov,* occurs only here in the Bible in this sense, thought it will become the standard term for "holiday" in rabbinic Hebrew.

were passing as Jews. The verb here is the reflexive form of the root *y-h-d,* *yehudi,* "Jew." It is unlikely that it means conversion to Judaism, as it would in later Hebrew, because there was no procedure of religious conversion in the fifth century BCE and also because the Book of Esther shows not the least concern with religion. What the verb seems to imply in context is that the sundry peoples pretended to be Jews, or perhaps aligned themselves with the Jews, in order to avoid attack.

for the fear of the Jews had fallen upon them. This sweeping military triumph of the Jews is not presented in any way as a miracle, but it is clearly another element of fantasy in this fantastic tale, as Adele Berlin notes, underlining its carnivalesque genre. The Jews, after all, were a small minority in the Persian empire, and the authorization by the emperor for them to take up arms against their assailants does not plausibly mean that they could overwhelm their enemies and strike terror among them. This turnabout, then, is a resolution of the fairy-tale plot: the beautiful queen has successfully interceded to save her people; the tables are turned on those who meant to wipe out the Jews; and as the great victory is celebrated, a Jew in royal finery becomes first minister to the king.

CHAPTER 9

On the twelfth month, which is the month of Adar, on the thirteenth day therein, when the king's command and his rule came to be enacted, on the day when the enemies of the Jews hoped to dominate them and, on the contrary, it was the Jews who dominated their foes, the Jews assembled in their cities in all the provinces of King Ahasuerus to lay hands on those who sought to do them harm, and no man could stand before them, for the fear of them had fallen on all the peoples. And all the ministers of all the provinces and the satraps and the governors and those who carried out the king's tasks were raising up the Jews, for the fear of Mordecai had fallen upon them. For great was Mordecai

---

1. *on the contrary.* This expression—in the Hebrew, *wenahafokh hu'*, "and it was the opposite"—makes verbally explicit the entire series of neatly antithetical reversals with which the story concludes.

2. *the Jews assembled.* As before, the verb suggests a drawing together of forces for effective military action against the assailants.

3. *for the fear of Mordecai had fallen upon them.* As Berlin aptly notes, while the populace fears the armed weight of the Jews, the high-ranking officials of the imperial bureaucracy fear Mordecai because they see that he has been given extraordinary power in the court. This point is underlined in the next words of the text, "For great was Mordecai in the house of the king."

in the house of the king, and his fame was going about through all the
5 provinces, for the man Mordecai was becoming ever greater. And the
Jews struck down all their enemies with a blow of the sword and with
killing and destruction, and they did to their enemies what they willed.
6 And in Shushan the capital the Jews killed and destroyed five hundred
7,8 men. And Parshandatha and Dalphon and Aspatha and Poratha and
9 Adalia and Aridatha and Parmashta and Arisai and Aridai and Vaizatha
10 the ten sons of Haman son of Hammadatha foe of the Jews did they
11 kill, but they did not lay hands on the spoil. On that day, the number of

---

4. *his fame was going about.* The writer makes abundant use of what amounts
to a progressive tense, relatively rare in earlier biblical Hebrew, to indicate an
unfolding process.

the man Mordecai. This epithet is unusual, and the writer may have in mind
the characterization in Exodus of Israel's great lawgiver as "the man Moses."

6. *five hundred men.* Though biblical narrative typically uses highly inflated
casualty figures, this one sounds plausible: the fighting in Shushan appears to
have involved only a few thousand, with five hundred slain. Perhaps the proximity to the palace discouraged large numbers from attempting to implement the
murderous decree of the disgraced and executed Haman.

7. *And Parshandatha and Dalphon . . .* The writer seems to revel in this sheer
Persian foreignness of all these names, as elsewhere he delights in studding his
Hebrew with Persian loanwords.

10. *but they did not lay hands on the spoil.* The decree promulgated by Mordecai
in fact allowed them to take the booty, but they choose to limit themselves to
killing their enemies in self-defense. Berlin proposes that this gesture is a reversal of King Saul's taking spoils from the Amalekites ruled by Agag, Haman's
putative ancestor (1 Samuel 15).

the slain in Shushan the capital came before the king, and the king said 12
to Queen Esther, "In Shushan the capital the Jews killed and destroyed
five hundred men and the ten sons of Haman, and in the rest of the
king's provinces, what have they done? And what is your petition, and
it will be granted to you, and what more is your request and it will be
done!" And Esther said, "If it please the king, let it be granted to the 13
Jews who are in Shushan tomorrow as well to do according to today's
rule, and let Haman's ten sons be impaled on stakes." And the king 14
spoke to have it done thus and to have a rule given out in Shushan
and to impale Haman's ten sons. And the Jews who were in Shushan 15

---

12. *in the rest of the king's provinces, what have they done?* Fox and Levinson see
in this question a satiric jab at the king, who is more concerned as he speaks to
Esther with body counts than with whether her people has been saved. But the
question may also reflect Ahasuerus's habitual ignorance about what is going on
around him: Do those fallen number only a few hundred here and there, as in
Shushan, or many thousands? Why he thinks Esther should have a command
of the casualty figures is a puzzle.

And what is your petition. The king mechanically repeats the formula he has
used twice before in speaking to Esther, though it is unclear why he should
think she has still another petition. Has the feared monarch become an uxorious husband, constantly asking his wife what he can do for her?

13. *let it be granted to the Jews who are in Shushan tomorrow as well.* The narrative logic of this request is not altogether evident because after the five hundred
killed and the killing of Haman's ten sons, it is not terribly likely that there
would be further attacks on the Jews in the capital. Some scholars have proposed that the rationale for the request is etiological—to provide an explanation
for the fact that this new carnivalesque holiday was in some places celebrated
for two days.

let Haman's ten sons be impaled on stakes. They have already been killed, so
this is a clear indication that impalement often followed execution, as a means
of humiliating the dead by exposing their bodies.

assembled as well on the fourteenth day of the month of Adar and killed
three hundred men in Shushan, but they did not lay hands on the spoils.
16 And the rest of the Jews who were in the king's provinces assembled and
defended their lives and had respite from their enemies and killed their
17 foes, seventy-five thousand, but they did not lay hands on the spoils, on
the thirteenth day of the month of Adar, with respite on the fourteenth
18 day therein, and they made it a day of banqueting and rejoicing. And the
Jews who were in Shushan assembled on the thirteenth day therein and
on the fourteenth day therein, with respite on the fifteenth day therein,
19 and they made it a day of banqueting and rejoicing. Therefore do the
village Jews, who dwell in unwalled towns, make the fourteenth day of
the month of Adar rejoicing and banqueting and holiday and the send-
20 ing of portions of food to each other. And Mordecai wrote down these
things and sent missives to all the Jews who were in all the provinces of

---

16. *had respite from their enemies*. This expression evokes an older Hebrew
idiom that indicates the state of calm and relief after the consummation of a
military victory.

 seventy-five thousand. Now the number of fallen enemies moves to the kind
of hyperbolic scale one would expect in ancient narrative.

17. *and they made it a day of banqueting and rejoicing*. The grounding of the new
holiday in this story is now pointedly emphasized, with a careful stipulation of
the day in Adar when it is to be observed. As before, the word for "banquet" or
"banqueting" highlights drinking.

19. *Therefore*. The Hebrew *'al-ken* is a standard locution for introducing etiolo-
gies. Virtually everything that follows is a kind of epilogue that explains how the
festival of Purim came to be celebrated on this date.

 the village Jews, who dwell in unwalled towns. In practical terms, this would
eventually apply to almost all Jews, who therefore celebrate the holiday one
day only. The sole clear candidate for a currently inhabited city that was walled
in ancient times is Jerusalem, where a second day of Purim, called "Shushan
Purim," is observed.

20. *And Mordecai wrote down these things and sent missives . . .* The preoccupation of this narrative with the sending of written documents as the instrument
for carrying out policy continues to the end of the story. One should note that

King Ahasuerus, near and far, to fix for them that they should make the 21
fourteenth day of the month of Adar and the fifteenth day therein every
single year like the days when the Jews had respite from their enemies, 22
and the month that was turned for them from sorrow to joy and from
mourning to holiday, to make them days of banqueting and rejoicing
and sending of portions of food to each other and gifts to the poor, and 23
for the Jews to accept all that they had begun to do and that Mordecai
had written to them. For Haman son of Hammedatha the Agagite foe 24
of the Jews had schemed against the Jews to destroy them and had cast
a *pur*, which is a lot, to panic them and to destroy them. And when she 25
came before the king, he said, with the missive, "Let the evil schemes
that he hatched against the Jews turn back on his own head." And they
impaled him and his sons on stakes. Therefore have they called these 26
days Purim, by the name of the *pur*. Therefore by all the words of this
epistle and what the king had seen concerning this and what had come
upon them, the Jews fixed and accepted for themselves and for their 27

---

this verse initiates a sprawling run-on sentence that goes all the way to the end
of verse 23. This is an especially egregious example of the syntactic looseness
of the book's Hebrew style.

25. *And when she came before the king.* The referent of "she" would be Esther.
Some interpreters read this as "it" (Hebrew has no neuter pronoun), referring to
Haman's plot or news of his plot, but that construction is problematic because
there is no noun in the preceding sentence, feminine or otherwise, that could
serve as antecedent to the proposed "it."

   with the missive. This phrase *'im hasefer* is rather obscure and may reflect
a scribal error. The word *sefer*, "missive, document, or scroll," occurs so frequently that it would not be surprising if a scribe inadvertently repeated it here
out of place.

27. *the Jews fixed and accepted.* The language in these closing verses is pointedly
legalistic: the Jews enter into a binding agreement that they will scrupulously
observe the terms of their new holiday for all time. The writer is treading on
dangerous ground because he is arguing for the legitimacy of a holiday that has
no warrant among the sundry festivals listed in the Torah. Consequently, he
wants to make it clear that there is national consent for all the conditions of this
newly minted holiday. One might note that no religious justification is given for

seed and for all who joined with them, never to be violated, to make
these two days, as they were written and according to their time, in
28 every single year, and that these days should be remembered and done
in every generation, clan by clan, province by province, city by city, and
that these days of Purim should not pass away from the midst of the
Jews, and their remembrance should not come to an end from among
29 their seed. And Queen Esther daughter of Abihail with Mordecai the
Jew wrote with full authority to confirm this Purim epistle once more.
30 And missives were sent to all the Jews, to the hundred twenty-seven
31 provinces of the kingdom of Ahasuerus, words of peace and truth, to

---

the holiday: it is not commanded by God but instituted to commemorate the
people's victory over those who sought to destroy it.

for all who joined with them. Though some see these as the Persians who
"passed as Jews," it is more likely that the expression refers to fellow travelers
of the Jews, Judaizing foreigners who are probably not quite formal converts.
The anonymous prophet of the return to Zion (Isaiah 56:3, 6) uses this same
verb in this sense.

28. *that these days of Purim should not pass away from the midst of the Jews.* The
phrasing here continues the terminology of binding legal agreement for the
establishment of the holiday.

29. *Queen Esther daughter of Abihail.* She is so identified here near the end of
the book to underscore her Jewish lineage—she is both Queen of Persia and
daughter of Abihail.

30. *And missives were sent.* The Hebrew appears to say "and he sent missives,"
but the third-person singular verb is often used as the equivalent of a passive
(somewhat like the *on* construction in French).

words of peace and truth. This is the literal sense of the Hebrew, a collocation that occurs a few times elsewhere. It may well be a hendiadys, meaning
something like "true peace." After all the violence, real peace would indeed be
welcome.

fix these days of Purim in their times as Mordecai the Jew and Queen Esther had fixed for them, and as they had fixed for themselves and for their seed just as they had fixed for themselves matters of fasts and their supplication. And Esther's dictum fixed these matters of Purim and was 32 written out in a missive.

---

31. *matters of fasts and their supplication.* The literal sense of the word rendered as "supplication" is "cry," as the King James Version shows. The mention of fasts and supplication at the end of this festive narrative may seem at least momentarily puzzling. The point is that just as the Jews have been punctilious in observing their sundry fast days, they are now to be equally punctilious in celebrating this holiday of merrymaking. The introduction of this comparison between somber and joyous holidays accords nicely with the previously mentioned transition "from sorrow to joy, from mourning to holiday."

32. *Esther's dictum . . . was written out in a missive.* The first noun, *ma'amar,* suggests speech, something said, but as throughout the book, it takes on the full weight of authority only when it is written out in a scroll or missive, *sefer.* The fact that here it is Esther, not Mordecai, who has the decree written reinforces the understanding that in verse 29 it is Esther who does the writing (the Hebrew grammar indicates "she wrote"), with Mordecai merely reinforcing her effort.

CHAPTER 10

1 And King Ahasuerus imposed forced labor on all the land and on the
2 coastlands. And all the acts of his authority and his might and the
account of Mordecai's greatness to which the king raised him, are they
not written in the Book of the Acts of the Kings of Media and Persia?
3 For Mordecai the Jew was second to King Ahasuerus and great over the
Jews, in favor with his many brothers, seeking the good of his people and
speaking peace for all its seed.

---

1. *forced labor.* In the ancient Near East, conscripting subjects for service in
corveés was a common form of taxation. The notation of the king's taxation at
the end looks a little odd, but it is perhaps introduced to indicate that after the
violent upheavals caused by Haman's nefarious plot, Ahasuerus imposed order
on his realm and took steps to ensure its economic stability.

the coastlands. In later Hebrew, *'iyey hayam* means "islands of the sea," but in
biblical usage it refers to far-flung places that may be either along the shore of
the Mediterranean or actual islands. Here the idiom stands instead of phrases
used earlier for the vast extent of the empire.

2. *are they not written in the Book of the Acts of the Kings of Media and Persia?*
The wording of this entire verse pointedly imitates a recurrent formula in the
Book of Kings, where it refers to one of two actual sets of annals of the kings of
Judah and Israel, respectively. This is an effort to impart an effect of authentic
history to a narrative that is actually woven of fantastic invention.

3. *its seed.* Many interpreters understand this as "his seed." But a declaration
at the very end of Mordecai's status and virtues would surely not conclude by
saying that he looked after his own offspring. Rather, he seeks the good of his
people and creates conditions of harmonious existence for all its posterity.

THE BOOK OF JONAH

TO THE READER

W E KNOW NOTHING about the author of the Book of Jonah or his geographic location, and only a rough approximation can be made of the time of the book's composition. The main evidence for dating is linguistic: there are quite a few turns of phrase that indicate this is Late Biblical prose, a kind of Hebrew not written till after the return from the Babylonian exile in the fifth century BCE. The book's universalist theology probably also argues for a relatively late date because one does not find this sort of rigorously world-embracing monotheism until Second Isaiah, the anonymous sixth-century prophet of the Babylonian exile. It is possible that the book's author drew on an earlier folktale, as some scholars have conjectured, though there is no way of proving that, and the fabulous elements of the story in their very extravagance have a look more of literary invention than of a naïve folk imagination.

The name Jonah son of Amittai is drawn from a passing reference in 2 Kings 15 to a prophet so designated who delivered God's word during the reign of Jereboam II and about whom nothing more than that is said. Since our story—which has no clear historical moorings, apart from the vague invocation of Assyria—was almost surely composed centuries later (despite some unconvincing dissent on the issue of dating from a few biblical scholars), the protagonist is surely not identical with the prophet mentioned in 2 Kings. The writer may have adopted the name because the patronym *amittai* suggests *'emet*, "truth," in Hebrew. The first name, *yonah*, means "dove," which could have an ironic application here because this Jonah is an unwilling agent who ends up averting a punitive cataclysm, in approximate analogy to Noah's dove, which signals the restoration of life after a punitive cataclysm. Alternately, the writer might simply have chosen this particular prophet's name as a convenient hook on which to hang a fable about prophecy precisely because nothing more is known about the prophet in question.

Though the Hebrew narratives composed in the First Temple period utilize heterogeneous materials, they exhibit a great deal of uniformity in regard to narrative conventions and the general purposes for which narratives are framed. By contrast, what characterizes the narratives of the Late Biblical period is a vigorous experimentation with genre and an impulse to move beyond the governing procedures of earlier biblical narrative. Perhaps the most distinctive hallmark of Jonah's relatively late composition is that it tells a story altogether unlike those of earlier biblical literature. The recalcitrance of the prophet is a recurring feature of the classic call narratives of the prophets, as with Jeremiah, Isaiah, and Moses himself, but nowhere else do we have a person summoned to prophecy who actually tries to flee to the other end of the known world. Similarly, though one prophet, Amos, is sent from his Judean home to prophesy in the northern—and not very friendly—kingdom of Israel, the two realms are still, after all, within the family, and only in Jonah is a man called to deliver a prophecy to the general populace of an altogether foreign, and hostile, nation.

The two instances just mentioned offer a clue to Jonah's relation to its literary antecedents. It picks up certain hints or precedents from earlier biblical narrative but pushes them to an extreme where they play a role in what amounts to a different genre. The narratives originating in the First Temple period, despite exhibiting some miraculous events and some spectacular episodes of divine intervention, are by and large "history-like," as Hans Frei has aptly called them, from the Patriarchal tales to the stories of David and the later kings. Jonah, on the other hand, is a manifestly fabulous tale. Though earlier Hebrew narrative offers one anomalous instance of a talking animal, Balaam's she-ass, that is the exception that proves the rule, an invention introduced to sharpen the satire on the pagan soothsayer who is blind to what his visionary beast can plainly see. Jonah's fish does not speak, but it follows God's instructions dutifully, first swallowing Jonah and then, when it gets the word, vomiting him up on dry land. Its capacity, moreover, to keep Jonah three days in the dark wet prison of its innards is an even more fantastic contrivance than according Balaam's ass the momentary gift of speech. This peculiar performance of the fish, serving as God's obedient instrument, is in keeping with the cattle and sheep in Nineveh, bizarrely required to don sackcloth and fast together with the human beings and, in the deliberately ambiguous wording of the Hebrew, seen as if consciously covering themselves with sackcloth and as if crying out to God along with the human denizens of Nineveh.

All this has led scholars to scramble for labels to describe Jonah. It has been called everything from a Menippean satire to an allegory, but none of these identifications of Jonah is entirely convincing. I would see Jonah as its own kind of ad hoc innovative narrative. It aims to recast traditional Israelite notions of prophecy in a radically universalist framework. The prophets of Israel all work in an emphatically national context. Their messages are addressed to the people of Israel, often with explicitly political concerns, and the messages are manifestly directed to the fate of the nation—its imminent destruction by foreign powers if it fails to mend its evil ways, the fulfillment of its hope for national restoration after the disaster has occurred. The medium of the prophets is generally poetry, where all the powerful, expressive resources of the Hebrew language could be summoned to convey the prophetic vision to the people. That may be one reason why Jonah is accorded no verbal prophetic message, only that single brief prediction of catastrophe which, if one is supposed to think of such considerations, he would have spoken not in Hebrew but in the language of the Assyrians.

Jonah engages with no Israelites in the story. First he has an exchange with the polytheistic mariners, then he addresses the Ninevites, and his closest connection is with two presumably insensate living things, a very large fish and a leafy plant. The God with whom he has such difficulties because of his Israelite nationalist mindset is not chiefly the God of Israel but the God of the whole world, of all creatures large and small. He is not a God you can pin down to national settings. Though He initially addresses Jonah somewhere within the Land of Israel, perhaps even in Jerusalem, where the temple, evoked in Chapter 2, stands, His fullest dialogue with Jonah is on a promontory overlooking Nineveh. Though He does rebuke Jonah, as the God of earlier Hebrew narratives and poems rebukes wayward people, the rebuke itself is oddly formulated, in keeping with the wonderful strangeness of this book. God exercises magisterial control over storm winds, fish, livestock, and plants as well as over human beings of all tribes and nations, and He asks the recalcitrant prophet why he should "have pity" for an ephemeral plant and not for a vast city of clueless human beings and their beasts. It is beautifully appropriate that the story ends with the beasts, and with a question. It is in no way clear how Jonah will respond to this question. Will God's challenge lead him to a transformative insight about God's dominion over all things and all peoples, or will it prove to be a challenge that is quite beyond the myopia of his ingrained prejudices? The trembling balance of this concluding ambiguity perfectly focuses the achievement of the Book of Jonah both as an enchanting story and as the shaking up of an entire theological world.

CHAPTER 1

And the word of the LORD came to Jonah son of Amittai, saying, "Get 1,2
up, go to Nineveh the great city, and call out against it, for their evil has
risen before Me." And Jonah got up to flee to Tarshish from before the 3

---

1. *came to Jonah.* The literal meaning of the Hebrew verb is "was to Jonah."

2. *Nineveh the great city.* The entirely fabulous proportions of its vastness will
become clear in Chapter 3. Though there are a couple of rare instances, in the
Book of Kings, of an Israelite prophet going on a mission to a foreign country,
the call to go to Nineveh is anomalous and hardly historical. Nineveh is the
capital of the Assyrian empire, no longer existent by the likely time of Jonah's
composition but remembered as the power that entirely destroyed the northern
kingdom of Israel and that later seriously threatened the southern kingdom of
Judah as well. To send a Hebrew prophet to Nineveh would be rather like sending a Jewish speaker to deliver moral exhortation to the Germans in Berlin in
1936. Though Jonah's words to God in 4:2 make it clear that he does not want
to undertake the mission because he foresees that the Ninevites will repent
and that God will forgive them, he might well also be afraid to go to Nineveh.

3. *And Jonah got up to flee.* For a brief moment, he might seem to be heeding
God's command to get up and go to Nineveh, but this momentary illusion is
broken by the infinitive "to flee."
   Tarshish. This location, mentioned in a variety of biblical texts, has been
identified with various places from Asia Minor to Spain. In any event, it is far
to the west, in the opposite direction from Nineveh.

LORD to Jaffa and found a ship coming from Tarshish, and he paid its
fare and went down with them to go to Tarshish from before the LORD.
4 And the LORD cast a great wind upon the sea, and there was a great
5 storm on the sea, and the ship threatened to break up. And the sailors
were afraid, and each man cried out to his god, and they cast the gear
that was in the ship into the sea to lighten their load. And Jonah had
come down into the far corners of the craft and had lain down and
6 fallen deep asleep. And the captain approached him and said, "What
are you doing deep asleep? Call out to your god. Perhaps the god will
7 give some thought to us, that we may not perish." And they said to each

---

Jaffa. This port city, more or less on the site of present-day Tel Aviv, was probably not under Israelite control. The rest of Jonah's story will unfold entirely
among foreigners.

went down. We are not informed about Jonah's hometown, but it would
likely be up in the hill country, perhaps even Jerusalem, for Israelite habitation
in the coastal plain was sparse. First Jonah goes down to Jaffa, then into the
ship. His trajectory is a series of goings down as he is cast into the sea and then
into the belly of the fish.

4. *the ship threatened to break up.* The term *hishvah* reflects a root that in earlier
biblical Hebrew means "to plan, to devise, or to reckon." Jack Sasson argues
that it is a deliberate personification and thus he renders it as "expected," but
"threatened" is personification enough and more idiomatic in context.

5. *And the sailors were afraid.* Their fear will mark this entire episode, taking on
a new meaning at its end.

to lighten their load. The literal sense of the Hebrew is "to lighten from upon
them."

Jonah had come down. This is the third occurrence of this thematically
fraught verb, marked here as a pluperfect (subject before the verb, verb in the
qatal form).

the far corners of the craft. This is presumably the hold, but the phrase *yarketey hasefinah* plays on *yarketey bor,* "the far corners of the pit" (that is, death),
and perhaps also, as James Ackerman has proposed, on *yarketey tsafon,* "the far
corners of Tsafon" (the dwelling place of the gods in Canaanite mythology).

6. *will give some thought to us.* The Hebrew *yit'ashet* is unique to this text. The
translation follows the proposal of some medieval exegetes that is related to
'eshtonot, "thoughts."

other, "Let us cast lots that we may know on whose account this evil is
upon us." And they cast lots, and the lot fell on Jonah. And they said to 8
him, "Tell us, pray, you on whose account this evil is upon us, what is
your work and from where do you come? What is your land, and from
what people are you?" And he said to them, "I am a Hebrew and the 9
LORD God of the heavens do I fear, Who made the sea and the dry land."
And the men feared greatly, and they said to him, "What is this you have 10
done?" For the men knew that he was fleeing from before the LORD, for
he had told them. And they said to him, "What shall we do that the sea 11
calm for us?" For the sea was storming more and more. And he said to 12

---

7. *Let us cast lots.* The lot is divinatory device, especially for determining guilt.
See Joshua 6 and 1 Samuel 14.

8. *you on whose account.* The "you" is merely implied in the Hebrew.
what is your work. Most passengers would have been merchants, but Jonah
has brought no merchandise on board. The noun has a specific connotation of
designated task, so they may be asking Jonah what he is up to.
What is your land. Jaffa, probably a polyglot city where traders embarked
and disembarked, would give them no clue as to the national identity of this
passenger.

9. *I am a Hebrew.* This is regularly the designation used by foreigners for Israelites and so it makes sense that Jonah would choose it to identify his nationality
to the ship's crew.
and the LORD *God of the heavens do I fear, Who made the sea and the dry land.*
Although this declaration of faith serves the thematic purposes of this story,
the effect is almost comic: Jonah, who has run away from God's command, as
though a geographic escape from God were possible, now announces his reverence for the universal God of sky, sea, and earth. His declaration would surely
at first have baffled the polytheistic sailors, for whom there would have been a
separate deity for each of these realms.

11. *For the sea was storming more and more.* As the story continues, there is an
indication in the verbal form used, *holekh weso'er*, of a constant increase in the
intensity of the storm, which was powerful to begin with.

them, "Lift me up and cast me into the sea that the sea calm for you,
13 for I know that on my account this great storm is upon you." And the
men rowed to get back to the dry land and were not able, for the sea was
14 storming upon them more and more. And they called out to the LORD
and said, "Please, O LORD, pray let us not perish on account of the life of
this man, and do not exact from us the blood of the innocent, for You, O

---

12. *Lift me up and cast me into the sea.* Jonah means simply that if they get rid
of his jinxing presence on board, the storm will cease to pound the ship. The
crew, however, may well have construed this as casting an offering to appease
the raging sea god.

13. *And the men rowed to get back to the dry land.* They are reluctant to follow
Jonah's instructions, which they of course understand as condemning him to
almost certain death. But rowing toward the shore (the ship would have been
equipped with both oars and sails) is a strategy of desperation because in a
fierce storm, approaching the shore would have most likely led to a catastrophic
shipwreck.

14. *And they called out to the LORD.* They may not have been transformed into
monotheists, but Jonah's testimony to them has clearly convinced them that
in the present dire circumstances, the LORD, YHWH, is a powerful deity who
controls the urgent situation.
    let us not perish on account of the life of this man. This might mean that they
do not want to be the target of God's punishing wrath together with Jonah, who
is on the ship with them. But the reference to the blood of the innocent in the
next clause may rather suggest that they are praying not to be condemned for
killing Jonah by throwing him overboard.

LORD, as You desire You do." And they lifted up Jonah and cast him into 15 the sea, and the sea ceased from its fury. And the men feared the LORD 16 greatly and offered sacrifices to the LORD and made vows.

---

16. *And the men feared the LORD greatly.* This is exactly the phrase used for their fear of the storm in verse 10. Now it appears in its other meaning of showing reverence through worship (the sacrifices and vows at the end of this verse) for a deity, though the first sense of terror still lingers—they revere the LORD because they have witnessed His awesome power in the terrible storm and in His causing it to suddenly stop. Again one needn't assume that they have become perfect monotheists, like the Aramean general in 2 Kings miraculously cured of his skin disease, for they might simply be recognizing that Jonah's deity is the one who has manifested awesome control over the storm that almost destroyed them. In any case, the turning of the hearts of these pagans to the God of Israel anticipates the response of the Ninevites to Jonah's message.

offered sacrifices to the LORD and made vows. There is some evidence that ships in the ancient world actually carried animals which could be sacrificed on board at urgent or propitious moments. The "vows" are pledges to offer further, votary sacrifices after their safe return to land.

CHAPTER 2

¹ And the LORD set out a great fish to swallow Jonah, and he was three
² days and three nights in the innards of the fish. And Jonah prayed to the
³ LORD his God from the innards of the fish. And he said:

> "I called out from my straits
>   to the LORD, and He answered me.

---

1. *And the* LORD *set out.* This term (*m-n-h*) recurs in the subsequent story,
highlighting God's supervisory control over all living constituents of creation—
animal, vegetable, and human.

a great fish. Though this could conceivably be a whale, as traditional under-
standings of the story imagine—perhaps most vividly in *Moby-Dick*—the
Hebrew employs the unspecific generic term for sea creature.

three days and three nights. Many events in biblical narrative are said to occur
in precisely this time span. What is distinctive here is the emphatic addition of
three nights to three days, inviting us to envisage Jonah's terror imprisoned in
the dark belly of the big fish three long nights and three long days, during which
he of course has no way of distinguishing between day and night.

2. *the* LORD *his God.* Now, as if to confirm Jonah's declaration of faith to the
mariners, the LORD is reported to be his God.

3. *I called out from my straits / to the* LORD, *and He answered me.* As is the regular
practice in biblical narrative, a poem is inserted that was originally composed
for another context (compare Hannah's thanksgiving psalm, 1 Samuel 2:1–10).
This poem is a psalm of thanksgiving, exhibiting many of the formulas and
metaphors of that genre. It fits the narrative situation somewhat imperfectly
because, though it is introduced as Jonah's prayer from the belly of the fish,
it is not actually a plea for deliverance but the rendering of thanks to God for

From the belly of Sheol I cried out—
    You heard my voice.
You flung me into the deep, in the heart of the sea,   4
    and the current came round me.
All your breakers and waves
    streamed over me.
And I thought: 5
    I am banished from before Your eyes.
Yet again will I look
    on Your holy temple.

---

having already delivered the speaker, as this opening line at once makes clear. The image of almost drowning in the depths of the seas as a metaphor for near death (often because of a grave illness) is conventional in thanksgiving psalms, but here it is made to apply literally to Jonah's desperate aqueous plight. Not surprisingly, the inserted psalm makes no mention of being swallowed by a fish because the maws of gigantic fish do not figure in thanksgiving psalms. Nevertheless, the poem does incorporate several relevant points of connection with Jonah's story.

You heard my voice. Having first referred to God in the third person, the speaker now intimately addresses Him directly.

4. *All Your breakers and waves / streamed over me.* This vivid image of drowning invokes, as noted, a conventional trope of the thanksgiving psalm.

5. *And I thought: / I am banished from before Your eyes.* Death is the ultimate separation from God in the biblical worldview. But the psalm also provides a geographical orientation for Jonah's story: fleeing God's presence, which has its territorial focus in the Jerusalem temple on Mount Zion, Jonah finds himself in the watery depths, at the antipodes from God's holy place. He has manifestly "gone down"—compare verse 7, "to the roots of the mountains I went down"— from Jerusalem.

Yet again will I look / on Your holy temple. The speaker expresses faith against odds that he will live and return to worship God in His temple. Jonah, who has fled from the divine presence, now affirms the desire to return and enjoy it.

6   Water lapped about me to the neck,
        the deep came round me,
           weed was bound round my head.

7   To the roots of the mountains I went down—
        the underworld's bolts against me forever.
    But You brought up my life from the Pit,
        O Lord my God.

8   As my life-breath grew faint within me,
        the Lord did I recall,
    and my prayer came unto You,
        to Your holy temple.

---

6. *weed was bound round my head.* This strong image of the head entrammeled in seaweed amplifies the conventional metaphor of sinking into the depths. The clause is rhythmically compact and assonant in the Hebrew—*suf ḥavush lero'shi*—an effect the translation tries to emulate.

7. *underworld's . . . the Pit.* Because the sea as a site of drowning is the metaphorical equivalent of death, the poem naturally moves from the watery abyss to the underworld, just as it began by placing the speaker in "the belly of Sheol."

8. *my prayer came unto You, / to Your holy temple.* The temple is where prayer is most readily heard by God. We have here a cosmic reach from the roots of the mountains, the bottom of the sea, to the temple on Mount Zion.

Those who look to vaporous lies   9
      will turn away from their mercy.
And I with a voice of thanksgiving   10
      let me sacrifice to You.
What I vowed let me pay.
      Rescue is the LORD's."

And the LORD spoke to the fish, and it vomited Jonah onto the dry land. 11

---

9. *Those who look to vaporous lies.* This phrase replicates a phrase that occurs in Psalm 31:7.

will turn away from their mercy. The wording in the Hebrew is cryptic and has encouraged diverse interpretations. The least strained, which this translation seeks to register, is that the idol worshipers (clearly the reference of "those who look to vaporous lies") at some point will be compelled to recognize that the purported deities from whom they seek mercy are mere illusions, and thus they will abandon their futile worship. The possessive pronoun "their" (in Hebrew merely a suffix) attached to "mercy" would refer to the idols. In all this, as both medieval and modern commentators have noted, there is some relevance to Jonah and the sailors: each of the mariners calls upon his own God, but to no avail; after hearing Jonah's words, they implore YHWH instead, Who in the end saves them.

10. *And I with a voice of thanksgiving.* One of the conventions of the thanksgiving psalm is to announce thanks or acclamation (*todah*, which is also the designation of the thanksgiving sacrifice) at the end of the poem.

let me sacrifice . . . let me pay. Existing translations render this as a simple future, but that misses the nuance of the Hebrew because both verbs show the suffix that is the marker of the optative mode. What the speaker declares is that he *wishes* to offer sacrifice. Presumably, he will carry out his desire, but that is different from a simple statement of the future tense.

11. *And the LORD spoke to the fish.* Just as He assigns the fish to swallow Jonah at the beginning of the episode, now He gives word to the fish to spew out Jonah. God's omnipresent control of all things is again manifest.

vomited. As Sasson observes, this unpleasant verb is perfectly appropriate for a kind of indignity to which Jonah is subjected in the very act of being rescued.

CHAPTER 3

^{1, 2} And the word of the LORD came to Jonah a second time, saying, "Get up, go to Nineveh the great city and call out to it the call that I speak
³ to you." And Jonah got up and went to Nineveh according to the word

---

2. *Get up, go to Nineveh the great city and call out to it.* God repeats verbatim His initial command to Jonah, rightly anticipating that after Jonah's terrifying experience of God's power on the ship and in the belly of the fish, the prophet will now be prepared to carry out the mission. The one small difference from the opening words of Chapter 1 is that instead of the preposition *'al,* "against," God uses *'el,* "to," perhaps suggesting that Jonah's message may not have an altogether hostile purpose. If that is so, it is a clue Jonah does not pick up, as we shall see.

3. *And Jonah got up and went to Nineveh.* All we know about his location is that, after having been spewed out by the big fish, he is somewhere on the eastern coast of the Mediterranean. In a move characteristic of biblical narrative, his journey to Nineveh, which would have taken weeks, is compressed into four Hebrew words, with all circumstantial detail suppressed.

of the LORD. And the Nineveh was a great city of God's, a three days'
walk across. And Jonah began to come into the city, one day's walk, and 4
he called out and said, "Forty days more, and Nineveh is overthrown."

---

a great city of God's. The Hebrew has been variously understood as "a great
city to God," "a great city before God," and even as "a super-great city" (with
'elohim serving merely as an intensifier). But this preposition *le* in biblical
Hebrew (including many inscriptions on pottery, seals, and the like) often
means "belonging to." That meaning makes sense in terms of the theology of
the book: Nineveh, like everything else in the world, is God's possession, and
thus God is appropriately concerned about the behavior of its inhabitants and
their fate.

a three days' walk across. "Across" is merely implied in the Hebrew. But the
dimensions of the city vividly reflect the fabulous nature of the story: clocking
roughly three miles an hour, a walker could cover as much as thirty miles in a
day. A city ninety miles across would be considerably larger than contemporary
Los Angeles, and needless to say, no actual city in the ancient Near East could
have been anywhere near that big. This three days' walk also has the consequence that it will take Jonah three days—a formulaic unit in biblical narrative,
as we have seen in the instance of the sojourn in the fish's belly—to proclaim
his message throughout the city.

4. *Forty days more, and Nineveh is overthrown.* The number is formulaic, as
in the forty days of the Flood, the forty days Moses spends on the mountain,
and the forty years of wandering in the Wilderness. Unless we are to construe
Jonah's prophecy as a highly elliptical report, it is unconditional: in forty days,
Nineveh is to be utterly devastated (and Jonah uses the participial form, not
the future, to heighten the immediacy), with the verb "overthrown" the same
one that is applied to Sodom. But as the next verse makes clear, the people of
Nineveh understand this dire prediction as implying a reversal of the disaster
if they change their ways.

5 And the people of Nineveh trusted God, and they called a fast and
6 donned sackcloth, from the greatest of them to the least. And the word
reached the king of Nineveh, and he rose from his throne and took
off his mantle and covered himself in sackcloth and sat upon ashes.
7 And he had it proclaimed and he said in Nineveh: "By the authority of
the king and his great men, saying, man and beast, cattle and sheep,
shall taste nothing. They shall not graze and they shall not drink water.

---

5. *And the people of Nineveh trusted God.* That is, they trust God's word delivered by Jonah that they will be annihilated unless they turn back from their evil
ways. This translation avoids the use of "believe" for the Hebrew term because
the general meaning of this word in the Bible—as opposed to the postbibli-
cal usage of *he'emin*—suggests an act of trust, not of belief. One should not
imagine that the Ninevites have become monotheists but rather that they have
taken seriously the word of YHWH that He is prepared to destroy the city.
The claim of some scholars that this verb, when followed by the preposition
be, means "believe" does not stand up under analysis. The few cases where it
occurs with this preposition are at best ambiguous, and in Micah 7:5 the usage
is unambiguously a statement about trust, not belief: "Do not trust in evil,"
and then in the poetic parallelism, "nor place confidence [*tivtehu*] in a leader."

6. *And the word reached the king of Nineveh.* First, a wave of penitence sweeps
through the populace as Jonah continues his three days' walk through the city,
crying out his grim prophecy; then word of it comes to the king in his palace.

   his mantle. Elsewhere the noun *'aderet* can be any sort of mantle or cloak,
but here it is clearly a royal mantle, with the designation perhaps playing on the
word *'adir*, "majestic," that might be discerned in its root.

7. *had it proclaimed.* Literally, "caused to be shouted."

   By the authority. The term *mita'am* is appropriate for the introduction of
a royal decree and also is one of the reflections in our text of Late Biblical
Hebrew.

   man and the beast, cattle and sheep, shall taste nothing. The bracketing, a
virtual equation, of man and beast becomes a thematic thrust of the story. It is,
of course, bizarre that a fast should be imposed on animals, another reflection
of the fabulous character of the story, and that bizarreness will be heightened
in the next verse.

   graze. Though this word ordinarily applies only to the animals, here it seems,
almost comically, to refer to humans as well.

And man and beast shall cover themselves with sackcloth, and they 8
shall call out to God with all their might, and every man of them shall
turn back from his evil way and from the outrage to which they hold fast.
Who knows? Perhaps God will turn back and relent and turn back from 9
His blazing wrath, and we shall not perish." And God saw their acts, that 10
they had turned back from their evil way, and God relented from the evil
that He said to do to them, and he did not do it.

---

8. *And man and beast shall cover themselves with sackcloth.* The translation
closely follows the wording of the Hebrew, which intimates an image, against
all logic, of the beasts voluntarily covering themselves with sackcloth. In the
next clause, though "call out" should refer to the humans only, its syntactical
placement comes close to inviting us to imagine the beasts calling out as well.
All this amounts to a kind of hyperbolic farcical representation of the penitence of Nineveh: after Jonah's message, the city is so caught up in a profound
impulse of penitence that a fast with sackcloth is imposed on beasts as well as
on human beings.

　　turn back. The verb *shuv,* repeated three times in two verses, becomes the
thematic focus of this episode: the people turn back from evil, and God then
turns back from His baleful intentions.

10. *God relented from the evil that He said to do to them.* "Evil" here means
"harm," as often elsewhere in biblical usage, but it is a measure-for-measure
response to the evil of the Ninevites, and thus the translation follows the repetition of the word in the Hebrew. As in the previous episode, God is seen first
as a wrathful God—sending the terrible storm that threatens the sailors' lives
as well as Jonah's—and then as a merciful God—rescuing Jonah from the belly
of the fish to give him a second chance as a prophet, and now canceling the
decree to destroy Nineveh.

CHAPTER 4

1, 2   And the thing was very evil for Jonah, and he was incensed. And he prayed to the LORD and said, "I beseech You, LORD, was it not my word when I was still in my land? Therefore did I hasten to flee to Tarshish, for I knew that You are a gracious and compassionate God, slow to anger and

---

1. *And the thing was very evil for Jonah.* Various translations seek to reconcile this clause with English idiomatic usage by representing Jonah here as "dejected," "depressed," "displeased." But the repetition of the term *ra'ah*, "evil," is important for the writer's purpose. When the Ninevites decide to turn away from evil, their very repentance so upsets Jonah that it becomes, ironically, an evil, which is to say, a bitter vexation for him.

2. *hasten.* The basic meaning of the Hebrew for *qidem* is to anticipate something by acting before it can happen. As Sasson notes, there is an interplay between this term and *miqedem*, "to the east of," in verse 5, as well as with the "east wind," *ruaḥ qadim*, in verse 8.
   You are a gracious, compassionate God, slow to anger and abundant in kindness. These words are a direct quotation of Exodus 34:6. One may infer that by the late moment of the writing of Jonah, the Torah was already canonical and these words were familiar as a kind of doxology. Jonah, knowing God's compassionate nature from such an authoritative text, did not want to undertake the prophetic mission because he did not want to be an instrument in saving Israel's hated arch-enemies from destruction. At this late point in the story, he remains an unreconstructed Israelite nationalist, in contradiction to the universalist outlook of the book.

abundant in kindness and relenting from evil. And now, LORD, take my 3
life, pray, from me, for better my death than my life." And the LORD said, 4
"Are you good and angry?" And Jonah went out of the city and sat down 5
to the east of the city and made himself a shelter there and sat under it in
the shade till he might see what would happen in the city. And the LORD 6
God set out a *qiqayon* plant, and it rose up over Jonah to be a shade over
his head to save him from his evil plight. And Jonah rejoiced greatly over
the *qiqayon*. And God set out a worm as dawn came up on the morrow, 7

---

3. *take my life.* Facing the galling fact that he has enabled the despised Ninevites to survive, which was God's intention all along but not his, Jonah does not
want to go on living. This becomes the story of a prophetic mission that is a
great success (unlike those of the historical prophets), with the success being
intolerable to the prophet.

4. *Are you good and angry?* God's response in this first exchange with Jonah is
scarcely a response, only a provocation that leaves Jonah simmering.

5. *see what would happen in the city.* Either Jonah hopes that the Ninevites will
yet abandon their repentance and suffer cataclysmic destruction, with him as
a privileged spectator, or he will be confirmed in what he must see as God's
perverse compassion as he watches Nineveh prosper. Jonah must be situated
on a hilltop or promontory, so he has gone up after the repeated and emphatic
goings down. The verb "to go up" will be repeated in this episode, but it is not
attached to Jonah.

6. *qiqayon plant.* The term appears only here. The King James Version renders
this as "gourd," which is as good as anybody's guess, but since the plant has not
been confidently identified, it seems prudent to preserve the Hebrew name in
the translation. Why does Jonah need the *qiqayon* if he has already set up a
shelter to give him shade? The most reasonable explanation is that the shelter,
assembled no doubt from the materials he could scrape together from what was
on hand, provided rather imperfect shade, whereas the *qiqayon*, miraculously
sprung up overnight, offered luxuriant foliage.

7. *God set out.* God in this story repeatedly assigns elements of nature to do His
bidding, alternately protecting and destroying.

8 and it struck the *qiqayon* and it withered. And it happened, as the sun
   rose, that God set out a slashing east wind, and the sun struck Jonah's
   head, and he grew faint and wanted to die, and he said, "Better my death
9 than my life." And God said to Jonah, "Are you good and angry over the
10 *qiqayon*?" And he said, "I am good and angry, to the point of death." And
   the LORD said, "You—you had pity over the *qiqayon*, for which you did
   not toil and which you did not grow, which overnight came and over-
11 night was gone. And I, shall I not have pity for Nineveh the great city,
   in which there are many more than 120,000 human beings who do not
   know between their right hand and their left, and many beasts?"

---

8. *slashing*. The adjective *harishit* occurs only here. Because it appears to recall
the verb *heherish*, "to be silent," one understanding, which becomes ensconced
in later literary Hebrew, is that it means "silent" here. But that scarcely accords
with the present context because the wind—the hot wind called the *hamsin*
that blows from the eastern desert—has an obviously devastating effect. The
translation guesses, picking up a cue from some of the medieval Hebrew exegetes, that the adjective is related to the verb *harash*, "to plow" and perhaps by
extension "to shear or cut through something."

   the sun struck Jonah's head. What happened to the shade of the shelter?
Sasson plausibly suggests that the shelter was swept away by the powerful east
wind.

9. *Are you good and angry over the qiqayon?* God repeats the words he spoke in
the earlier exchange, adding "over the *qiqayon*."

   I am good and angry, to the point of death. Jonah bounces back to God the
provoking words He has just spoken, adding, in a pattern of incremental repetition, "to the point of death."

10. *You—you had pity over the qiqayon*. God points an emphatic vocative finger
at Jonah by using the second-person singular pronoun, normally not required in
front of the conjugated verb. With similar pronominal emphasis, He contrasts
"I, shall I not" at the beginning of the next verse. The choice of the verb "pity"
is pointedly not quite appropriate. Jonah not does pity the plant for withering;
rather, he is furious that he has been stripped of its vitally necessary shade. His
"pity" for the *qiqayon* is by no means disinterested, whereas God's pity for all
the living creatures of Nineveh flows from His compassion.

THE BOOK OF DANIEL

TO THE READER

ANIEL IS SURELY the most peculiar book in the Hebrew Bible. It is also clearly the latest. Whereas the dating of most biblical books is no more than a series of rough approximations, often hotly debated by scholars, it is almost certain that the second half of Daniel was written between 167 and 165 BCE because it refers in detail to the persecutions initiated by Antiochus IV Epiphanus and his suppression of the temple cult in those years and to no subsequent events. Given this late date, it is not surprising that Daniel more closely resembles the apocalyptic texts of the Apocrypha and of the Dead Sea Scrolls, which were written around the same time or a little afterward, and the Book of Revelation in the New Testament, which draws on Daniel, than earlier biblical books.

The apocalyptic vision of history has abundant anticipations in the Hebrew Prophets, but it is a similarity with crucial differences. The Prophets, whose usual vehicle of expression was biblical poetry with its system of intensifications from one part of the line to the next and, often, from one line to the next, sometimes conjured up a landscape of catastrophe in which the world would revert to the state of chaos that obtained before creation or, alternatively, imagined a landscape of redemption in which all peoples would come to Mount Zion to imbibe the LORD's teaching. But these prophecies, however extravagant, were ultimately dystopian or utopian visions of some actual historical future, cast in vivid poetic hyperbole. The writer of Daniel, on the other hand, seems to be pushing toward a notion of an era that will come at the end of familiar historical process, something he thought to be imminent after the intolerable violations by Antiochus IV that his people were then suffering. The prospect of the resurrection of the dead, certainly new to biblical writing in such a literal form, is an intrinsic element in this end-time, when all things would radically change.

In regard to literary form as well, Daniel is quite different from previous biblical literature. There are narrative segments in the first seven chapters but no real characters of the sort we encounter in the earlier biblical books. Daniel and his three friends are little more than exemplary figures of piety, without nuance or psychology, who are moved by the writer through miracle stories that make manifest to all the supreme power of their God. Daniel himself, beyond being the object of miraculous intervention, operates as the interpreter of visionary dreams and, in the last half of the book, as the one to whom vision is vouchsafed. As a high-ranking courtier interpreting the dreams of a king, he is of course modeled on Joseph in Pharaoh's court, but again this is a similarity with a difference. Pharaoh's dreams, like Nebuchadnezzar's here, are a communication from God about what will befall his kingdom, and Joseph then proposes that certain measures can be taken to avert the disastrous consequence of what is about to unfold. In Daniel, no such human intervention is possible because the dreams and the visions are part of an inexorable deterministic system—a hallmark of the apocalyptic view. Daniel seems less an interpreter than a decipherer of divine codes, which sometimes have a numeric aspect, in which the details of God's plans for humankind are encrypted. It is no wonder that both Christians and Jews used the Book of Daniel as their point of departure for intricate calculations about the end of days. In the Christian canon, Daniel is placed with the Prophets because, from his purported location in the Babylonian Persian period, he prophesies what will happen in future times. The Hebrew Prophets, however, though they evoke future possibilities, are for the most part not strictly predictive, and certainly not in the minutely circumstantial way we find in Daniel. The placement of Daniel in the Jewish canon in Ketuvim, or Miscellaneous Writings, is more in keeping with the anomalous nature of this text.

The other unusual feature of the book is that it is written in two languages. The opening is in Hebrew—the first chapter and the four initial verses of Chapter 2. At this point, the text switches to Aramaic, the language in which it continues uninterrupted till the end of Chapter 7. The rest of the book is in Hebrew. By this late date, Aramaic had for the most part replaced Hebrew as the Jewish vernacular. It was by then the established language of international diplomacy in the Near East, and the Aramaic used here is the so-called imperial Aramaic, somewhat more formal and different in certain usages from the rabbinic Aramaic that was emerging, in which the Talmud and much of the Midrash would be written over the next few centuries. Aramaic is a Semitic language closely cognate with Hebrew, the distance between the two languages being something like the distance between French and Italian. Grammatical structures are analogous, and many primary terms in the two languages are the same, only slightly different in form. Thus, Hebrew *melekh*, "king," is matched by Aramaic *malka'*; Hebrew *lehem*, "bread," by Aramaic *lahma'*. Many other terms are distinctively Aramaic, though, for understandable reasons, hundreds upon hundreds of these words would be absorbed into the evolving rabbinic Hebrew, and some Aramaic loanwords already appear in the poetry of Job and in Esther, though, for a reason I shall explain, hardly at all in the Hebrew of Daniel.

The Hebrew of this book is in fact even stranger than its quasi-narrative form and its apocalyptic character. This Hebrew writer (there might have been more than one) was clearly quite familiar with the Pentateuch and the Prophets, though it is hard to say what else he might have known of earlier Hebrew scripture. He manifestly sought to make his own Hebrew sound prophetic (though perhaps "vatic" might be a more appropriate term), and that is probably why, for the most part, he resisted Aramaic usages and other conspicuous features of Late Biblical Hebrew. The impulse to sound prophetic led to some deliberate obscurity in expression. This obscurity was probably compounded by scrambled scribal transmission at a good many points. But I would like to propose that this author, though he knew earlier Hebrew writings, was fully comfortable in Aramaic and not in Hebrew. Much of what he produced can be fairly characterized as bad Hebrew prose. The syntax is often slack, at points unintelligible; parts of speech are sometimes inappropriate; the idioms not infrequently sound odd or perhaps are simply wrong. The writer overworks certain Hebrew terms, as though he did not have other more apt ones available: the verbs, for example, *'amad*, "stand," and *heheziq*, "hold, make strong," are awkwardly used over and over, in quick sequence, in a number of different senses, some of them unwarranted by earlier Hebrew.

The Book of Daniel, then, is an imperfect composition. In style, its Hebrew sections are seriously flawed. Its narrative is primarily a vehicle for laying out tales of miraculous aid that demonstrate God's power, or for setting the circumstances for elaborately coded revelations of the future course of history that require deciphering. In strictly literary terms, it is a book that falls far below what earlier biblical texts, both narrative and prophetic, would lead us to expect. And yet Daniel is also a book fraught with religious importance for its age and beyond. As the latest text of the Hebrew canon, it is a hinge work between the Hebrew Bible proper and the intertestamental period as well as the New Testament. Earlier Hebrew writers had assumed an essential element of contingency in historical process: human action, for better or for worse, would determine the future course of events. Daniel sees things differently: some people are written in the Book of Life and some are not; a plan dictated from on high is unfolding step by step, replete with precise numerical indications and mystifying symbolic prefigurations. Daniel points the way forward to many aspects of the New Testament, to a series of Jewish false messiahs from the Middle Ages to the seventeenth century, to the Christian chiliastic sects of the sixteenth and seventeenth centuries as well as earlier, and to much else. Daniel imposes a heavy burden on both Jewish and Christian history that in some ways we may still be carrying. Its strange and enigmatic visions are something with which we continue to grapple.

CHAPTER 1

In the third year of the kingship of Jehoiakim king of Judah, Nebu- 1
chadnezzar king of Babylonia came to Jerusalem and lay siege against
it. And the Lord gave Jehoiakim king of Judah into his hand and the 2
best of the vessels of the house of God, and he brought them to the
land of Shinar, to the house of his god, and the vessels he brought to

---

1. *In the third year of the kingship of Jehoiakim.* This historical-sounding notation at the beginning of the book in fact betrays its pseudohistorical character.
The third year of Jehoiakim was 606 BCE, and there is no evidence that Nebuchadnezzar besieged Jerusalem then. On the contrary, extrabiblical documents
show that he and his army were occupied elsewhere at that time. He did make
an incursion into Jerusalem and took Jehoiakim captive nine years later.

2. *the best of the vessels.* The Hebrew *miqtsat* can mean either "some of" or "the
best of," but it seems more likely that the conquering king would plunder the
choicest vessels.
   the land of Shinar. This is an old name for Babylonia.

3   his god's treasure-house. And the king said to the majordomo head of
his eunuchs, to bring from the Israelites and from the royal seed and
4   from the nobles young men who were without blemish and goodly in
appearance and discerning in all wisdom and possessing knowledge and
understanding matters, and who had the strength to serve in the king's
palace, to teach them book learning and the language of the Chaldeans.

---

3. *eunuchs.* The Hebrew term, a loanword from the Akkadian, can mean either
"eunuch" or "high official" (as in the case of Potiphar, who is married, in Genesis 39). Some have inferred from his being placed over Daniel and his friends
that they were castrated, but this is surely contradicted by the stipulation that
they must be "without blemish," as Ibn Ezra and many others have noted. In
any case, eunuchs often served in the Persian court, and our story evinces some
intermingling of Babylonian and Persian elements.

    to bring from the Israelites and from the royal seed and from the nobles. Some
have detected here a general Babylonian practice of conscripting young exiled
noblemen for court service, perhaps to demonstrate the universal command of
the empire, but the whole idea of educating the adolescent Israelites for the
court may more likely be a storytelling contrivance to set up a situation in which
Daniel's superior wisdom can be exhibited.

4. *young men who were without blemish and goodly in appearance.* The sprawling
sentence, which begins in the previous verse, shows a certain stylistic slackness in the Hebrew, with loose syntactic links and some inert synonymity. The
looseness of the prose may reflect a tendency in Late Biblical Hebrew (as in
Esther), or could be the consequence of the translation from Aramaic that
many scholars have detected in this chapter.

    to serve. The literal meaning of the Hebrew is "to stand." The same idiom
occurs in verse 19.

    the language of the Chaldeans. The young men would have been speakers
of Aramaic (and perhaps Hebrew as well). The language of the Chaldeans
is Akkadian, written in cuneiform. The mastery of both the written and the
spoken form of the language would have been necessary for the young men to
serve in the Babylonian court.

And the king apportioned for them for each day from the king's royal 5
provisions and from his drinking wine, to rear them for three years, that
the best of them should serve in the king's presence. And among them 6
from the Judeans were Daniel, Hananiah, Mishael, and Azariah. And 7
the chief of the eunuchs gave them names, and he made Daniel Belteshazzar, and Hananiah Shadrach, and Mishael Meshach, and Azariah
Abednego. And Daniel resolved that he would not defile himself with 8
the king's provisions and with his drinking wine, and he asked of the
chief of the eunuchs that he not have to defile himself. And God made 9
Daniel find grace and mercy in the presence of the chief of the eunuchs.
And the chief of the eunuchs said to Daniel, "I fear my master the king, 10
who has apportioned your food and your drink, for why should he see

---

5. *drinking wine.* This phrase, repeated in what follows, looks like a redundancy.
Either it is an idiomatic flourish, or it is meant to distinguish wine meant to be
drunk from libation wine.

for three years. Persian documents actually stipulate three years as the period
for educating young men coming of age.

the best of them. See the comment on "the best of the vessels" in verse 2.

7. *the chief of the eunuchs gave them names.* This is the first step in the process of acculturation—substituting Babylonian names for their given Hebrew
names. Mordecai and Esther, too, have names reflecting the host culture of
the exiles.

8. *he would not defile himself with the king's provisions.* These presumably would
have included prohibited meats such as pork and rabbit. One might note that
the exiled King Jehoiakim (2 Kings 25:29–30) is not reported to have any com-
punction about eating the Babylonian king's provisions; nor does this appear to
be a concern in Esther. It has been suggested that the concern about consuming prohibited foods was a special issue in the Hellenistic period.

9. *And God made Daniel find grace and mercy in the presence of the chief of the
eunuchs.* Although the idioms used here are different, the general formulation
is reminiscent of Joseph's finding favor in the eyes of Potiphar, then of the
prison warden, in Genesis 39. Other allusions to the Joseph story will follow.

you downcast among the young men of your age? And you would make
11 me guilty to the king." And Daniel said to the overseer whom the chief
of the eunuchs had set over Daniel, Hananiah, Mishael, and Azariah,
12 "Test your servants ten days, and let them give us from the grains that
13 we may eat, and water that we may drink. And let our appearance be
seen before you together with the appearance of the young men who eat
14 the king's provisions, and as you see, so do with your servants." And he
15 heeded them in this matter and tested them ten days. And at the end
of the ten days their appearance was seen to be better and plumper in
16 flesh than all the young men who had eaten the king's provisions. And
the overseer kept bearing away their provisions and their drinking wine
17 and giving them grains. And to these young men, the four of them, did
God give knowledge and discernment in all books and wisdom, and
18 Daniel understood all visions and dreams. And at the end of the time
that the king had said to bring them, the chief of the eunuchs brought

---

12. *the grains.* The Hebrew noun is related to the word for "seed." Some construe this as "legumes" or "vegetables." In any case, it is obviously a spartan vegetarian diet.

15. *their appearance was seen to be better and plumper in flesh.* This is a minor miracle, that they should flourish on a diet of grains and water, and greater miracles will follow. The Hebrew phrase for "plumper in flesh" is the same one used in Pharaoh's dream of the seven fat cows in Genesis 41, making this another allusion to the Joseph story.

17. *and Daniel understood all visions and dreams.* This faculty sets him apart from his three friends, whose wisdom is limited to books and bodies of knowledge. Joseph, too, is an expert interpreter of dreams, though visions are not part of his story.

18. *at the end of the time.* This is the three-year period stipulated by the king for the education of the young men.

them before Nebuchadnezzar. And the king spoke with them, and none 19
of all of them was found like Daniel, Hananiah, Mishael, and Azariah,
and they entered the service of the king. And in every matter of discern- 20
ing wisdom that the king asked of them, he found them ten times better
than all the soothsayers and wizards who were in all his kingdom. And 21
Daniel was there until the first year of King Cyrus.

---

19. *none of all of them.* There is a sizable group of noble young Judeans who
have undergone the course of education, but Daniel and his three friends stand
out among them.

20. *all the soothsayers and wizards.* The first term, *ḥartumim*, is an Egyptian
loanword that appears several times both in the Joseph story and in the story of
Moses's confrontation with Pharaoh in Exodus. The second term, *'ashafim*, is
an Akkadian loanword. Thus, the wisdom of the young Hebrew noblemen far
exceeds that of the professional sages of these two empires, renowned for their
expertise in astrology, soothsaying, and related arts conceived as instruments of
knowledge in the ancient world.

21. *the first year of King Cyrus.* Cyrus was the Persian emperor who overthrew
the Babylonians. Emperors come and go, but Daniel remains.

CHAPTER 2

1   And in the second year of Nebuchadnezzar's kingship, Nebuchadnezzar dreamed dreams, and his heart pounded and his sleep was ruined.
2   And the king said to all the soothsayers and the wizards and the magicians and the Chaldeans to explain the king's dreams to him, and they
3   came and stood before the king. And the king said to them, "I have
dreamed a dream, and my heart pounded, wanting to know the dream."

---

1. *in the second year of Nebuchadnezzar's kingship.* This notation is a much
discussed contradiction because in Chapter 1, it is in the third year of Nebuchadnezzar's reign that Daniel and his three friends are sent off for three years
of education, after which they are brought back to the court. None of the pro-
posals for resolving this difficulty is entirely convincing.

   his heart pounded. Literally, "his spirit pounded." This is the same phrase
used for Pharaoh's response to his two dreams and constitutes a clear allusion.

   his sleep was ruined. This translation links the verb *nihyatah* with the noun
howah, "disaster." Others emend it to read more smoothly *nadedah*, the verb for
"wandering" sleep, that is, insomnia.

2. *the Chaldeans.* Because the Chaldeans were famous for their skills in soothsaying and divination, the ethnic name came to indicate those who practice
these arts.

3. *wanting to know the dream.* The simplest reading is that he wanted to know
the meaning of the dream, though some interpreters understand this, with a
mind to his subsequent dialogue with the sages and Daniel, that he cannot
remember the dream.

And the Chaldeans spoke to the king in Aramaic, "May the king live 4
forever! Say the dream to your servants and we shall tell its meaning."
The king answered and said, "The matter has been determined by me: 5
if you do not explain to me the dream and its meaning, you will be cut
to pieces and your houses will be turned into dung-heaps. But if you 6
tell the dream and its meaning, gifts and presents and great honor you
shall receive from me. Therefore tell me the dream and its meaning."
They answered a second time and said, "Let the king say the dream to 7
his servants and we shall tell its meaning." The king answered and said, 8
"Indeed, I know that you are buying time because you have seen that
the matter was determined by me. For if you do not explain the dream 9
to me, there is but one decree for you, and you have prepared a false and
lying word to say to me until time passes. Therefore say to me the dream
and I shall know that you have told me its meaning." The Chaldeans 10
answered before the king and said, "There is no man on earth who can
tell the word of the king because no great and powerful king has asked a
thing like this of any soothsayer or wizard or Chaldean. And the matter 11

---

4. *And the Chaldeans spoke to the king in Aramaic.* This looks like an editorial
contrivance to mark the transition from Hebrew to Aramaic. Afterward, everything is in Aramaic until the end of Chapter 7. Aramaic, which by the sixth
century BCE was the lingua franca of the region, would have been the native
tongue of the Chaldeans. It is unclear what language we are supposed to imagine was being spoken in the dialogues before this point—perhaps Akkadian but
surely not Hebrew.

8. *I know that you are buying time.* Though this idiom may sound excessively
contemporary in English, it is the precise literal sense of the Aramaic.

10. *There is no man on earth who can tell the word of the king.* They have asked
that he report his dream to them so that they can interpret it, but he has confronted them with an absolutely unheard of challenge: he expects them to know
the contents of his dream without the slightest prompt from him and then to
provide an interpretation. This is why they go on to say that only the gods who
are not flesh and blood could answer such a challenge. In the event, it is Daniel's God who will reveal to him both the contents of the dream and its meaning.

that the king has asked is grave, and there are no others that can tell
it before the king except the gods, whose dwelling is not with flesh."
12 Because of this the king raged and was very angry and thought to put to
13 death all the sages of Babylonia. And a decree was issued that the sages
14 were to be killed, and Daniel and his friends were to be killed. Then did
Daniel respond with counsel and insight to Arioch, chief of the king's
15 executioners, who had gone out to call the sages of Babylonia. He spoke
out and said to Arioch, the king's regent, "For what is this severe decree
16 from the king?" Then Arioch informed Daniel of the matter. And Daniel
went and asked of the king that time be given him to tell the meaning
17 to the king. Then Daniel went to his house and informed Hananiah,
18 Mishael, and Azariah his friends of the matter to ask mercy of the God
of the heavens about this mystery, that Daniel and his friends not perish
19 with the rest of the sages of Babylonia. Then was the mystery revealed
to Daniel in a night vision. Then Daniel blessed the God of the heavens.
20 Daniel spoke out and said, "May the name of God be blessed forever
21 and forever, for wisdom and strength are His. And He changes the times
and the seasons, takes kings away and raises up kings, gives wisdom to

---

13. *the sages were to be killed, and Daniel and his friends were to be killed.*
Although the forms of the two verbs are different (the latter employs an auxil-
iary verb joined to "killed" in the reflexive infinitive), both must be construed, in
light of what ensues, as actions about to happen but not yet performed. Daniel
and his friends are on the list of those to be executed because they have joined
the group of the country's sages.

16. *that time be given him.* Though the sages have been accused by the king of
buying time, Daniel now needs a brief span of time to pray to God that he be
granted knowledge of the dream.

19. *the mystery revealed.* The two words, *raza' gali,* recur with variations throughout the story. They constitute an Aramaic equivalent of the etymological sense of
"apocalypse" in Greek, and the dream itself proves to be incipiently apocalyptic.

21. *He changes the times and the seasons.* Just as God's power is manifested
cosmically in the changing cycles of time and seasons, it is manifested politi-
cally as he "takes kings away and raises up kings." The dream will be about the
displacement of one kingdom by another.

the wise and knowledge to those who know discernment. He lays bare 22
the deep and hidden things, knows what is in darkness, and light dwells
with Him. To You, God of my fathers, I give thanks and praise that You 23
have granted me wisdom and strength, and now You have made known
to me that which we asked of You, for the matter of the king You have
made known to us." Because of this Daniel came to Arioch, whom the 24
king had appointed to put to death all the sages of Babylonia. He went
and thus he said to him, "Do not put to death the sages of Babylonia.
Bring me before the king and I will tell the meaning to the king." Then 25
did Arioch rush to bring Daniel before the king, and thus he said to him,
"There is a man of the exiles from Judah who will explain the meaning to the king." The king answered and said to Daniel, whose name 26
was Belteshazzar, "Can you explain to me the dream that I saw and its
meaning?" Daniel answered before the king, "The mystery of which the 27
king has asked, sages, wizards, soothsayers, and diviners cannot tell
the king. But there is a God in the heavens Who reveals mysteries and 28
has made known to the king what will be in the latter days, your dream
and the visions in your head as you lay asleep, this is it. You, king, your 29

---

24. *Bring me before the king.* Here Daniel observes court protocol. In verse 16,
he appears to have come into the royal presence uninvited, unless one infers
an ellipsis there.

25. *There is a man . . . who will explain the meaning.* One of several indications
that this is not a story that adheres to any realistic logic is that this high court
official should be certain that a young Judean exile can interpret the dream
solely because he says he can.

26. *whose name was Belteshazzar.* This notation is introduced because Daniel
would be called by his Babylonian name when brought before the king.

28. *there is a God in the heavens.* This designation, *'ita 'elah bishemaya,* or simply,
'elah shemaya, is Daniel's way of referring for the benefit of the polytheist king
to the one God of heaven and earth.
    in the latter days. The phrase *'aharit yomaya* draws directly from the Hebrew
'aharit hayamim. Although later this phrase comes to mean the eschatological
"end of time," its biblical sense is something like "in time to come."

thought has risen as you lay asleep of what will be in the time to come, and the Revealer of Mysteries has made known to you what will be.
30 As for me, not through wisdom that is in me more than all living men has the mystery been revealed to me but in order to make known to
31 the king the meaning, that you may know your heart's thoughts. You, king, were seeing, and look, a huge statue. This statue was great and its brilliance was abundant. It was standing before you and its appearance
32 was fearsome. That statue, its head was goodly gold, its chest and arms
33 were silver, its loins and its thighs were bronze. Its legs were iron and its
34 feet part iron and part clay. You were watching till a stone hewed not by hands struck the statue on its feet of iron and clay and shattered them.

---

30. *that you may know your heart's thoughts.* There is an odd congruence here with the Freudian notion of dreams. The dreaming mind is a theater of vital revelation, but the dreamer himself cannot understand the meaning of the dream. For that he needs an expert interpreter.

31. *and look, a huge statue.* Going beyond Joseph, his prototype in Genesis, Daniel is able to envisage exactly what the king saw in his dream, just as the king had demanded of his sages.

32. *gold . . . silver . . . bronze . . . iron.* As we go down the body of the statue, the metals progressively decrease in value. The four metals linked with four ages obviously correspond to the progressive decline in Hesiod's *Works and Days.* Though it is possible that our late author actually read Hesiod (elsewhere in Daniel, Greek loanwords appear), the myth of the four ages and four kingdoms is equally attested in old Iranian literature, and it seems likely that it had some currency throughout the eastern Mediterranean and the Near East. In its Iranian version, the first kingdom is Assyria, but Daniel substitutes Babylon because it is the empire that subdued the kingdom of Judah. The other three, then, would be Media, Persia, and Greece. (Rashi and Ibn Ezra see Rome as the fourth kingdom, in keeping with rabbinic historical typology, but Rome would be too late for inclusion in Daniel.)

33. *part iron and part clay.* The clay, of course, is the origin of the English idiom, "feet of clay." The odd mixture of iron and clay suggests both that the fourth kingdom is powerfully destructive and easily broken.

34. *a stone hewed not by hands.* This is clearly a supernatural stone, one that in verse 35 will become a great mountain and fill all the earth.

Then altogether the iron, clay, bronze, silver, and gold were shattered 35
and became like chaff from the summer threshing floor, and no place
was found for them. And the stone that struck the statue became a great
mountain and filled all the earth. This is the dream, and its meaning we 36
shall say before the king. You are king, even king of kings, to whom the 37
God of the heavens has given power and might and honor. And wherever 38
human beings, beasts of the field, and fowl of the heavens live, He has
given them in your hand and caused you to rule over them all. You are
the head of gold. And after you shall arise another kingdom, inferior to 39
yours, and a third kingdom, of bronze, that shall rule over all the earth.
And a fourth kingdom shall be strong as iron because iron shatters and 40
splinters all things, and like smashing iron, all these shall it shatter and
smash. And as to the feet and the toes you saw, part potter's clay and part 41
iron, the kingdom shall be split, and it shall have of the strength of iron
because you saw iron mixed with clay from the soil. And as to the toes, 42
part iron and part clay, some of the kingdom shall be strong and some
of it fragile. And as to your seeing iron mixed with clay from the soil, 43
they shall be mixed with human seed and shall not hold together just
as iron does not mix with clay. And in the days of these kings the God 44

37. *You are king, even king of kings, to whom the God of the heavens has given power and might and honor.* The opening words make Nebuchadnezzar sound virtually divine, but the words that follow put him in his place in the theological scheme of things—it is God alone who has granted this greatness to the king.

40. *iron shatters and splinters all things.* The terrific destructive force of the fourth kingdom reflects Alexander the Great's establishment through military might of a world empire and perhaps also the armed power of his warring heirs.

43. *they shall be mixed with human seed.* This clause is enigmatic. Some understand it to mean "they shall be mixed in marriage," referring to a matrimonial alliance between the Seleucids and the Ptolemys, but *zera'* plainly means "seed," not marriage.
  and shall not hold together. This definitely looks like a reference to the splitting of Alexander's empire, wrought in fierce iron, into three competing kingdoms, hence frangible as potter's clay.

of the heavens shall establish a kingdom that shall never be destroyed. To another people it shall not be abandoned. It shall shatter and put an

45 end to all these kingdoms, and it shall stand forever. Because you have seen that from a mountain a stone was hewed not by hands and smashed the iron, bronze, clay, silver, and gold, the great God has made known to the king what will be after this, and the dream is true, its meaning

46 certain." Then did King Nebuchadnezzar fall on his face, and he bowed down to Daniel, and he said to offer to him grain offering and incense.

47 The king answered Daniel and said, "In truth, your god is the God of gods and master of kings and revealer of mysteries, for you were able to

48 reveal this mystery." Then did the king make Daniel great, and he gave him many great gifts and caused him to rule over all the province of Babylonia and made him chief governor over all the sages of Babylonia.

---

44. *a kingdom that shall never be destroyed.* The establishment by God of an eternal kingdom on earth is a strongly messianic idea.

46. *he bowed down to Daniel.* This prostration before a human being, followed by offering to him grain and incense, may be understandable after Daniel has demonstrated such astounding visionary wisdom, but it looks suspect from a monotheistic point of view. The text, however, does not intimate any negative judgment of the act.

47. *In truth, your god is the God of gods.* The king appears to be a virtual convert to monotheism, though his phrasing may rather suggest that he acknowledges Daniel's god as superior to all others—the God of gods, just as he himself has been said to be the king of kings.

48. *all the province of Babylonia.* As in Esther, *medinah* (a Persian loanword) does not mean "kingdom" or "state" but "province." Babylonia is the principal province of the empire, but there are others.

And Daniel asked of the king, and he appointed Shadrach, Meshach, 49
and Abednego over the work of the province of Babylonia. And Daniel
served in the king's gate.

---

49. *over the work of the province of Babylonia.* They appear to have responsibility
over public projects, corvée labor, and the like, whereas Daniel is supervisor of
the sages and operates in the court.

And Daniel served in the king's gate. "In the king's gate," *bitraʿ malkaʾ*, essentially means in the palace. The verb used here in the Aramaic is literally "was,"
for which "served" has been substituted in the translation to indicate that he is
performing a function. Serving in the palace, Daniel is an intimate counselor
of the king.

CHAPTER 3

1 Nebuchadnezzar made a statue of gold, sixty cubits high and six cubits wide.
2 He set it up in the Dura Valley in the province of Babylonia. And Nebuchadnezzar sent out to assemble the satraps, the governors and officials, the counselors, the treasurers, the judges, the commanders of the camps, and all the administrators of the provinces to come for the dedication of
3 the statue that King Nebuchadnezzar had set up. Then did the satraps, the governors and officials, the counselors, the judges, the commanders of the

---

1. *a statue of gold, sixty cubits high.* Herodotus and other ancient sources in fact report monarchs erecting monumental statues to Zeus and other gods. In this case, the deity is not specified. Sixty cubits would make the statue in question about ninety feet high. The width is too narrow to be proportionate, but the writer probably did not trouble himself about such details. It is often assumed that "gold" means gold-plated, but given the folktale quality of the whole story, perhaps we are intended to imagine that this fabulously extravagant statue was solid gold. The editorial placement of this story here may have been dictated by the statue with the gold head in the previous episode.

2. *the satraps, the governors and officials, the counselors* . . . The author of this story clearly revels in lists, first this one indicating the elaborate network of the royal bureaucracy and then the pomp and circumstance of the list of the musical instruments to be played at the dedication ceremony. Unlike classical biblical narrative, where with very few exceptions repetitions appear with significant and subtle swerves from the verbatim, here the lists are repeated exactly (one might say, mechanically). One should note that most of the bureaucratic titles here are Persian loanwords, and there are no borrowings from the Greek. Since Jews in the Hellenistic period were quite familiar with the titles of imperial functionaries and many of these terms are then reflected in the Talmud and the Midrash, it seems likely that the core of this particular story was formulated in the Persian period.

camps, and all the administrators of the provinces assemble for the dedication of the statue that Nebuchadnezzar had set up, and they were standing
before the statue that Nebuchadnezzar had set up. And the herald called 4
out loudly: "To you, is it said, peoples, nations, and tongues! When you hear 5
the sound of the horn, the pipe, the lute, the zither, the lyre, the flute, and
all kinds of music, you shall fall down and worship the gold statue that
King Nebuchadnezzar has set up. And whoever does not fall down at once 6
shall be cast into the furnace of blazing fire." Therefore, when they would 7
hear the sound of the horn, the pipe, the lute, the zither, the lyre, the flute,
and all kinds of music, all the peoples, nations, and tongues would at once
worship the gold statue that King Nebuchadnezzar had set up. Because of 8
this, at that time Chaldean men came forward and denounced the Jews.
They spoke out and said to King Nebuchadnezzar, "O king, may you live 9
forever! You, O king, put out a decree that any man who heard the sound 10

5. *the horn, the pipe, the lute, the zither* . . . The first two items in this list of
instruments are indigenous Aramaic, but the next three are borrowings from
the Greek. If the basic narrative of assembling all the officials for the dedication of the statue antedates Alexander's conquest of the Near East, the elabo-
ration concerning the musical performance at the ceremony must have been
composed in the Hellenistic period. These are wind and string instruments
but no percussion instruments, though it is unclear whether that reflects the
actual composition of orchestras in this period. The exact identification of all
the instruments is not entirely clear. The fifth term in the list, *pesantrin*, was
adopted in modern Hebrew as the word for "piano." The sixth term, *sumponia*,
originally meant "musical harmony" in Greek, though it obviously names a
musical instrument in this list, and "flute" in the translation is one guess among
many that have been made.

fall down and worship the gold statue. There is no evidence here of Nebuchadnezzar's conversion to monotheism after Daniel's interpretation of his
dream. This is one indication that this is an originally independent story.

6. *whoever does not fall down at once shall be cast into the furnace of blazing
fire.* Such lethal cultic coercion was not generally practiced by pagan kings.
Some commentators have detected here a reflection of the religious coercion
of the Jews by Antiochus Epiphanes in the 160s BCE, but as John J. Collins
has argued, that is not a necessary inference, especially since the edict is not
directed specifically at the Jews. Instead, this may be a parable of the dangers
of cultic assimilation in the situation of diaspora.

of the horn, the pipe, the lute, the zither, the lyre, the flute, and all kinds
11 of music must fall down and worship the gold statue. And whoever did
not fall down and worship would be cast into the furnace of blazing fire.
12 There are certain Jewish men whom you have appointed over the work of
the province of Babylonia, Shadrach, Meshach, and Abednego. These have
paid no heed to you, O king. They do not serve your god, and they do not
13 worship the gold statue that you set up." Then did Nebuchadnezzar say in
anger and fury to bring Shadrach, Meshach, and Abednego. Then were
14 these men brought before the king. Nebuchadnezzar spoke out and said
to them, "Is it true, Shadrach, Meshach, and Abednego, that you are not
15 serving my god, and are not worshipping the gold statue that I put up? Now,
if you are ready, when you hear the sound of the horn, the pipe, the lute,
the zither, the lyre, the flute, and all kinds of music, and you worship the
statue that I have made, [all will be well]. And if you do not worship, you
will at once be thrown into the furnace of blazing fire, and who is the god
16 who can save you from my hands?" Shadrach, Meshach, and Abednego
answered and said to King Nebuchadnezzar, "We do not need to answer
17 you about this matter. If our God, Whom we serve, is able to save us from
the furnace of blazing fire and from your hand, O king, He shall save us.
18 And if not, let it be known to you, O king, that we will not serve your god,

---

12. *There are certain Jewish men.* Since Daniel and his three friends have been
presented as a tight group and all four have been given administrative posts in
the imperial bureaucracy, the absence of Daniel's name here and throughout
the chapter is another reflection that this story was not originally connected
with the Daniel narrative.

15. *all will be well.* These words are supplied in the translation because there
is a conditional clause in the Aramaic that appears to break off at this point.

17. *If our God . . . is able to save us . . . He shall save us.* The three young men
are not entirely sure that they will be saved, but their devotion to God is so
absolute that they are prepared to suffer the pangs of fiery death if divine rescue
is not forthcoming. In all this, Shadrach, Meshach, and Abednego are scarcely
"characters," with an individual psychology, a personal history, and an intimated
inner life like the characters in classical Hebrew narrative, but are rather exemplary figures on a didactic tale, perfect embodiments of unswerving allegiance
to the one God. The willingness to accept martyrdom is also a new emphasis.

and we will not worship the gold statue that you have set up." Then was 19
Nebuchadnezzar filled with wrath, and the look of his face changed because
of Shadrach, Meshach, and Abednego. He spoke out and said to stoke the
furnace seven times hotter than it was wont to be stoked. And to the valiant 20
warriors of his army, he said to bind Shadrach, Meshach, and Abednego in
order to throw them into the furnace of blazing fire. Then were these men 21
bound in their trousers, their tunics, their headgear, and their garments
and were thrown into the furnace of blazing fire. Therefore because the 22
king's word was severe, and the furnace was intensely stoked, those men
who had brought up Shadrach, Meshach, and Abednego did the fire's flame
kill. And these three men, Shadrach, Meshach, and Abednego, fell bound 23
into the furnace of blazing fire. Then was King Nebuchadnezzar astounded 24
and arose in haste. He spoke out and said to his counselors, "Did we not
throw three men bound into the fire?" They answered and said to the king,

---

20. *to bind Shadrach, Meshach, and Abednego.* This gratuitous command will
compound the miracle. The death of prisoners flung into a fiery furnace would
have been in any case certain, but these three are bound so that they can
scarcely move about as they are—presumably—burned to a crisp.

21. *their trousers, their tunics, their headgear.* There is some ambiguity about
the identification of these items of apparel. In any case, they are probably their
wardrobe as court officials, now to be consigned to the fire together with their
bodies.

22. *those men who had brought up Shadrach, Meshach, and Abednego did the
fire's flame kill.* This is not only a stroke of retribution against the henchmen
of the pagan king, but also another compounding of the miracle that is about
to occur: the excessively stoked furnace sends flames shooting out its aperture
that burn to death the royal agents, whereas the three Judean exiles will prove
to be unhurt in the very heart of the flames.

25 "Indeed, O king." He answered and said, "Why, I see four men walking
unbound within the fire, and there is no hurt in them, and the appearance
26 of the fourth is like a divine being!" Then did Nebuchadnezzar approach
the gate of the furnace of blazing fire. He spoke out and said, "Shadrach,
Meshach, and Abednego, servants of the most high God, come out!" Then
27 did Shadrach, Meshach, and Abednego come out from within the fire. And
the satraps, governors, officials, and the king's counselors were assembled
and saw these men, that the fire had no power over their bodies, and the hair
on their heads was not singed, and their trousers were in no way different

---

25. *I see four men walking unbound within the fire.* Although there are from
time to time miraculous events in earlier biblical narrative, this late text drastically steps up the supernatural nature of the miracle. The prophet Elijah does
ascend to heaven in a fiery chariot, but that is, after all, a translation from
earthly existence to something beyond. In this story, on the other hand, human
figures living in the here-and-now walk about in the intense flames, accompanied by a divine being, as though they were going for an evening stroll. Their
bonds as well have miraculously disappeared, and even their garments, item-
ized above, have not been singed.

a divine being. The literal sense of the Aramaic is "son of God," but as with
its Hebrew equivalent, which appears frequently in earlier biblical texts, the
idiom does not suggest filial connection with God but rather belonging to the
general category of celestial figures.

26. *the gate of the furnace.* Though most translations render this as "the door of
the furnace," the Aramaic *tera'* clearly means "gate." What the writer may have
envisaged is something like an iron grillwork gate over the front of the furnace.
Apertures in the gate world have allowed the king and his entourage to enjoy
the spectacle of the victims writhing as they are burnt. Verse 25 indicates that
the king can see what is going on inside the furnace, which would argue for a
gate, not a solid door. It is perhaps through the apertures of the gate that flames
shoot out to kill the men who have brought Shadrach, Meshach, and Abednego
to the furnace.

the most high God. The Aramaic *'ehaha 'ili'a* is a translation of the Hebrew
'el 'elyon. *'Elyon* was originally the name of the Canaanite sky-god, but by this
late period that origin was entirely obscured and the simple meaning of *'elyon*
as "high" or "lofty" was firmly in place.

and the smell of fire had not touched them. Nebuchadnezzar spoke out and 28
said, "Blessed be the God of Shadrach, Meshach, and Abednego, Who has
sent His messenger and saved His servants who trusted in Him and defied
the king's word and submitted their bodies, for they would not serve nor worship any god except their God. And let a decree be set out by me that any 29
people, nation, or tongue that speaks ill of the God of Shadrach, Meshach,
and Abednego shall be cut to pieces and their house shall be turned into a
dung-heap, for there is no other god that can rescue like this." Then did the 30
king exalt Shadrach, Meshach, and Abednego in the province of Babylonia:

---

27. *and the smell of fire had not touched them.* This last detail reflects what
might be characterized as the hyperbolic representation of the miraculous: not
only were their bodies and their garments completely undamaged by the fire,
but even the acrid smell of the fire had not attached itself to them.

28. *Blessed be the God of Shadrach, Meshach, and Abednego.* Perhaps one should
not infer that the king had become a monotheist, owing fealty only to the God
of the heavens Who is the God of Israel. His language seems to suggest that this
particular deity has manifested extraordinary power and therefore should be
the object of reverence. (Compare the wording of the edict in the next verse.)

Who has sent His messenger. The king concludes that the mysterious fourth
figure in the fiery furnace is a divine emissary who has saved the three young
men.

29. *for there is no other god that can rescue like this.* The king's words seem to say
that he recognizes the unique power of the God of Israel to effect miraculous
salvation; but he does not necessarily renounce the belief in other gods, only
concedes that they would not be as powerful as the God of the three exiled
Judeans.

31 "King Nebuchadnezzar, to all his people, nations, and tongues that dwell in
32 all the earth, may your well-being abound. The signs and wonders that the
most high God has performed with me, it pleases me to tell.

33   His signs, how great they are,
               and His wonders, how powerful!
        His kingdom is an everlasting kingdom,
               and his dominion for all generations."

---

31. *King Nebuchadnezzar, to all his people, nations, and tongues that dwell in all the earth.* This is the formal heading of the decree that the king promulgates. The phrase "that dwell in all the earth" is a hyperbolic flourish: Nebuchadnezzar of course knows that there are other kingdoms, but the extent of his empire is so vast that it is as if it embraced all the earth.

may your well-being abound. These words of well-wishing conclude the formal heading of the edict.

32. *it pleases me to tell.* This phrase constitutes an appropriate introduction to the poem praising God that concludes the royal decree.

33. *His signs, how great they are.* The poetic flourish at the end is also a pointing of the moral in this theologically didactic tale: the most high God is to be praised because He manifests signs and wonders that are tokens of His everlasting dominion.

His kingdom is an everlasting kingdom / and his dominion for all generations. This line is an Aramaic translation of Psalms 145:13.

CHAPTER 4

"I, Nebuchadnezzar, was tranquil in my house and flourishing in my ₁
palace. I saw a dream and it frightened me, and thoughts upon my couch ₂
and visions in my head panicked me. By me has an edict been issued ₃
for all the sages of Babylonia to come before me, that they may make
known to me the meaning of the dream. Then did the soothsayers, wiz- ₄
ards, Chaldeans, and diviners come, and I said the dream to them, but
its meaning they did not make known to me. And latterly, Daniel came ₅
before me, whose name is Belteshazzar, like the name of my god, and in
whom the spirit of the holy gods resides, and I said the dream to him:
'Belteshazzar, master soothsayer, of whom I know that the spirit of the ₆
holy gods resides in you and no mystery is withheld from you, these are

---

1. *I, Nebuchadnezzar* . . . Despite the late medieval chapter divisions, most
modern scholars plausibly conclude that the epistolary formulation of 3:31–33
is actually the beginning of the royal message to the people of the realm that
continues here. The first-person narrative that follows is a form that would have
been unusual in earlier biblical literature.

3. *for all the sages of Babylonia to come before me.* The setup of this story is
patently devised as a parallel to the story of the interpretation of the king's
dream in Chapter 2, where after all the sages of the realm are summoned
and prove unable to interpret the dream, Daniel is brought in and provides an
authoritative interpretation.

5. *whose name is Belteshazzar, like the name of my god.* The king of course refers
to and addresses Daniel with his Babylonian name. Underscoring Daniel's Babylonian acculturation, the king asserts, in what is actually a false etymology, that
the beginning of the name is derived from Bel, the Babylonian god.

7 the visions of my dream that I saw, and say its meaning. And the visions in my head upon my couch I saw, and, look, there was a tree in the earth

8 and its height was great. The tree grew and became mighty, and its top

9 reached the heavens and its branches to the end of all the earth. Its foliage was lovely and its fruit great, and there was food for all in it. Beneath it the beasts of the field were shaded, and in its branches the birds of

10 the heavens dwelled, and all flesh was nourished from it. I saw among the visions in my head, and, look, a holy emissary came down from the

11 heavens, calling out loudly and thus saying, "Cut down the tree, hack off its branches. Shake loose its foliage and scatter its fruit. Let the beasts

12 go off from underneath it and the birds from its branches. But leave one of its roots in the ground and with a chain of iron and bronze be it set in the grass of the field, and by the dew of the heavens be it moistened

13 and with the beasts its portion in the grass of the earth. Its heart shall

---

7. *the visions in my head upon my couch I saw.* Though the formulation sounds a little odd to modern ears, the fixed assumption in the Bible is that dreaming is above all a visual experience, so that a person is said to "see a dream."

8. *The tree grew and became mighty, and its top reached the heavens.* Behind this vision are ancient Near Eastern traditions of a cosmic tree. In this instance, however, the tree represents Nebuchadnezzar's kingdom, which in fact was characterized hyperbolically by the sundry Babylonian emperors as reaching the heavens and extending to the ends of the earth. "Mighty" may seem to be a strange adjective for a tree but is influenced by the reference to empire.

its branches. The Aramaic *ḥazoteih* seems to mean "appearance," which does not make the best sense in context, but there is a homonym with the same root, also attested in Hebrew, that means something like "tangle of branches."

10. *a holy emissary.* Many modern interpreters read the noun here, *'ir*, as "watcher," deriving it from *'er*, "awake." The grounds for this understanding are not conclusive. It is at least as likely that *'ir* is an Aramaic cognate of the Hebrew *tsir*, "emissary." (Phonetically the Hebrew consonant *tsadeh* converts to the Aramaic *'ayin*.)

12. *with a chain of iron and bronze be it set in the grass.* It is altogether unclear what a metal chain is doing tied to the root of a tree, and attempts to rescue the meaning of the received text are unconvincing. One suspects that a small fragment from a different vision extrudes in the text here.

be changed from humankind, and a beast's heart shall be given to it, and seven seasons shall pass over it. By the decree of the divine emissaries is 14 the word, and the utterance of the holy ones is the pronouncement, so that the living may know that the Most High rules over the kingdom of man, to whom He wills he gives it, and the lowliest of men He shall raise up over it." This is the dream that I, King Nebuchadnezzar, saw, and 15 you, Belteshazzar, say its meaning, for all the sages of my kingdom have not been able to make its meaning known to me, but you can, for the spirit of the holy gods resides within you.'" Then Daniel, whose name 16 was Belteshazzar, was astounded for about an hour, and his thoughts panicked him. The king spoke out and said, "Belteshazzar, let not the dream and its meaning panic you." Belteshazzar answered and said, "My lord, may the dream be for your enemies and its meaning for your

---

13. *Its heart shall be changed from humankind.* One should keep in mind that in the biblical view the heart is primarily the seat of understanding, so what is indicated is a loss of reason.

seven seasons. The time span marked by the Aramaic *'idanin* is not altogether clear, but though it is not the ordinary word for "years," it probably refers here to a period of seven years during which the king is to be reduced to a condition of bestial irrationality.

14. *so that the living may know that the Most High rules over the kingdom of man.* This is the great recurring theme of Daniel, an idea nurtured when the Jews were under the dominion of overpowering empires—Babylonian, Persian, Greek. Human dominion is transient and contingent, a mere mirage in comparison with the dominion of God.

15. *the spirit of the holy gods.* As above, the king uses appropriate polytheistic language, though he will ultimately be compelled to recognize the undisputed supremacy of "the Most High."

16. *Daniel . . . was astounded for about an hour.* Unlike his earlier act of dream interpretation, at first he is daunted by the enigmatic character of the dream, and only after taking some time to collect his exegetical powers and after being encouraged by the king does he propose the interpretation.

the dream be for your enemies and its meaning for your foes. This is a diplomatic way of saying that the portent of the dream is a disaster, and one wishes it had been for Nebuchadnezzar's enemies and not for him.

17 foes. The tree that you saw, which was great and mighty and its height
18 reached the heavens and its branches in all the earth, and its foliage was
lovely and its fruit great, and food for all in it, beneath it dwelled the
beasts of the field and in its branches rested the birds of the heavens,
19 you are the king, who has become great and mighty, and your greatness
has grown and reached to the heavens and its branches to all the earth.
20 And as to your seeing, O king, a holy emissary coming down from the
heavens and saying, 'Cut down the tree and destroy it but leave one of
its roots in the ground, and with a chain of iron and bronze [set it] in the
grass of the field and by the dew of the heavens let it be moistened and
with the beasts of the field its portion, until seven seasons pass over it,'
21 this is its meaning, O king, and the decree of the Most High that is to
22 come upon my lord the king. And you shall they banish from men, and
your dwelling shall be with the beasts of the field, and grass like the ox

---

17. *which was great and mighty and its height reached the heavens . . .* The narrative here again follows the procedure we have observed before in the verbatim
repetition of details.

22. *you shall they banish from men.* This is the heart of the prophetic meaning
of the dream. It is also the point at which it becomes clear that this whole story
was not originally about Nebuchadnezzar. There are no ancient reports of Nebuchadnezzar's leaving his throne for an extended period. There are, on the other
hand, such reports about his successor several decades later in the sixth century
BCE, Nabonides. He seems to have been incapacitated from exercising kingship
for a period of about ten years, which here, in accordance with the general use of
formulaic numbers in the Bible, is rounded down to seven ("seasons" or "times,"
but very likely in the sense of "years"). Further confirmation is offered by a frag-
mentary text found at Qumran that scholars call "The Prayer of Nabonides." In
this text, Nabonides prays to be healed from an evil disease with which he has
been stricken. If the details of Daniel 4 reflect something of the historical facts,
Nabonides would have been suffering from some psychological illness, a kind of
long psychotic break that took away his reason. The author of our story interprets
this episode of mental disturbance as a powerful demonstration of God's ability
to bring the mighty low, to reduce to bestiality or raise up again the most imposing of monarchs. An editor probably substituted the name of Nebuchadnezzar
for Nabonides in order to align this story with the previous episodes. The moral
is spelled out at the end of verse 22 and in the king's confession of faith in the
power of the Most High in verses 31–32.

shall they feed you, and from the dew of the heavens shall they give you drink. And seven seasons shall pass over you until you know that the Most High rules over the kingdom of man and to whom He chooses He gives it. And as to their saying to leave one of the roots of the tree, your 23 kingdom shall endure for you once you know that the heavens rule. And 24 yet, O king, let my counsel be pleasing to you, and redeem your offenses through righteousness, in showing kindness to the poor, let your tranquillity be prolonged. All this is to come upon King Nebuchadnezzar." At 25,26 the end of the twelve months he was walking up on [the roof of] the royal palace of Babylon. The king spoke out and said, "Is not this the great 27 Babylon that I have built as the house of the kingdom in the might of my power and for the honor of my glory?" The word was still in the mouth 28 of the king when a voice fell from the heavens: "To you they say, King Nebuchadnezzar, the kingship has turned away from you. And from man 29

---

24. *through righteousness.* Many scholars contend that *tsidqah* (Hebrew *tsedaqah*) here shows the rabbinic use of the word to mean "charity," as the parallel phrase, "showing kindness to the poor," may indicate. It is worth noting that many of the formulations in this episode are framed in semantically parallel statements that are close to poetry, and some scholars in fact set out much of the king's epistle as formal verse.

26. *he was walking up on [the roof of] the royal palace.* The preposition in the original is clearly "on," so the implication is that he was walking on the roof. The roof would have given him a vantage point to look out upon the splendors of his royal city, as in fact he does in the next verse.

27. *the great Babylon.* The Aramaic is *Bavel rabta'*. The Hebrew cognate of this adjective is several times attached to great cities elsewhere in the Bible. Nebuchadnezzar was in fact famous for his grand building projects, which here he contemplates.

28. *The word was still in the mouth of the king.* The king's pride in the imposing edifices he has put up is a manifestation of hubris, and so this is the propitious moment for him to be stricken in the fashion that has been prophesied in his dream.

they shall banish you, and with the beasts of the field your dwelling, grass like the ox they shall feed you, and seven seasons shall pass over you until you know that the Most High rules over the kingdom of man
30 and to whom He chooses He gives it." At that very moment the word was fulfilled upon Nebuchadnezzar, and from man he was banished and he ate grass like the ox, and from the dew of the heavens his body was moistened until his hair grew like eagles and his nails like birds.
31 And at the end of many days: "I, Nebuchadnezzar, raised my eyes to the heavens and my mind returned to me, and I blessed the Most High and praised and extolled the Eternal One, whose dominion is an eternal
32 dominion and His kingdom for all generations. And all earth's dwellers are counted as naught, and as He chooses He does with the array of the heavens and earth's dwellers, and there is none who can protest against
33 Him and say to Him, 'What have You done?' At that very moment my mind returned to me, and the glory of my kingdom, my grandeur and my splendor, returned to me, and me did my counselors and my nobles seek out, and I was set up over my kingdom, and exceeding greatness

---

30. *from man he was banished and he ate grass like the ox.* The writer hews to his commitment to repeat verbatim what has been said before (said twice): his is a world of oracular predictions and perfect fulfillments, and the exact repetition expresses this absolute correspondence between the two. In Daniel's world, there is really no wiggle room for human freedom; everything plays out according to God's predestined plan that is an essential aspect of the apocalyptic worldview. The only textual detail here that goes beyond repetition is the wild growth of the king's hair and nails, which simply elaborates the idea that there is no distance between him and the beasts.

31. *at the end of many days.* This would be at the end of the seven seasons or years, when the king through his purgatorial experience comes to recognize his subservience to God.

32. *with the array of the heavens and earth's dwellers.* God's unchallenged dominion, he now sees, extends not only over all the earth but even over the heavens, where He commands the heavenly armies, which are both the stars and the angels.

was added to me. Now I, Nebuchadnezzar, praise and exalt and glorify 34
the King of the Heavens, all of Whose acts are truth and Whose paths
are justice, and Who can bring low those who go about in pride."

---

34. *Now I, Nebuchadnezzar, praise and exalt and glorify the King of the Heavens.*
This whole concluding speech is often characterized as a doxology. The term
is apt, for this story, like the others in Daniel, turns on creating circumstances
that drive the character to a formal affirmation of a theological principle. There
is very little that resembles this in earlier biblical narrative, where complexities
and ambiguities of character preclude this sort of flat confession of faith.

CHAPTER 5

1 King Belshazzar made a great feast for a thousand of his nobles, and
2 before the thousand he drank wine. With the wine on his tongue,
Belshazzar said to bring the vessels of gold and silver that Nebuchadnezzar his father had taken away from the temple in Jerusalem so that
the king and his nobles, his wives and his concubines might drink from
3 them. Then did they bring the vessels of gold that had been taken away
from the temple of the house of God in Jerusalem, and the king and

---

1. *King Belshazzar made a great feast.* As with other details of court life in the
early chapters of Daniel, this feasting with extravagant consumption of wine
sounds more Persian than Babylonian.

2. *With the wine on his tongue.* The literal sense of the Aramaic is "in the taste
of the wine."

the vessels of gold and silver. To use the sacred vessels from the Jerusalem
temple for drunken carousing is, of course, an act of sacrilege, and it will spell
the king's doom.

Nebuchadnezzar his father. This is another instance of the scrambling, or
perhaps schematization, of the royal line in Daniel. Belshazzar was the son
of Nabonides, and he actually was never king, only regent during his father's
ten-year absence from the court. Nabonides, not Belshazzar, was the last Babylonian king. In fact, the two were not descendants of Nebuchadnezzar: after
the death of Nebuchadnezzar's son-in-law, who had succeeded him, Nabonides
assumed the throne in a palace coup.

his nobles, his wives and his concubines, drank from them. They drank 4
the wine and praised the gods of gold and silver, bronze, iron, wood,
and stone. At that very moment, the fingers of a man's hand came out 5
and wrote before the lampstand on the plaster of the wall of the king's
palace, and the king saw the palm of the hand that was writing. Then 6
did the king's countenance change and his thoughts panicked him, and
the cords of his loins went slack and his knees knocked together. The 7
king called out loudly to bring in his magicians, Chaldeans, and diviners.
The king spoke out and said to the sages of Babylonia, "Whichever man
reads this writing and tells me its meaning shall wear royal purple and
have a golden collar round his neck and rule over a third of the kingdom."

---

4. *praised the gods of gold and silver, bronze, iron, wood, and stone.* There is a
small irony in their worshipping gods of gold and silver as they drink from the
sacred vessels fashioned from gold and silver. The catalog of materials from
which idols are made then proceeds in descending order of value to bronze,
iron, wood, and stone.

5. *the fingers of a man's hand.* Though the "finger of God" appears in the Exodus
story, it is essentially metaphorical. This sort of spooky, quasi-magical appari-
tion is not characteristic of earlier biblical narrative.
   before the lampstand. The likely reason for this detail is that the writing on
the wall is thus fully illuminated, so the visual legibility of the letters is not the
issue.

6. *countenance.* The literal sense is "radiance," and the term is probably related
to the rabbinic *ziw panim*, "radiance of the face."
   the cords of his loins went slack and his knees knocked together. The loins are
imagined in biblical usage as the seat of strength. This physical realization of
the king's dismay is unusual and virtually satiric.

7. *reads this writing and tells me its meaning.* Throughout the story, there are
two challenges—reading the writing and saying what it means. Since the
sages would surely have been able to read the alphabet shared by Aramaic and
Hebrew, it may be that this supernatural inscription used a cryptic script.
   a golden collar. This probably alludes to the regal ornament placed around
Joseph's neck in Genesis 41:42. To judge by Egyptian paintings and archaeo-
logical finds, that was a kind of collar, coming down over the upper chest, and
not a chain.

8 Then did the king's sages come in, but they could not read the writing
9 nor make its meaning known to the king. Then did King Belshazzar
greatly panic and his countenance changed, and his nobles were con-
10 founded. Because of the words of the king and his nobles, the queen
came into the banquet hall. The queen spoke out and said, "May the
king live forever! Let not your thoughts panic you, nor your countenance
11 change. There is a man in your kingdom in whom the spirit of the holy
gods resides, and in your father's days enlightenment and understanding
and wisdom like the wisdom of the gods were found in him. And King
Nebuchadnezzar your father raised him up as master of the soothsayers,
12 the magicians, the Chaldeans, the diviners because exceeding spirit and
knowledge and understanding to interpret dreams and explain enigmas
and untie knotty matters were found in Daniel, to whom the king gave
the name of Belteshazzar. Now, let Daniel be called and he will tell its
13 meaning." Then was Daniel brought in before the king. The king spoke
out and said, "You are Daniel, who is of the exiles from Judah whom my
14 father brought from Judah. And I have heard of you that the spirit of the
gods resides within you and that enlightenment and understanding and
15 exceeding wisdom are found within you. And now, the sages and the
magicians were brought in before me, that they should read this writing

---

10. *the queen.* Since it seems improbable that the queen would know about
Daniel while the king would not, this is in all likelihood the queen-mother. (In
the false genealogy of the story, she is Nebuchadnezzar's wife and Belshazzar's
mother, who would have known firsthand of Daniel's wisdom through the previous episodes.)

May the king live forever! This is the same blessing Bathsheba pronounces
to the aged and decrepit David. It turns into an irony here because he dies that
night.

12. *untie knotty matters.* The same idiom *meshare' qitrin* that was used for the
slackening of the cords of the king's loins (verse 6) is now used antithetically to
express not weakness but strength in unraveling mysteries.

14. *And I have heard of you . . .* Once again, our writer exhibits his proclivity
for verbatim repetition by deploying virtually the same string of epithets for
Daniel's wisdom that the queen-mother used.

and make its meaning known to me, but they could not tell the thing's meaning. And I have heard of you that you can interpret meanings and 16 untie knotty matters. Now, if you can read the writing and make its meaning known to me, you shall wear royal purple and a golden collar shall be round your neck, and over a third of the kingdom you shall rule." Then did Daniel speak out and say before the king, "Let your gift 17 be yours, and your presents give to another. I shall read the writing and the meaning I shall make known to the king. You, O king, the Most 18 High God gave kingship and greatness and honor and glory to Nebuchadnezzar your father. And because of the greatness that He gave him, 19 all people, nations, and tongues were trembling and fearful before him. Whom he would will he would slay and whom he would will he would let live, and whom he would will he would raise up and whom he would will he would bring low. And when his heart was overweening and his spirit 20 grew mighty in defiance, he was taken down from his royal throne and his glory was removed from him. And he was driven from humankind, 21 and his heart was leveled with the beasts and his dwelling was with the wild asses. Grass like the oxen they fed him, and from the dew of the heavens his body was moistened, until he knew that the Most High God rules over the kingdom of man, and whom He will He raises over it. And you, his son Belshazzar, your heart has not been humbled though 22

---

17. *Let your gift be yours.* That is, keep all your gifts; my sole interest in deciphering the writing on the wall is to act as a mouthpiece for the Most High and to display the special wisdom He has implanted in me.

19. *Whom he would will he would slay and whom he would will he would let live.* Since these phrases and the ones that follow are typically attached to God in Psalms and elsewhere, it sounds as though the king were exercising godlike power. In the event, his successor to the throne will prove powerless before God.

20. *he was taken down from his royal throne and his glory was removed from him.* This and what follows in the next verse correspond to the story told in Chapter 4, which applies historically not to Nebuchadnezzar but to Nabonides.

23 you have known all this. And against the LORD of the heavens you have
exalted yourself, and you brought the vessels of His house before you,
and you and your nobles, your wives and your concubines drank wine
in them, and you praised gods of silver and gold, bronze, wood, and
stone, who do not see and do not hear and do not know. And the God
in Whose hand is your life-breath and all your ways are His, you did not
24 glorify. Then before Him was sent the palm of a hand and this writing
25 was inscribed. And this is the writing that was inscribed: *mene mene*
26 *teqal ufarsin*. This is the meaning of the word: *mene*, God has numbered
27 your kingship and brought it to an end. *Teqal*, you have been weighed

---

23. *who do not see and do not hear and do not know.* This mocking characterization of the inert idols is a near-quotation of Psalms 115:5–6.

24. *Then before Him was sent the palm of a hand.* This formulation of indirect
agency with the passive mode of the verb reflects a growing tendency in the
Late Biblical period to avoid attributing anthropomorphic acts directly to God:
it is God's initiative, but the disembodied hand is somehow "sent" from before
the divine presence.

25. *this is the writing that was inscribed.* Daniel's wording suggests that the
script itself was not intelligible to others, so he begins by reading out the four
words. Since *mene* is repeated, there are actually only three words, but in all
likelihood the writer wanted four in order to make the prophecy correspond to
the paradigm of the four kingdoms.

26. *mene.* This is a recognizable Aramaic verb that means "to count" or "to
number." But it has been widely recognized since the nineteenth century that
the three words point to a prophecy that is not mainly focused on Belshazzar's
personal fate. The three words are the names of three ancient coins: the *mina*,
a valuable coin worth sixty shekels; the shekel (*teqal* is the Aramaic equivalent
to that Hebrew term, *sh* in Hebrew converting to *t* in Aramaic); *peras*, which is
a half-shekel (the verbal root, as is evident in Daniel's interpretation, means "to
break apart"). In rabbinic Hebrew, this verbal stem is used for breaking bread.

on the scales and found wanting. *Peras*, your kingdom has been broken 28
apart and given to Media and Persia." Then Belshazzar spoke, and they 29
clothed Daniel in royal purple and put a golden collar round his neck and
proclaimed of him that he should rule over a third of the kingdom. On 30
that very night Belshazzar king of the Chaldeans was slain. And Darius 6:1
the Mede received the kingdom when he was sixty-two years old.

---

28. *your kingdom has been broken apart.* In the paradigm of the four kingdoms,
forced though it may be here, Nebuchadnezzar is the high-value *mina*, Belshazzar is the shekel, and when Babylonia is conquered, the kingdom breaks into
two parts, Persia and Media (which does not entirely fit the historical facts).
The form of the fourth term (dropping the prefix *u* for "and") as Daniel reads it
was *parsin*; now it is modified to *peras* to bring it close in form to the Hebrew
and Aramaic name for Persia.

29. *they clothed Daniel in royal purple.* It may seem odd that he should be
rewarded rather than beheaded for bringing so dire a message to the king. Of
course, our story needs a happy ending from the Jewish point of view, but perhaps we are to infer that Belshazzar is exercising an honorable sense of fairness:
he promised all this grandeur to the person who succeeded in telling him the
meaning of the writing on the wall, and this Daniel has managed to do, however
ominous the writing.

30. *On that very night Belshazzar king of the Chaldeans was slain.* As John Collins notes, this instant fulfillment of Belshazzar's punishment has a folkloric
look. The ancient Greek historians do report that Babylonia was overwhelmed
by a surprise attack. In any case, the defeated king was Nabonides

6:1. *And Darius the Mede received the kingdom.* This notation of the transfer of
power clearly marks the end of this story, despite its later editorial placement
at the beginning of a new chapter. The attribution of the conquest of the Babylonian empire to Darius is still another confusion. Cyrus was the conqueror,
and in any case Darius was a Persian, not a Mede. The writer needs to insert a
Mede in order to arrive at four kingdoms, and he has in mind biblical prophecies (e.g., Jeremiah 51:11) that the Medes destroyed Babylonia.

sixty-two years old. The historical Darius was considerably younger when he
began his reign.

CHAPTER 6

₂ It pleased Darius to raise up one hundred twenty satraps to be through-
₃ out his kingdom, and above them three overseers, of whom Daniel was
one, to whom these satraps would report, that the king should not be
₄ troubled. Then was this Daniel preeminent among the overseers and
the satraps, for there was exceptional spirit in him, and the king thought
₅ to raise him up over the whole kingdom. Then the overlords and the
satraps were seeking to find some pretext against Daniel in regard to
the kingdom, but no pretext nor corruption could they find, for he was
₆ faithful, and no fault nor corruption was found in him. Then these men
said that "no pretext was found against this Daniel, but we have found
₇ one against him in the law of his god." Then did these overseers and

---

2. *one hundred twenty satraps*. Herodotus reported that there were twenty
satraps. The inflated number recalls the formulaic 120 years that is the ideally
long life-span, that of Moses.

4. *Then was this Daniel preeminent among the overseers*. The ascendancy in the
royal administration of a man perceived to be a foreigner clearly kindles the
jealousy of the overseers and the satraps and gives them a motive to do away
with Daniel.

5. *was found in him*. One might note the rather flaccid repeated use of the
serve-all verb "was found." The author of this story is not a great Aramaic stylist.

6. *the law of his god*. The word for "law" or "rule" is a Persian loanword, *dat*, that
is also used frequently in Esther. Collins renders it here as "religious practice,"
and the present context does in fact seem to edge the term in the direction of
its meaning in later Hebrew, "religion."

satraps come in a crowd to the king and thus said to him, "King Darius, live forever! All the overseers of the kingdom, the governors and the 8 satraps and counselors have resolved to issue a royal vow and to enforce a binding edict that for thirty days whoever asks a petition of any god or man other than you, O king, shall be thrown into the lions' den. Now, 9 O king, you should issue the binding edict and put it down in writing that is not to be changed, according to the law of Media and Persia that shall not be transgressed." Because of this, King Darius indited the writ 10 of the binding decree. And when Daniel knew that the writ was indited, 11 he went into his house, and it had windows in its upper chamber open toward Jerusalem, and three times daily he would fall to his knees and

---

8. *All the overseers of the kingdom, the governors and the satraps and counselors have resolved.* The notion that irrevocable royal edicts could be initiated by government bureaucrats in the Persian empire is historically quite unlikely.

for thirty days whoever asks a petition of any god or man other than you. This is another historical improbability. Darius never claimed divine status for himself and so was unlikely to have denied his subjects the right to petition their gods, not to speak of petitioning a person who held power over them. And if in fact Darius was to be treated as the godlike monarch of all he surveyed, why limit the ban to thirty days?

the lions' den. The Aramaic *guba'* (cognate to the Hebrew *geiv*) is actually a pit, but the translation respects the proverbial force of "Daniel in the lions' den."

9. *that is not to be changed.* As with the authorization to massacre the Jews in Esther, this story turns on the fiction that no royal decree in the Persian empire could be revoked. Such a practice is extremely unlikely, and the writer may have picked up the idea from Esther.

11. *windows in its upper chamber open toward Jerusalem.* This is the only moment when anything other than diaspora existence is envisaged. Jews to this day face toward Jerusalem when they pray, and the present text suggests the practice may go back to the Late Biblical period. Facing Jerusalem, of course, does not necessarily mean going back there.

three times daily he would fall to his knees. Three daily prayers became the standard practice in later Judaism, but it is unclear whether the notation here reflects the beginning of that practice or is merely meant to indicate Daniel's persistent piety.

pray and give thanks before his God just as he had done in time past.
12 Then did these men come in a crowd and find Daniel petitioning and
13 imploring his God. Then they approached and said before the king,
"About the binding edict, O king, did you not indite a binding edict that
any man who petitioned any god or man for thirty days other than you,
O king, should be thrown into the lions' den?" The king answered and
said, "The word is right according to the law of Media and Persia, which
14 cannot be transgressed." Then did they answer and say before the king
that "Daniel, who is of the exiles of Judah, has paid no heed to you, O
king, nor to the binding edict that you indited, and three times daily he
15 makes his petition." Then when the king heard the word, it was very dire
for him and he set his mind on Daniel to save him, and till sunset he
16 was striving to rescue him. Then these men came in a crowd to the king
and said to the king, "Know, O king, that it is a rule of Media and Persia
that any binding edict or vow that the king issues cannot be changed."

---

14. *Daniel, who is of the exiles of Judah.* As Collins observes, they do not mention his office but only the fact that he is a foreigner.

15. *it was very dire for him.* Literally, "It was very evil for him." The king likes
and admires Daniel, but he has been trapped by his counselors because the
royal decree is irrevocable, as his officials emphatically point out to him in the
next verse.

   till sunset he was striving to rescue him. What this must mean is that he was
trying to think of some way out of the terrible quandary.

Then the king said, and they brought Daniel and threw him into the 17
lions' den. The king spoke out and said to Daniel, "Your god whom you
always worship will save you." And a stone was brought and placed over 18
the mouth of the den, and the king sealed it with his signet and with the
signet of his nobles, that nothing should be changed regarding Daniel.
Then did the king go to his palace and fast through the night, and no 19
banquet table was set before him, and his sleep went wandering from
him. Then did the king rise with the light at dawn and in a rush went to 20
the lions' den. And as he approached the den, he shouted to Daniel with 21
a sad voice, the king spoke out and said to Daniel, "Daniel, servant of
the living God! Your God whom you worship always, can He have saved
you from the lions?" Then did Daniel speak with the king: "O king, live 22
forever! My God sent His messenger and he shut the lions' mouths and 23
they did not harm me because I was found innocent before Him, and

---

18. *the king sealed it with his signet.* Presumably, the king's seal on the stone is
a sign that no man may dare to roll the stone away.

19. *banquet table.* The Aramaic *daḥawan* is obscure. The idea that it refers to
a table goes back to Rashi and is supported by some modern scholars; others
think it may mean "diversions" or even "dancing girls."

   his sleep went wandering from him. This is the vivid literal sense of the Aramaic (and Hebrew) idiom for insomnia.

20. *rise with the light at dawn.* This early rising of the sleepless king is clearly
an expression of his acute anxiety about Daniel's fate.

21. *as he approached the den, he shouted to Daniel.* The king is sorely afraid that
Daniel has been torn to shreds, and so he shouts to Daniel as he comes near,
hoping against hope that he will get a response. If not, he may choose not to
have the stone rolled back.

23. *My God sent His messenger and he shut the lions' mouths.* Efforts to explain
this naturalistically—for example, the king may have had the lions fed before
Daniel was thrown into their den—are dubious. As with the Ten Plagues in
Exodus, the writer manifestly wants to present this event as a miracle, enabled
by an emissary sent by God.

24 also before you, O king, no harm have I done." Then was the king very
content, and he said to bring up Daniel from the den. And Daniel was
brought up from the den, and no harm was found in him, for he had
25 trusted in his God. And then the king said, and they brought those men
who had slandered Daniel and they threw them into the lions' den, them
and their children and their wives. They had barely touched the bottom
of the den when the lions overwhelmed them and crunched all their
26 bones. Then King Darius wrote to all the peoples, nations, and tongues
27 that dwelled in all the land: "Great peace to you! By me an edict has
been issued that in all the realm of my kingdom people shall fear and
tremble before the God of Daniel,

for He is the living God
and endures forever,
and His kingdom shall not be destroyed,
and His dominion until the end.

---

24. *Then was the king very content.* Literally, "then was it very good for the king."
   bring up Daniel from the den. The verb used is a clear indication that the
den is conceived as a pit.

25. *them and their children and their wives.* The retribution, as in the story of
Achan's violation of the ban in Judges 7, is swift and savage: not only are the
scheming counselors fed to the lions but so are their entire families.

27. *in all the realm of my kingdom people shall fear and tremble before the God
of Daniel.* The monotheistic wish-fulfillment fantasy is especially prominent at
this point. Unlike the previous stories, the king in this instance does not merely
recognize the supreme power of Daniel's God but enjoins the worship of this
God on all his subjects. There is, of course, no way in which such an act could
have a historical basis.
   for He is the living God / and endures forever. In the ceremonial flourish of the
royal edict, the language moves into formal verse, using in the Aramaic epithets
for God that appear frequently in the Hebrew poetry of the Bible. The rhythms
of the next verse, which concludes the edict, are looser, and so that sentence
has not been set out as poetry in this translation.

He saves and rescues and does signs and wonders in the heavens and on   28
earth, Who has saved Daniel from the lions." And this Daniel prospered   29
in the reign of Darius and in the reign of Cyrus the Persian.

---

29. *in the reign of Darius and in the reign of Cyrus the Persian.* The order of
the two emperors suggests that Cyrus came after Darius, though in point of
historical fact, Cyrus preceded him. The reason for this reversal is that the
writer wants to preserve the paradigm of the four kingdoms: Darius is supposed
(falsely) to be a Mede, which is why Cyrus is then identified as "the Persian."

CHAPTER 7

1 In the first year of Belshazzar king of Babylonia Daniel saw a dream and the visions in his head on his couch. Thus he wrote down the dream, the 2 beginning of the words he said. Daniel spoke out and said: "I was seeing in my vision by night, and, look, the four winds of the heavens were rip- 3 pling the Great Sea. And four great beasts were coming out of the sea,

---

1. *Daniel saw a dream.* This marks a new stage in the book. Though the present chapter shares with previous ones enigmatic dream-symbols and the paradigm of the four kingdoms, here Daniel is the recipient of the dream-vision and not the interpreter of the king's dream. In the next verse, Daniel will become the first-person narrator of his dream, another feature that sets this apart from what has preceded. As we shall see, the nature of this dream also differs from the previous dreams.

the beginning of the words he said. This is a literal rendering of the Aramaic. The sense appears to be: he began to speak.

2. *the four winds of the heavens.* The phrase also indicates the four directions of the compass. It sets the scene in cosmic terms.

3. *four great beasts were coming out of the sea.* The ultimate background of this moment is Canaanite cosmogonic myth, which our author would have known only through intermediaries, whether cultic or literary. This is precisely the case for the Job poet, who makes abundant use of Canaanite mythology. In the Canaanite myth, a fearsome sea-monster (Lotan-Leviathan, Yamm) rises to do battle with the weather-god of the land. Here the beast is multiplied to four in order to correspond to the four kingdoms. The strong scholarly consensus is that the four beasts represent, in chronological order: Babylonia, Media, Persia, and Greece.

each different from the others. The first was like a lion, and it had eagle's 4
wings. I was watching till its wings pulled apart and it was lifted from
the earth and made to stand on its legs like a man, and a man's heart was
given to it. And, look, a second beast resembling a bear, and on one side 5
it was made to stand, and three ribs were in its mouth between its teeth,
and thus were they saying to it: 'Arise, consume much flesh.' After this 6
I was watching, and, look, another like a leopard, and it had four bird's
wings on its back, and the beast had four heads, and dominion was given
to it. After this I was seeing among the visions of the night, and, look, 7
a fourth beast, fearsome and terrifying and exceedingly powerful, and,
it had great iron teeth. It was devouring and mangling, and the remains
at its feet it trampled, and it was different from all the beasts before it,
and it had ten horns. I was watching the horns, and, look, another small 8
horn came up among them, and three of the previous horns were torn
out before it, and, look, eyes like a man's eyes were in this horn and a

---

4. *a lion.* The first three beasts are all beasts of prey, suggesting the power and
destructive force of these empires. But the lion and the leopard are also regal
heraldic animals, emblems of the glory of empire.

6. *four bird's wings on its back.* Like the lion with eagle's wings, this image of a
sphinxlike winged beast is a common element in ancient Near Eastern iconog-
raphy from Egypt to Mesopotamia.
   four heads. The imagery of the beasts becomes progressively phantasmagoric
(by comparison, the image of the bear with ribs between its teeth is relatively
realistic). This movement will culminate in the utterly fantastic fourth beast.

7. *fearsome and terrifying and exceedingly powerful.* This most menacing of
the beasts represents Greece, with the persecutions of the Jewish population
around 167 BCE particularly in mind, according to the view of most scholars.
Hence the iron teeth and the devouring and mangling and trampling.
   ten horns. At least some interpreters conclude that these are ten successive
Seleucid kings.

8. *another small horn came up among them.* The last horn probably represents
Antiochus Epiphanes, the perpetrator of the persecutions and the suppressor of
the Jewish cult. Collins proposes that the adjective "small" is a gesture of contempt.
   three of the previous horns were torn out before it. These are three claimants
to the throne eliminated and supplanted by Antiochus Epiphanes.

9 mouth uttering overweening things. I was looking, until thrones were cast down and the Ancient of Days took His seat. His garment was like white snow and the hair of His head like pure wool, His throne tongues
10 of flame, its wheels burning fire. A river of fire was flowing and went out before Him. Thousands upon thousands ministered to Him, and myriad upon myriad stood before Him. The court was seated and the
11 books were opened. I was looking—then from the sound of the over-weening words that the horn was uttering I looked till the beast was
12 slain and its body destroyed and consigned to the burning fire. As to the remaining beasts, their dominion was taken over, and an extension of
13 life was given to them for a time and season. I was seeing in the visions of the night and, look, with the clouds of the heavens one like a human being was coming, and he reached the Ancient of Days, and they had

---

9. *the Ancient of Days took His seat.* At this point, in contrast to the earlier dream-visions, the scene becomes explicitly apocalyptic. God Himself enters the picture, seated on a throne, clothed in glorious white raiment, to mete out judgment. History is to take a decisive and irreversible turn through spectacular divine intervention. The apocalyptic note aligns this chapter with the second half of Daniel, while its being written in Aramaic—all that follows will be in Hebrew—serves as a bridge between the first half of the book and the second.

10. *Thousands upon thousands ministered to Him.* All this celestial glory consti-tutes an implicit rejoinder to the power of earthly empires that has just been symbolically evoked: the court of even the greatest emperor is a mean and minuscule thing in comparison with the court of the Ancient of Days, with its untold thousands of celestial ministrants, its throne with wheels of fire, the river of fire that flows out from it.

11. *the beast was slain.* The last and most vicious of earthly kingdoms is anni-hilated by God.

13. *one like a human being.* The translation avoids "like the son of man" because of its strong, and debatable, tilt toward a messianic interpretation. If tradi-tional Christian interpreters have understood this is a reference to Christ, some Jewish interpreters have seen it as a collective representation of the Jewish people, which is equally unlikely. Collins, after a thorough and scrupulous survey of all the possible readings, plausibly concludes that the term refers to

him approach before Him. And to him were given dominion and honor 14
and kingship, and all the people, nations, and tongues did serve him.
His dominion is an everlasting dominion that will not pass away and
his kingdom will not be destroyed. I, Daniel, my spirit was downcast 15
within me and the visions within my head panicked me. I approached 16
one of those standing there and asked of him the truth about all this,
and he spoke to me and made known to me the meaning of the things.
'These great beasts, which are four—four kings shall rise up from the 17
earth, and the holy ones of the Most High shall receive the kingdom and 18
take possession of the kingdom forever and forever.' Then I wanted the 19
truth about the fourth beast that was different from all of them, exceedingly fearsome—its teeth of iron and its claws of bronze, consuming and

---

an angelic being, most likely Michael, descending onto the scene "with the
clouds." This would explain the force of "like"—this figure looks like a human
being but is more than that.

14. *His dominion is an everlasting dominion.* This is an apocalyptic motif par
excellence: history as we know it, with its cycles of empires, comes to an end,
and the divinely effected kingdom, championing God's people, is instated
instead.

16. *and made known to me the meaning of the things.* Here we see clearly how
Daniel as an apocalyptic text differs in its use of symbolism from biblical prophecy. Though the vision of the four beasts has a certain affinity with Ezekiel's
vision of the celestial chariot, it is more phantasmagoric and bewildering—the
beast with ten horns, the little horn that emerges, and so forth—and in its very
enigmatic character cries out for decoding, which one of the ministering angels
now proceeds to do, at least in part.

18. *the holy ones of the Most High.* The most likely reference is to angels. The
"Most High" here has a plural ending, but that is probably a plural of majesty.

19. *different from all of them, exceedingly fearsome.* This horrendous iron-toothed
beast, mangling and trampling, reflects the frightening oppressive power of the
Seleucid kingdom under Antiochus Epiphanes.

20 mangling and trampling what remained with its feet. And concerning the ten horns that were on its head and another that came up and three fell before it, and that horn had eyes and a mouth uttering overweening

21 things, and its appearance was greater than its fellows. I was watching, and that horn did battle with the holy ones and prevailed over them.

22 Until the Ancient of Days came and meted out justice for the holy ones of the Most High, and the time came when the holy ones took posses-

23 sion of the kingdom. Thus did he say: 'The fourth beast is the fourth kingdom that shall be on the earth, which shall be different from all the kingdoms and shall consume all the earth and shall harrow it and grind

24 it to dust. And the ten horns from that kingdom, ten kings shall arise, and another shall arise after them, and he shall be different from those

25 before him, and three kings shall he bring low, and he shall utter words against the Most High and afflict the holy ones, and he shall think to change the times and the law. And they shall be given in his hand for

---

21. *that horn did battle with the holy ones.* This is an apocalyptic war, essentially between the forces of darkness and light (even if those terms, which appear in the Qumran scrolls, are not mentioned). The armies of evil at first prevail, as the Greeks did in 167 BCE, but then God intervenes (verse 22) to bring about a decisive victory.

24. *another shall arise after them, and he shall be different from those before him.* The author of this vision writes in the conviction that Antiochus Epiphanes, arising out of a line of ten kings and displacing three contenders to the throne before him, is different in his pernicious nature from all who preceded him.

25. *he shall utter words against the Most High.* This might refer, as Collins notes, to Antiochus's practice of stamping on some of his coins "God manifest" with his image.

he shall think to change the times and the law. This sibylline formulation in all likelihood refers to the decree of Antiochus Epiphanes suppressing the traditional Jewish cult and imposing pagan worship in the Jerusalem temple.

a season, a season, and a half-season. And the court shall be seated, and 26
they shall take away his dominion, destroying and expunging to the end.
And the kingdom and the dominion and the greatness of all kingdoms 27
under the heavens shall be given to the people of the holy ones of the
Most High. Its kingdom is an everlasting kingdom, and all dominions
shall serve it and obey it. This marks the end of the matter.' I, Daniel, 28
my thoughts sorely panicked me and my countenance changed, and I
kept the matter in my heart."

---

a season, a season, and a half-season. The writer continues to hew to the
murky style of oracular pronouncement, but this probably means two and a
half years.

26. *And the court shall be seated.* Heavenly judgment of the forces of evil is
indicated by this.

27. *all dominions shall serve it and obey it.* The downtrodden people of Israel will
now exercise unending dominion. This theme may owe something to the poetic
hyperboles in Second Isaiah, where the kings and queens of the nations are said
to serve Israel, but that idea is recast here as a ringing apocalyptic declaration
of the radical transformation of history.

28. *my thoughts sorely panicked me.* Though the vision ends with a grand pronouncement of the ultimate triumph of the forces of light, the bewildering
vision bristles with terrifying elements, so at the end Daniel feels overwhelmed
by it all.

CHAPTER 8

I n the third year of King Belshazzar a vision appeared to me, Daniel,
after what had appeared to me before. And I saw in the vision, and it
happened when I saw, that I was in Shushan the capital, which is in
the province of Elam by the brook of Ulai. And I raised my eyes and
saw, and, look, a ram was standing before the brook, and it had two
horns, and the horns were high and one was higher than the other, and
the higher one sprouted last. I saw the ram, and, look, it was butting
to the west and to the north and to the south, and all the beasts could
not stand up before it, and none could save from its power, and it did

---

1. *In the third year.* The language now switches from Aramaic to Hebrew and
will continue in Hebrew till the end of the book. But, as noted above, the form
and content of this chapter are closely related to those of the previous chapter.

2. *Shushan the capital.* This is the royal city of the Persian empire and the
theater in which most of the action takes place in the Book of Esther. Daniel's
fictional location, we should recall, is in the Babylonian, then Persian, empire.
Many modern interpreters understand the noun rendered here as "capital" to
signify "fortress city."

3. *two horns.* These are the kingdoms of Media and Persia, with Persia being
the "higher" horn that sprouts after the other horn.

4. *to the west and to the north and to the south.* Though one ancient version sup-
plies the fourth direction, these are in fact the directions in which the Persian
empire chiefly expanded.

as it pleased and grew great. And I was pondering, and, look, a he-goat 5
came from the west over all the earth and was not touching the ground,
and the goat had a jutting horn between its eyes. And it came up to the 6
ram with the two horns that I had seen standing before the brook and
ran toward it in the fury of its strength. And I saw it reaching the ram, 7
and it attacked it and struck down the ram and shattered its two horns.
And the ram did not have the strength to stand up before it, and it flung
the ram to the ground and trampled it, and there was none to save the
ram from its power. And the he-goat became very great, and as it grew 8
mighty, the large horn was broken and four jutting ones sprouted in its
stead to the four corners of the heavens. And from one of them came 9
out a puny horn, and it grew exceedingly toward the south and toward

---

5. *a he-goat came from the west.* This is the Greek empire, which invaded the
Near East from the west.

and was not touching the ground. It is unnecessary to assume that this makes
the he-goat a winged beast. The obvious indication is of the breathtaking swift-
ness of Alexander's conquest.

a jutting horn. The Hebrew collocation *qeren ḥazut* is peculiar, and Hebrew
usage will become still stranger as the vision proceeds. Most interpreters
understand the second term to reflect a verbal root that means "to see," thus
indicating something like "highly visible." It is on that assumption that the present translation uses "jutting," but this is somewhat conjectural.

7. *it attacked it and struck down the ram.* This is an image of Alexander's devastating frontal assault on the Persian empire.

8. *the large horn was broken and four jutting ones sprouted in its stead.* This is a
symbolic representation of the death of Alexander in 323 BCE and the breakup
of the vast empire he had established into four smaller empires.

9. *a puny horn.* This repeats the derogatory Aramaic reference in 7:8 to Antiochus Epiphanes.

10 the east and toward the Splendid Land. And it grew up to the host of the heavens and brought down some of the stars from the host and trampled
11 them. And up to the Commander of the Host it grew, and from it the daily offering was taken away, and the firm place of His sanctuary was
12 flung away. And a host was criminally set against the daily offering, and
13 it flung truth to the ground and prospered in what it did. And I heard a certain holy one speaking, and the certain holy one said to whoever was speaking, 'Till when is the vision—the daily offering and the desolating
14 crime giving the sanctum and the host to be trampled?' And he said to

---

10. *And it grew up to the host of the heavens and brought down some of the stars.* The host (or "array") of the heavens is both God's celestial army and the stars. Though the imagery sounds apocalyptic, the reference is probably to the violation of the temple cult by Antiochus, which is understood as an assault on God.

11. *the daily offering was taken away.* This formulation directly invokes the suppression of the temple cult in late 167 BCE. The "Commander of the Host" would have to be God, so the profanation of the temple is seen as affecting God Himself.

12. *And a host was criminally set against the daily offering.* The Hebrew of this entire verse is crabbed and opaque, whether through mangling in scribal transmission or because the writer, perhaps more comfortable in Aramaic than in Hebrew, had an imperfect sense of the language. As a result, any translation at this point is somewhat conjectural.
    prospered in what it did. The Hebrew is again problematic: both "prospered" and "did" are conjugated as feminine verbs, but the word for "host" is masculine. "Truth" is a feminine noun, but it makes no sense for that to be the subject of the verbs.

13. *a certain holy one.* This is clearly an angel.
    the daily offering and the desolating crime giving the sanctum and the host to be trampled. Although the reference has to be again to the desecration of the temple by Antiochus, this whole clause reads like word salad in the Hebrew— literally: the daily offering and the desolating crime give and holiness and host trampling.

me, 'Two thousand three hundred evenings and mornings, and the sanctum will be made right.' And it happened when I Daniel saw the vision 15
that I sought understanding, and, look, standing before me was as the
likeness of a man. And I heard a human voice in the midst of the Ulai, 16
and it called out and said, 'Gabriel, make that one understand what is
seen.' And he came to where I stood, and when he came, I was terrified 17
and fell on my face. And he said to me, 'Understand, O human, that the
vision is for the end-time.' And as he spoke to me I fell into a trance, my 18
face on the ground, and he touched me and made me stand up. And he 19
said, 'I am about to make known to you what will be in the latter time
of the wrath, for it is the appointed time for the end. The ram that you 20

---

14. *Two thousand three hundred evenings and mornings.* The daily offering was
made each evening and morning. Thus the time envisaged during which the
temple cult is suppressed comes to slightly more than three years.

will be made right. Alternately, "will be justified." It is an anomalous use of
the verb *ts-d-q.*

15. *as the likeness of a man.* This is another way of referring to an anthropomorphic celestial being.

16. *a human voice in the midst of the Ulai.* The voice, that is, comes as human
speech, but the speaker is more than human, addressing Daniel from the midst
of a watercourse, where no ordinary human would be.

Gabriel. It is only in this late period that angels are given names.

17. *O human.* The Hebrew *ben-'adam,* which some render, misleadingly, as "son
of man," is a term of address used by the divine for the human that is borrowed
from Ezekiel.

18. *I fell into a trance.* As Abraham does in his face-to-face covenant with God
in Genesis 15:12.

19. *the latter time of the wrath.* The most probable reference of this murky
formulation is to the end of the period of persecution initiated by Antiochus.

21 saw with the horns is the king of Media and Persia. And the he-goat is
the king of Greece, and the great horn that is between its eyes is the first
22 king. And the one broken and four stood in its stead are the four king-
23 doms that rose up from a nation and not through its power. And in the
latter time of his kingdom, when the crimes are fulfilled, an impudent
24 king will rise up, who understands enigmas. And his power will grow
mighty but not through his own power, and he will lay waste wondrously
and prosper in what he does and lay waste to mighty ones and to the
25 people of the holy ones. And with his shrewdness he will prosper in the
deceit he possesses, and in his mind he will grow great and lay waste
to many unawares, and he will stand against the prince of princes, but
26 he will be broken effortlessly. And the portent of evening and morning

---

21. *the first king.* This, of course, is Alexander the Great.

23. *when the crimes are fulfilled.* The meaning is obscure. Some have compared
it to Genesis 15:16, when it is said "for the iniquity of the Amorites is not yet
full"—that is, once the balance sheet of all their crimes is full, they will be
destroyed.

   an impudent king . . . who understands enigmas. Antiochus is impudent but
also exercises a certain cunning or shrewdness.

24. *lay waste to mighty ones.* Collins understands these to be the three pretend-
ants to the throne whom Antiochus eliminated.

25. *shrewdness.* The Hebrew *sekhel* also has a more positive sense ("insight,"
"intelligence"), but the present context surely calls for a negative term for
acumen.

   unawares. Antiochus took Jerusalem in a surprise attack.

   effortlessly. More literally, "without a hand" (others, "not by human hands").
Collins suggests that in this the author of the vision dissociates himself from
the Maccabean rebellion against Antiochus.

that was said is truth. As for you, keep the vision a secret, for it is for
a long time off.' And I Daniel, I was devastated and stricken for a long 27
time, and I arose and did the king's tasks and was dumbfounded over
the vision, and none understood."

---

26. *keep the vision a secret, for it is for a long time off.* It is doubtful that this text,
or any other in Daniel, was hidden as esoteric doctrine in its own time, but one
must remember that this prophecy is purportedly revealed to Daniel back in
the Persian period, in the third year of the reign of Belshazzar.

27. *devastated.* The translation follows Rashi in deriving the verb *nihyeiti* from
the noun *howah*, "disaster."
    did the king's tasks. Daniel returns to his responsibilities as a high-ranking
royal bureaucrat.
    and none understood. The meaning of the portent has been revealed to
Daniel but to no other person.

CHAPTER 9

¹ In the first year of Darius son of Ahasuerus from the seed of Media, who
² was made king over the kingdom of the Chaldeans, in the first year of his
reign, I, Daniel, came to understand in the books the number of years
that according to the word of the LORD to Jeremiah the prophet were to
³ fulfill the devastation of Jerusalem—seventy years. And I turned to the
Master God to petition in prayer and supplication, in fasting and sack-
⁴ cloth and ashes. And I prayed to the LORD my God and confessed and
said, "O Master, great and fearsome God, Who keeps the covenant and

---

1. *Darius son of Ahasuerus.* This is still another confusion of Persian dynastic
names. Ahasuerus was not the father of Darius, but he appears to be plugged
in here as a familiar Persian royal name.

2. *the books.* Daniel actually has in mind one book, Jeremiah, who prophesied
(Jeremiah 25:11) that "these nations shall be subject to the king of Babylonia
seventy years." The text from Jeremiah will surface in the exchange with the
angel Gabriel, verses 22–27, where it will be given a novel interpretation.

3. *the Master.* This chapter makes repeated use of 'adonay, "Master." That may
be a pious scribal substitution for YHWH, but YHWH is used in the next verse
and afterward in Daniel's prayer (and nowhere else in the book).
   in fasting and sackcloth and ashes. This paraphernalia of mourning is also
traditionally used for penitential prayers.

4. *I prayed to the LORD.* The form of the penitential prayer is unique to this
chapter. The language of the prayer is traditional (and somewhat different from
the Hebrew used elsewhere in Daniel), so this may have been an older prayer
adapted and inserted by the writer. This sort of literary collage is common in
biblical composition from its early stages.

faithfulness for those who love Him and keep His commands! We have ₅
offended and done wrong and acted wickedly and rebelled and swerved
from Your commands and from Your statutes. And we have not heeded ₆
Your servants the prophets, who spoke in Your name to our kings, our
nobles, our fathers, and to all the people of the land. Yours, O Master, is ₇
righteousness and ours the disgrace, the men of Judah and the inhabitants of Jerusalem and all Israel, far and near in all the lands to which
You have driven them for their betrayal that they committed against You.
Ours is the shame, O LORD, our kings', our nobles', and our fathers', for ₈
we have offended You. To the Master our God are compassion and for- ₉
giveness, for we have rebelled against Him. And we have not heeded the ₁₀
voice of the LORD our God to walk in His teachings that He set before
us through His servants the prophets. And all Israel have violated Your ₁₁
teaching and swerved away, not heeding Your voice. And the curse and
the imprecation written in the Teaching of Moses servant of God poured
down on us, for we have offended Him. And he fulfilled His word that ₁₂
He had spoken concerning us and concerning our judges who judged
us to bring upon us great evil, which has never been done under all the
heavens as was done against Jerusalem. As it is written in the Teaching ₁₃
of Moses, all this evil came upon us, yet we did not entreat the LORD
our God to turn from our wrongdoing and to find wisdom in Your truth.

---

5. *We have offended and done wrong and acted wickedly and rebelled.* The language of confession was adopted liturgically for the shorter confession of sins
in the Yom Kippur service.

6. *we have not heeded Your servants the prophets.* Heeding the prophets is of
paramount concern for Daniel because he is basing his vision of history on
Jeremiah.

7. *in all the lands to which You have driven them.* This formulation is in keeping
with the repeated declaration in Deuteronomy that exile comes as punishment
for violation of the covenant.

12. *great evil, which has never been done under all the heavens.* This hyperbolic
characterization of the national catastrophe that befell Judah (which of course
did not differ from the conquest of other peoples) echoes, perhaps consciously,
a repeated theme from Lamentations.

14 And the LORD was exacting about the evil and brought it upon us, for
the LORD our God is righteous in all His acts that He has done, but we

15 did not heed His voice. And now, O Master our God, Who brought Your
people out from the land of Egypt with a strong hand and made a name
for Yourself as on this day, we have offended, we have acted wickedly.

16 O Master, by all Your righteousness let Your wrath, pray, and Your fury
turn back from Your city Jerusalem, Your holy mountain, for through
our offenses and through the wrongdoing of our fathers, Jerusalem and

17 Your people are a disgrace to all around us. And now, listen, God, to the
prayer of Your servant and to his supplications, and let Your face shine

18 on Your desolate sanctuary for the sake of the Master. Bend Your ear, my
God, and listen. Open Your eyes and see our desolation and the city on
which Your name is called, for not because of our righteousness do we
pour out our supplication before You but because of Your great compas-

19 sion. O Master, listen. O Master forgive. O Master hearken, and do it,
do not delay, for Your sake, my God, for Your name is called on Your city

20 and on Your people." I was still speaking and praying and confessing my
offense and the offense of my people Israel and pouring out my sup-

---

16. *let Your wrath, pray, and Your fury turn back from Your city Jerusalem.* This formulation leads one to wonder whether this prayer may have originated before
the return to Zion in the middle of the fifth century BCE. At the time of the
composition of Daniel, the temple had long been rebuilt, and there was a substantial Jewish population in Jerusalem. But as we shall see, the catastrophe
of the destruction of Jerusalem and the razing of the temple is conflated with
a later and different disaster.

17. *Your desolate sanctuary.* The term *shamem,* "desolate," which originally
would have referred to the destroyed temple, will now be used to indicate a
different kind of desolation.

19. *O Master, listen. O Master forgive. O Master hearken.* These words constitute
a formal coda to Daniel's supplication.

20. *my offense and the offense of my people.* Although the confession of sin has
been in the first-person plural, Daniel, as spokesman for the people, must
include himself.

plication before the LORD my God for the holy mountain of my God, and I was still speaking in prayer, when the man Gabriel, whom I had 21 seen in the vision before, glided down in flight, reaching me at the hour of the evening offering. And he imparted understanding and spoke with 22 me and said, "Daniel, now have I come out to convey wisdom to you. At the beginning of your supplication the word was issued and I have 23 come to tell that you are beloved. And discern the word and understand the vision. Seven weeks of years are decreed for your people to work 24 out the crime and to finish offenses and to atone for wrongdoing and to bring everlasting justice and to seal vision and prophecy and to anoint

---

21. *the man Gabriel.* Although Gabriel is a divine being, he is designated "man" because his form is human.

glided down in flight. The term *biy'af*, rendered here as "in flight," is disputed, but it could easily derive from the verbal stem that indicates flying by a reversal of consonants. If so, this would be the first unambiguous instance of an airborne angel.

23. *the word was issued.* The likely reference is to the word of revelation or explanation that is here given to Daniel.

you are beloved. Hence, you are the privileged recipient of this revelation.

vision. Literally, "what is seen," that is, the vision. Elsewhere in Daniel another term is used for "vision."

24. *Seven weeks of years.* The Hebrew appears to say merely "weeks," but it becomes apparent in Daniel's calculations that these are weeks of years. That might be indicated by the otherwise odd masculine plural ending, whereas "weeks" in earlier Hebrew always has a feminine plural ending, though the word is masculine. It is also possible that a masculine plural ending is simply used as part of a general tendency of later Hebrew to regularize irregular forms. In any case, through this terminology, Jeremiah's "seventy years," which would approximately mark the time span from the moment of his prophecy to the beginning of the return to Zion, is transformed into 490 years—still not an exact number but bringing the elapsed time to just a few decades after the date of 167, when this vision is enumerated. Biblical Hebrew, with its attachment to formulaic numbers, often uses numerical indications only approximately.

to finish offenses. The received text reads "to seal," *lehatem*, but that is probably an inadvertent scribal duplication of that same verb which occurs later in the verse, and many manuscripts read *lehatem*, "to finish," "bring to an end."

25 the holy of holies. And you shall know and understand: seven weeks
of years from the issuing of the word to restore and rebuild Jerusalem
until the anointed prince, and in sixty-two weeks of years it will once
26 more be built, square and moat, but in a time of distress. And after the
sixty-two weeks of years the anointed one shall be cut off with none to
27 save him. And the troops of a prince who comes shall destroy the city
and the sanctuary, but his end shall come in a sudden rush, and till the

---

25. *from the issuing of the word.* This has to be Jeremiah's word.

the anointed prince. This is probably Antiochus Epiphanes. One should
remember that "anointed" in biblical Hebrew is the equivalent of "crowned"
and does not necessarily imply divinely sanctioned status.

in a time of distress. This is almost certainly a reference to the persecutions
ordered by Antiochus.

26. *the anointed one shall be cut off.* Though the reference, after the previous "anointed prince," is confusing, most commentators think this alludes to
Onias III, the high priest who was murdered around 171 BCE. Priests as well as
princes were anointed. After Onias III, there were no more legitimate Zadokite
priests.

with none to save him. "To save him" does not appear in the Hebrew but may
have been dropped in scribal transmission.

end of the decreed war, desolation. And he shall make a strong pact with 28
the many for one week of years, and for half a week of years he shall
put a stop to sacrifice and grain offering. And in its place there shall be
a desolating abomination until the decreed destruction is poured down
on the desolating thing."

---

28. *he shall make a strong pact with the many for one week of years.* What is
envisaged is the collaboration of the large population of Hellenized Jews in
Jerusalem with Antiochus in setting up a pagan cult in the temple. This alliance
is said to last seven years, and for three and a half years the traditional cult of
YHWH in the temple was violated.

in its place. The Masoretic text reads, incomprehensibly, "on the wing" (or
"corner"). The translation follows a commonly proposed emendation: instead
of *'al kenaf* we read *'al kano.*

a desolating abomination. Pointedly, Daniel cannot bring himself to mention
the vile, disgusting thing that has been placed in the temple. Some think it
may be the statue of a pagan god; others conclude that it is a special altar for
pagan sacrifice set up within the temple. On that altar (or perhaps, before that
statue), the animal sacrifices offered, as we know from other ancient sources,
included pigs—an animal toward which Jewish loyalists had a kind of visceral
revulsion, thus adding an associative coloration to the generalized language of
disgust that Daniel uses here.

CHAPTER 10

1 In the third year of Cyrus king of Persia a word was revealed to Daniel, whose name had been called Belteshazzar, and the word was true and the service great, and he understood the word and had understanding
2,3 of the vision. "At that time, I, Daniel, was mourning for three weeks. No fine bread did I eat, nor did meat and wine come into my mouth, and I was careful not to rub myself with oil until the three weeks were over.
4 And on the twenty-fourth day of the first month, I was by the great river,
5 which is the Tigris. And I raised my eyes and saw, and, look, there was a certain man dressed in linen and his loins were girt with pure gold,

---

1. *In the third year of Cyrus.* In 1:21, we are told that Daniel's mission continued only till the first year of Cyrus's reign. The discrepancy is unresolved.

the service. The more common meaning of *tsava'* is "army," but that is because one owes a term of service in the army. Presumably, the sense here is the great and arduous service as a recipient of vision.

3. *No fine bread did I eat . . .* Fasting, or partial fasting, as is evidently the case here, had become common in this period as a procedure for creating readiness for visionary experience.

not to rub myself with oil. The Hebrew uses a different verb from the one for anointing, and "anoint," adopted in almost all English versions, should be avoided because of its sacral or political associations. What is referred to here is the pleasurable and cosmetic rubbing of the body with soothing oil, a practice well attested in the ancient Mediterranean from Greece to the Fertile Crescent.

5. *dressed in linen.* Linen as angelic garb is a cue picked up from Ezekiel.

and his body was like chrysolite, and his face like the look of lightning, 6
and his eyes like fiery torches, and his arms and his legs like the color of
burnished bronze, and the sound of his words like the sound of a great
crowd. And I, Daniel, alone saw the vision, but the people who were 7
with me did not see the vision, yet a great trembling fell upon them
and they fled to hide. As for me, I remained alone, and I saw this great 8
vision, and no strength remained in me, and my bearing was shattered,
and I retained no strength. And I heard the sound of his words, and as I 9
heard the sound of his words, I was in a trance on my face, and my face
to the ground. And, look, a hand touched me and he pulled me to my 10
knees and to the palms of my hands. And he said to me, 'Daniel, beloved 11
man, understand the words that I speak to you and stand up where you
are, for now have I been sent to you.' And as he spoke this thing to me,
I stood up, shaking. And he said to me, 'Fear not, Daniel. For from the 12
first day that you set your mind to understand and to afflict yourself

---

6. *and his body was like chrysolite, and his face like the look of lightning . . .*
Though this figure, who must be Gabriel, has been described as "a certain man"
because his form is anthropomorphic, he is dazzling and monumental (like the
lover in Song of Songs 5:10–16) from his jewellike body and his refulgent face
and eyes to his roaring voice.

7. *yet a great trembling fell upon them.* Unlike Daniel, they are not privileged to
see the vision, but they sense some sort of numinous fearsome presence, which
strikes them with terror.

8. *my bearing.* The literal sense of the Hebrew noun is "glory." The word selection and, even more, the phrase that immediately follows, *nehpakh lemashhit*,
sound odd.

9. *a trance.* As before, the trance is a precondition to receiving the vision.

10. *a hand touched me.* Daniel, in a trance, with his face pressed to the ground,
is not in a position to see the angel, but now he feels a hand touching him and
raising him up with a shaking motion.

12. *to afflict yourself.* This reflexive verb often has the sense of "to fast" and in
Late Biblical and rabbinic Hebrew generates a cognate noun for fasting, *ta'anit.*

before your God, your words were heard, and I have come through your
13 words. And the prince of the kingdom of Persia was standing against
me twenty-one days, and, look, Michael, one of the leading princes,
was coming to help me, and I remained there by the king of Persia.
14 And I have come to let you understand what will befall your people in
15 the latter time, for there is yet a vision for the time.' And as he spoke
to me words of this sort, I put my face to the ground and I fell silent.
16 And, look, one in the likeness of a human being was touching my lips,
and I opened my mouth and spoke and said to him who stood before
me, 'My lord, in the vision my pangs overcame me and I retained no
17 strength. And how can this slave of my lord speak with my lord, and I,
18 strength will not stand in me and no breath is left me?' And again one
like the semblance of a human being touched me and made me strong.

---

13. *the prince of the kingdom of Persia.* The probable reference is not to the
Persian emperor but to a celestial *sar* who serves as an angelic patron of Persia.
Though there are a couple of episodic hints of such a notion in earlier biblical literature, it basically reflects a new concept of history: celestial agents do
battle with one another on behalf of the nations they patronize, and human
agency is thus drastically reduced.

　twenty-one days. These evidently correspond to the twenty-one days of Daniel's fast.

15. *I put my face to the ground.* Daniel's head had been raised when Gabriel
lifted him from his prostrate position, but as he is about to be told what will
befall his people in the time to come, he flings himself back down in fear.

16. *touching my lips.* Unlike the more general touch of verse 10, Daniel here is
specifically touched on the lips, an indication that he is to speak the prophecy
he will receive. In order to touch him on the lips, the angel would have had to
raise his head from the ground.

18. *made me strong.* Though some have linked Daniel's weakness with his
twenty-one days of partial fasting, what is much clearer is that the power of the
epiphany itself devastates or evacuates him, and so he needs to be strengthened.

And he said, 'Fear not, beloved man, it is well with you. Be very strong.' 19
And as he spoke with me, I grew strong and said, 'Let my lord speak, for
you have made me strong.' And he said, 'Do you know why I have come 20
to you? And now, I shall go back to do battle with the prince of Persia,
and as I go out, look, the prince of Greece is coming. But I shall tell you 21
what is inscribed in the writ of truth, and there is no one sustaining me
against all those save Michael your prince.'

And I in the first year of Darius the Mede, I took my stand to strengthen 11:1
and to be a bastion for him. And now the truth shall I tell you." 2a

---

19. *it is well with you.* Some render *shalom lakh* as a greeting, "peace be with
you," but given the context of Daniel's overwhelming weakness followed by his
regaining strength, the inevitable sense is "it is well with you"—don't worry,
you are all right now.

20. *I shall go back to do battle with the prince of Persia.* As in verse 13, this is a
battle between angelic patrons of the nations.
　　the prince of Greece is coming. In this theocentric vision of history, it is not
Alexander the Great but the celestial prince of Greece who approaches to
defeat the Persian empire.

21. *the writ of truth.* Though most translations render this as "the book of truth,"
the Hebrew noun *ketav* means anything that is written down, and it is worth
preserving the mysterious indeterminacy of the locution, which seems apt for
a prophetic revelation.
　　sustaining me. The reflexive Hebrew verb is the same one used in verse 19
for Daniel's "growing strong."
　　Michael your prince. Gabriel is speaking, but his celestial ally Michael is the
prince of the people of Israel.

11:1. *And I in the first year of Darius the Mede.* This translation follows the proposal of many scholars that the first verse and a half of chapter 11 are actually
the conclusion of the textual unit that begins with 10:1.
　　I took my stand. This is still another instance in which the Hebrew of Daniel
seems a little peculiar. The literal sense of the Hebrew is "my stance is to
strengthen and to be a bastion for him," but the context appears to require a
verb, not a noun, and that has been supplied in the translation.

CHAPTER 11

2b   Look, another three kings are to stand forth for Persia, and the fourth
shall grow rich with greater wealth than all, and with his wealth he
3   shall stir up all, even the kingdom of Greece. And a warrior king shall

---

2b. *another three kings are to stand forth for Persia*. As in all that follows in this
chapter, the three Persian kings plus one are cloaked in deliberately mystifying
anonymity, in keeping with the intended prophetic effect. Scholarship generally gives this the neutral label of *ex eventu* prophecy, though it may be more to
the point to call this pseudoprophecy. That is, Daniel, fictionally located in the
Persian empire, is represented as foreseeing the political events of the next century and a half—events that the author of the book, around 167 BCE, knew in
minute detail. In contrast, however, to the treatment of the wars and campaigns
in the Seleucid and Ptolemaic empires, the four Persian kings are schematic,
and the extraordinary wealth of the fourth is probably a literary invention.

    he shall stir up all, even the kingdom of Greece. The notion that the wealth
of the Persian emperor—probably Darius III—motivated Alexander to invade
is not strictly historical.

3. *a warrior king*. The dominant warrior king is of course Alexander the Great.

stand forth and rule very dominantly and do as he pleases. And when 4
he stands forth, his kingdom shall be broken and divided to the four
winds of the heavens and not to his offspring and not to the dominion
that he had ruled, for his kingdom shall be uprooted and be for others
besides these. And the king of the south shall be strong, but one of his 5
commanders shall prevail over him and shall rule, very dominant his
dominion. And at the end of some years they shall join together, and 6
the daughter of the king of the south shall come to the king of the north
to make a treaty, but she shall not retain strength, nor shall he retain
strength, and she shall be given over—she and those who brought her
and her begetter and her supporter in those times. And a shoot shall 7
stand forth from her roots in his place, and he shall come to the army

---

4. *And when he stands forth.* The verb here, repeated from verse 2, is obscure
in context and symptomatic of the use of awkward and unclear repetitions in
Daniel's Hebrew. In fact, the empire broke up not while Alexander was "standing" but after his premature death.

divided to the four winds of the heavens. Alexander's vast empire broke into
four parts, only two of which, warring over the Land of Israel, will be the object
of attention in what follows.

not to his offspring. Alexander had no biological heirs to the throne.

5. *the king of the south.* This is Ptolemy I Soter, who seized Egypt after Alexander's death.

one of his commanders shall prevail over him. This is Seleucus I Nicator, who
assisted Ptolemy around 312 BCE, then returned to Babylonia, where he cre-
ated an empire greater than Ptolemy's.

6. *the daughter of the king of the south.* Berenice, daughter of Ptolemy II Phila-
delphus, was married to Antiochus II Theos, the Seleucid emperor.

she shall not retain strength, nor shall he retain strength. Antiochus died suddenly, perhaps poisoned by his first wife, Laodice. Berenice and her child were
then murdered.

she shall be given over. The Hebrew is vague and obscure, like much of the
language in this chapter.

7. *a shoot shall stand forth from her roots.* This is Ptolemy III, Berenice's brother,
who was victorious in a campaign against Laodice's son, Seleucus II, in 246
BCE.

8 and enter the stronghold of the king of the north and prevail. And their gods as well with their molten images with their precious vessels of silver and gold he shall bring in captivity to Egypt, and for years he shall stand
9 away from the king of the north. And he, he shall come into the kingdom
10 of the king of the south and then return to his land. And his sons shall be stirred up and gather a crowd of many forces and surely come and sweep along and pass through. And again he shall be stirred up, as far
11 as his stronghold. And the king of the south shall be enraged and come out and do battle with him, with the king of the north, and he shall set
12 out a great crowd, and the crowd shall be given into his hand. When the crowd is borne off, his heart shall be haughty, and he shall bring down
13 tens of thousands, but he shall not be strong. And again shall the king of the north set out a crowd greater than the first, and at the end of some years he shall surely come with a great force and much paraphernalia.
14 And in those times many shall stand against the king of the south, and the lawless sons of your people shall be raised up to fulfill the vision,

---

8. *he shall stand away from the king of the north.* This is still another instance of an odd and unidiomatic use of the verb "stand."

9. *he shall come into the kingdom of the king of the south.* Seleucus II then counterattacked and regained the territory he had lost.

10. *his sons shall be stirred up.* These are Seleucus III (227–23 BCE) and Antiochus III (223–187 BCE). The latter dominated the region for three decades, exploiting the weakness of Ptolemy III.
   as far as his stronghold. The reference is obscure.

11. *the crowd shall be given into his hand.* Ptolemy IV defeated Antiochus in the battle of Rafia in 217 BCE. But he failed to take advantage of his victory and had to contend with uprisings of native Egyptians in his home territory.

13. *And again shall the king of the north set out a crowd greater than the first.* Antiochus recaptured eastern portions of his empire (212–205 BCE) and then attacked Egypt after the deaths of Ptolemy IV and his queen. By 200 BCE, the Seleucids had gained control of Judah.

14. *the lawless sons of your people.* The reference is disputed, but this may be a designation of the Jewish Hellenizers who allied themselves with the Seleucids.

but they shall stumble. And the king of the north shall come and build 15
a siege-work and capture the fortified city, and the powers of the south
shall not be able to withstand, not even his elite troops, and there shall
be no strength to withstand. And the one who comes against him shall 16
do as he pleases with none withstanding him, and he shall stand in the
Splendid Land, with all of it in his hands. And he shall set his face to 17
come in the might of all his kingdom, and make a treaty with him, and
give him a daughter in marriage to destroy him, but it shall not stand
and shall not be. And he shall turn his face back to the coastlands, and 18
capture many, and a consul shall put an end to his insults, even without
his insult, he shall requite him. And he shall turn his face back to the 19
strongholds of his land and stumble and fall and not be found. And there 20

---

15. *shall come and build a siege-work.* This is the siege of Sidon, in which Antiochus assaulted the Ptolemaic forces.

16. *he shall stand in the Splendid Land.* This is the notation, in pseudoprophetic
language, of Antiochus's conquest of Judah.

17. *give him a daughter in marriage.* Antiochus, in the interest of halting hostili-
ties, betrothed his daughter Cleopatra to Ptolemy V in 197 BCE.
   to destroy him. The Masoretic text reads "destroy her," but the Qumran
Daniel, more plausibly, shows a masculine suffix. Once again, the wording is
odd, but it probably refers to the idea that Cleopatra would pursue Seleucid
interests in the Ptolemaic court.
   it shall not stand and shall not be. Cleopatra failed to deliver, instead showing
loyalty to the Ptolemaic empire.

18. *he shall turn his face back to the coastlands.* Antiochus led his forces through
Asia Minor in the first years of the second century BCE.
   a consul shall put an end to his insults. The consul is the Roman officer
Lucius Cornelius Scipio, who defeated Antiochus at the battle of Magnesia in
190 BCE. But much of the wording is obscure.

19. *stumble and fall and not be found.* Antiochus perished at Elymaus in 187
BCE while attempting to sack the temple of Bel.

shall stand in his place one who makes a tribute collector pass through the glory of the kingdom, but in a few days he shall be broken, neither
21 in wrath nor in battle. And there shall stand in his place a contemptible man to whom the glory of the kingdom has not been given, and he shall
22 come stealthily and grasp the kingdom through smooth talk. And the sweeping powers shall be swept away before him and be broken, and
23 also the prince of the covenant. And after the joining with him he shall practice deceit, and he shall come up and grow mighty with a small
24 force. Stealthily shall he come into the richest provinces. He shall come and do what neither his father nor the fathers of his father had done, he shall despoil and take booty and distribute wealth to them, and against
25 fortresses he shall lay his plans, but for a time. And he shall rouse his strength and his heart against the king of the south, and the king of the south shall be stirred up for battle with a very great and mighty force, but

---

20. *one who makes a tribute collector pass through the glory of the kingdom.* Antiochus was succeeded by Seleucus IV. In financial straits, he dispatched one Heliodorus to collect taxes. Eventually Seluecus was killed in a plot hatched by Heliodorus. Though this took place after twelve years, it is referred to dismissively here as "a few days."

21. *a contemptible man.* This is Antiochus IV Epiphanus, the perpetrator of the desecration of the Jerusalem temple and hence Daniel's bête noir.
    to whom the glory of the kingdom has not been given. Antiochus IV usurped the throne from the Seleucid line after 175 BCE.

22. *the prince of the covenant.* The high priest, Onias III, was murdered at this point.

23. *after the joining with him.* This is still another vague locution, which must refer to political alliances made by Antiochus to strengthen his position.

25. *And he shall rouse his strength and his heart against the king of the south.* Antiochus invaded Egypt in 170 BCE.

he shall not withstand, for they shall lay plans against him. And those 26
who eat at his table shall break him and sweep away his army, and many
shall fall slain. And the two kings, their heart shall be for harm, and 27
on a single table, deceit; for there is still an end for the appointed time.
And he shall go back to his land with great wealth, and his heart against 28
the holy covenant. And he shall do his deeds and go back to his land.
At the appointed time, he shall again go into the south, but the second 29
time shall not be like the first. And ships from Kittim shall come against 30
him, and he shall be daunted and once again rage against the holy covenant, and do his acts and look to those who abandon the holy covenant.
And forces shall stand forth from him and profane the sanctuary, the 31
stronghold, and take away the daily offering and set up the desolating
abomination. And those who deal wickedly with the covenant he shall 32
flatter with smooth talk, but the people who know their God shall stand

---

26. *those who eat at his table shall break him.* Daniel attributes the defeat of
Ptolemy VI Philometor by Antiochus to bad counsel or a conspiracy by his
close advisers.

27. *on a single table, deceit.* Antiochus and Ptolemy VI negotiated, but in the
view of this author, Antiochus deceived the southern king through a pretense
of friendship and then seized control of Egypt.

29. *he shall again go into the south.* Antiochus, after having withdrawn from
Egypt, invaded it again in 167 BCE.

30. *ships from Kittim.* Kittim, an opaque geographic reference in Balaam's
oracle (Numbers 24:24), at this late period was often used to designate Rome,
as is clear in several Qumran documents. Antiochus, confronted by a Roman
ultimatum, had been forced to pull back from Egypt.

31. *the sanctuary, the stronghold.* Fortifications had been introduced into the
temple structure.
   the desolating abomination. This recurrent phrase, *hashiquts meshomem*,
which expresses Daniel's loathing of the object of idolatrous veneration set up
in the temple, may pun, as many scholars conclude, on *ba'al shamin*, the Baal
of the heavens, widely worshipped in the region. This could be a statue of Zeus
Olympius.

33 strong and act. And the discerning among the people shall make the
many understand, but they shall stumble for a time by the sword and by
34 flame, by captivity, and by despoiling. And when they stumble they shall
35 find little support, and many shall join them with smooth talk. And from
among the discerning shall people fall, to purge them and to refine and
36 to purify until the end, for it is still for the appointed time. And the king
shall do as he pleases, and he shall exalt himself and make himself great
over every god, and against the God of gods he shall speak wondrous
things, and he shall prosper till the wrath comes to an end, for what has
37 been decreed shall be done. And he shall not consider the gods of his
fathers nor the one beloved by women, nor shall any god be considered,

---

33. *the discerning among the people.* These are Daniel's own circle. Some commentators think they may be a kind of sect. In any case, it is clearly pious right
thinking rather than armed resistance that for Daniel constitutes the most
legitimate opposition to Antiochus.

    they shall stumble for a time by the sword and by flame. These words probably
refer to the martyrdom suffered by the "discerning" who kept the faith, as is
attested in Maccabees.

34. *they shall find little support.* The discerning ones remain an embattled
minority in the Jewish population, and even those who pretend to support them
(which might include the Maccabees) offer no more than lip service.

35. *to purge them and to refine and to purify.* The martyrdom of the discerning
may manifest a necessity to winnow out all those who are not sufficiently pure
of heart.

36. *he shall speak wondrous things.* The obvious sense is to speak arrogantly, but
the use of a root that means "wonder" is symptomatic of a certain imprecision
in the Hebrew vocabulary of Daniel.

    the wrath. The mostly likely reference is to the wrath of Antiochus.

37. *he shall not consider the gods of his fathers.* This statement might reflect
Antiochus's elevation of the cult of Zeus Olympius at the expense of the other
gods, but it is probably hyperbolic, intended to represent Antiochus as impious
even within his own polytheistic domain.

    the one beloved by women. Scholars generally understand this as the con-
flated figure of Tammuz-Adonis.

for over everything he shall make himself great. But he shall honor the 38
god of strongholds in his place, he shall honor a god that his fathers did
not know, with gold and with silver and with precious stones and costly
things. And he shall act for those who fortify the strongholds, the people 39
of an alien god whom he comes to know. He shall greatly honor them
and make them rule over many and share out land at a price. At the 40
end-time the king of the south shall join battle with him and the king of
the north shall storm against him with chariots and horsemen and many
ships, and he shall come into the lands and sweep through and pass on.
And he shall come into the Splendid Land, and myriads shall stumble, 41
but these shall escape from his hand—Edom and Moab and the lead-
ership of the Ammonites. And he shall reach out his hand against the 42
lands, and the land of Egypt itself shall not escape. And he shall rule 43
over the treasures of gold and silver and all the costly things of Egypt,
and the Libyans and the Nubians shall trail after him. But rumors from 44
the east and from the north shall alarm him, and he shall sally forth in

---

38. *the god of strongholds.* Collins plausibly suggests that this epithet is based
on "the hated Akra, the garrison established by Antiochus in the City of David."

39. *the people of.* The translation follows the widely accepted emendation of
Masoretic *'im,* "with," to *'am,* "the people of." These would be Seleucid soldiers
stationed by Antiochus in Jerusalem (and *'am* can also mean "troops").

40. *At the end-time.* These words indicate a move from pseudoprophecy to
actual prophecy. Daniel envisages an apocalyptic clash between the kingdom of
the north and the kingdom of the south, which in fact never occurred. After his
actions in Jerusalem, Antiochus turned his attention to the Persians in the east.

45 great rage to destroy and to slaughter many. And he shall pitch the tents
of his pavilion between the sea and the splendid holy mountain, and he
shall come to his end, with none to help him.

---

45. *he shall come to his end, with none to help him.* The concluding verses of
this chapter show many of the ingredients of apocalyptic vision. There is a
cataclysmic war (as in the battle between Gog and Magog). The representative
of the forces of evil triumphs for a time (what later rabbinic tradition would call
"the birth-pangs of the messiah"), and then he is suddenly rendered helpless
and perishes. This account, written around 167 BCE, has nothing to do with
Antiochus's death in Persia in 165, and word of his demise would not have
reached Jerusalem until 164.

CHAPTER 12

And in that time Michael shall stand up, the great prince who stands 1
over the sons of your people, and it shall be a time of distress the like
of which has not been since the nation came to be until that time.
And in that time your people shall escape, all who are found in the
book. And many of the sleepers in the deep dust shall awake—some 2
for everlasting life and some for disgrace and everlasting shame. And 3

---

1. *shall stand up . . . stands over.* The Hebrew of Daniel again exhibits a pro-
pensity to use the same word over and over again in different senses—not to
some subtle punning purpose, as in earlier Hebrew prose, but rather through
a certain stylistic slackness. The sense of "stand over" is to protect, Michael
being the guardian angel of the people of Israel.

all who are found in the book. The strong scholarly consensus is that this is
the book of life. There are some brief hints in earlier biblical literature of such
a book kept on high, but here it is made dramatically explicit.

2. *the sleepers . . . shall awake—some for everlasting life and some for disgrace
and everlasting shame.* This is, famously, the first and only clear reference to
the resurrection of the dead in the Hebrew Bible. There are a few possible
anticipations in the Prophets, but these may be either hyperbolic or metaphors
of national restoration. By the last biblical centuries, notions of an afterlife
had some currency in the Near East. Bodily resurrection after burial here is
accompanied by the idea of reward for the righteous and punishment for the
wicked, though "disgrace" for the latter rather than the tortures of hell is what
is expressed.

the deep dust. The literal sense of the Hebrew is "the soil of the dust," but
when two synonyms are joined this way in the construct state (*semikhut*), the
effect is an intensification. (Compare, among many instances, Exodus 10:22,
ḥosekh-'afeilah, "pitch dark.") The point is that the dead who are to rise are
buried deep in the ground.

the discerning shall shine like the splendor of the sky, and those who
4 guide the many to be righteous, like the stars, forever and ever. As for
you, Daniel, conceal the words and seal the book till the end-time. Many
5 shall roam about and knowledge shall abound. And I, Daniel, saw, and,
look, two others were standing, one on this bank of the river and one on
6 that bank of the river. And one said to the man dressed in linen, who
7 was over the water of the river, "Until when is the wondrous end?" And
I heard the man dressed in linen, who was over the water of the river,

---

3. *the discerning.* Once again, this is the term Daniel uses for the privileged
spiritual elite to which he belongs.

shine like the splendor of the sky. This phrase was later incorporated into the
Jewish prayer for the dead.

like the stars. Collins notes that the idea of astral immortality was current in
the Hellenistic world and may well have influenced this formulation.

4. *conceal the words and seal the book till the end-time.* In the first instance, this
command is dictated by Daniel's fictitious location in the Persian period—the
prophecy of the end must remain a secret until its time comes. But given the
apocalyptic freight of the prophecy, it needs to be a strictly esoteric revelation
even when its fulfillment is only three and a half years away.

Many shall roam about and knowledge shall abound. It is not necessary to
emend this sentence, as many scholars have done. The idea is that in the
end-time, many will go about in search of knowledge, which will then become
accessible.

5. *two others.* Two other angels, besides Michael.

the river. Though the Hebrew *ye'or* was initially an Egyptian loanword referring to the Nile, it became (usually in the plural) a poetic synonym for "river,"
and here it probably refers to the Euphrates.

6. *the man dressed in linen.* This is how the angel was described in 10:5.

the wondrous end. Many interpreters understand this as a reference to Antiochus's persecutions and so construe "wondrous," *niflla'ot*, against the grain of its
usual meaning, in a negative sense. (See the New Jewish Publication Society
translation, "awful things.") But it may be more plausible to understand this to
mean the end-time, when wondrous things will take place.

and he raised his right hand, and his left hand was toward the heavens, and he swore by the One who lives forever that at the appointed time of times and a half and at the end of the shattering of the power of the holy people, all these things shall be finished. And I heard and did 8 not understand, and I said, "My lord, what is the aftermath of these things?" And he said, "Go, Daniel, for the words are concealed and 9 sealed till the end-time. Many shall be sifted and purified and purged, 10 and the wicked shall act wickedly, and none of the wicked shall understand, but the discerning shall understand. And from the time the daily 11 offering was taken away and the desolating abomination was set up is a thousand two hundred and ninety days. Happy who waits and reaches 12

---

7. *he raised his right hand, and his left hand was toward the heavens.* The raising of the hand, or here both hands, is the gesture of making a solemn vow.

the appointed time of times and a half. The Hebrew here is a translation of the Aramaic phrase that appears in 7:25.

8. *aftermath.* Daniel pointedly uses the term *aḥarit,* "what comes after." That is, if all these things—perhaps in particular, the persecutions by Antiochus—are to come to an end, what will come afterward?

10. *Many shall be sifted and purified and purged, and the wicked shall act wickedly.* This is clearly a landscape of apocalypse: the righteous will be winnowed out from the chaff of evildoers, while the wicked will continue in their wicked ways until they are overtaken by perdition.

11. *a thousand two hundred and ninety days.* This makes three and a half years from the time Antiochus suppressed the temple cult in 167 BCE. But given the sweep of the language in this concluding section, beginning with the awakening of the sleepers in the dust, the writer seems to have in mind not merely the restoration of the daily sacrifices in a temple that has been cleansed but a radical transformation of existence.

13 a thousand three hundred and thirty-five days. As for you, go to the end
and you shall rest, and stand up for your destiny at the end of days."

---

12. *a thousand three hundred and thirty-five days.* There is, of course, a discrepancy of forty-five days between this figure and the one given in the previous
verse. The simplest explanation may be that this verse was written just after
the 1,290 days had passed and so another six and a half weeks were added in
hopeful expectation. In any event, subsequent Jewish and Christian interpreters used these verses to make intricate calculations for the coming of the end of
days, which manifestly had not taken place in the fourth decade of the second
century BCE, as Daniel had envisaged. An illuminating exposition of this activity
of calculating and recalculating the end-time is found in Frank Kermode's *The
Sense of an Ending.*

13. *go to the end.* This slightly odd expression must mean, as the rest of the
verse indicates, "go to await the end."
    you shall rest. The evident sense is: rest in the grave. The notion of Daniel's
death prior to his resurrection is probably another reflection of the fact that he
is supposed to be living in the Persian era, perhaps two centuries before the
prophesied end-time.
    stand up for your destiny. The translation preserves the literal sense of this
much-used Hebrew verb, though the meaning in context is "rise up." Given
that Daniel is preeminently one of the righteous, his destiny at the end-time
will surely be everlasting life.